James D. Strauss

Taking Every Thought Captive:

Essays in Honor of James D. Strauss

Edited by

Richard A. Knopp
and
John D. Castelein

 COLLEGE PRESS
PUBLISHING COMPANY
Joplin, Missouri

International Standard Book Number: 0-89900-668-X

Table of Contents

EDITORS' PREFACE

This book is a *festschrift*, a collection of essays expressing tribute, in honor of Dr. James D. Strauss, professor of theology and philosophy at Lincoln Christian Seminary from 1967 to 1994. It embodies the respect and gratitude of many around the world who have been touched by his preaching, teaching, and writing.

Professor Strauss has been described, with some legitimacy, as the "Einstein of the Restoration Movement." Indeed, few within the Stone-Campbell tradition can equal his intellect, in breadth or depth. Students, teaching colleagues, and administrators were constantly amazed at his proficiency in a remarkably wide range of disciplines. For example, the 1984-85 seminary catalog listed forty-seven courses taught by Dr. Strauss! His teaching load typically exceeded what seemed humanly possible. Yet students were always as impressed by *how* he taught as they were by how *much* he taught.

Occasionally, prospective students believed that "apologetics" was not sufficiently stressed at the seminary, since few of professor Strauss's courses directly mentioned apologetics. What many discovered, however, was that, for Dr. Strauss, it did not matter whether it was theology, anthropology, archaeology, psychology, sociology, biology, epistemology, logic, law, linguistics, literature, ethics, economics, physics, historiography, cults, the occult, hermeneutics, homiletics, Old Testament, or New Testament—it was *all* apologetics.

Surprisingly, professor Strauss's astonishing capacity to captivate student minds was surpassed by his ability to motivate student hearts. Many students came from small towns, but they left with a vision of the universe. Their self-professed (and diagnostically accurate) ignorance was overcome by constant encouragement regarding their potential when coupled with God's grace. Though they never equated the local church with the Kingdom of God, they clearly came to understand from their mentor that maintaining the "mind of Christ" means ministry in the church and missions in the world.

Dr. Strauss was more of a catalyst and questioner than a systematizer and answer-man. Because of his ever-expanding mind, students benefited from an open framework that enabled new and creative thought to build vigorously on that of the master himself. The chapters in this book represent the efforts of those who were privileged to sit at his feet, to see through his eyes, and to savor his hugging arms.

John D. Castelein   Richard A. Knopp

THE ANNOUNCEMENT OF THE
FESTSCHRIFT FOR DR. JAMES D. STRAUSS[1]

by Richard A. Knopp

Whose mind is faster than a speeding bullet and more powerful than a locomotive? Who can leap tall libraries at a single bound? Who has been disguised as a mild-mannered professor who fights for truth, justice, and the Christian way? If you thought of Dr. James D. Strauss, long-time professor of theology and philosophy at Lincoln Christian Seminary, you were undoubtedly not alone.

A number of years ago, I was drawn to the Emerald City of Lincoln, Illinois. I heard that a wizard lived and taught there—someone who knew best how to battle the wicked witches of secularism, existentialism, pluralism, pantheism, and relativism. He, I believed, could keep me on the narrow (and yellow-bricked) road.

Along with me, many little munchkins gathered around this wizard, and their lives were changed forever. This wizard of God was able to develop in others what he himself possessed by God's grace. For those straw men who longed for a brain, he turned them on to the mind of Christ which excludes no thought or practice from God's assessment. To those tin men who were often embraced by his arms, he gave the biggest heart in the world. And to those little lions who cowered in the face of a complex and threatening world, he gave the courage to defend and boldly proclaim the gospel of Christ in the church, on foreign mission fields, and within the intellectual strongholds of secular education.

In December of 1991, when Dr. Strauss lay in a hospital room with little worldly hope for survival, one

---

[1]This public announcement (slightly modified here) was initially given during the 50th anniversary celebration of Lincoln Christian College in 1994.

persistent thought crossed my mind: what a shame that so many of his colleagues and former students have not had the opportunity to express some notable appreciation for his incalculable influence. Dr. John Castelein and I were thinking along the same lines. Having completed Ph.D.'s in theology and philosophy respectively, John and I decided that one way to express our indebtedness was to edit a book as a tribute to our mentor, Jim Strauss.

The book will be entitled, "Taking Every Thought Captive: Essays in Honor of James D. Strauss." The contributors are among the finest of Christian servants and scholars—all of whom have been directly influenced by this wizard in the Emerald City of Lincoln. They are but a few who represent hundreds—even thousands—who have been touched by this man who has been a true prophet of God in the twentieth century.

The book will reflect the broad impact of Dr. Strauss—in biblical theology, preaching, the book of Revelation, philosophy, apologetics and the philosophy of science, ethics, cross-cultural missions, worldview studies, and cultural analysis and criticism. It will even have a chapter dealing with the value of books— something especially appropriate for one who is thought of as a "walking library." When the book is completed, it will be a proportionally small gesture of appreciation in relation to the contribution Jim Strauss has made to the life of Lincoln Christian College and Seminary and to the Kingdom of God at large.

As we think of the legacy of leadership at this institution, I am privileged to say that James D. Strauss is one among many who is the product of God's choice to bring something extra special to His world. I can think of nothing more appealing or more needed than to continue and extend the legacy of Jim Strauss. He has blessed me with his mind; he has motivated me with his heart; and he has challenged me with his courage. And I love him very much.

LETTERS FROM
EVANGELICAL SCHOLARS

✦ ✦ ✦ ✦ ✦ ✦ ✦ ✦

Twenty years ago Jim Strauss turned up at a class of mine on the theology of Rudolf Bultmann at Circle Campus of University of Illinois in Chicago. Right away I realized there was in my presence an immensely learned theologian. Subsequently I have never failed to be amazed at the breadth of his reading and by the creative connections he could make within the learning he commanded always for the sake of the Gospel. Yet for all this erudition, here was a humble servant of God who made no pretensions but revealed an eagerness to learn from any quarter. I found my friend Jim also to be an evangelical churchman of ecumenical openness and a believer of a most gracious disposition. I therefore honor him for work well done in the service of Christ and wish him well.

Clark H. Pinnock
McMaster Divinity College
Hamilton, Ontario

✦ ✦ ✦ ✦ ✦ ✦ ✦ ✦

Dr. Strauss has had a longtime interest in the Christian world-and-life view and has stressed in many classes the importance of theology and philosophy and their intertwining intellectual demands. No concerns could have been more opportune at this juncture of history, when evangelical enterprises have been tempted to exalt the emotional and to neglect the cognitive.

Carl F. H. Henry
Evangelical Theologian & Author

✦ ✦ ✦ ✦ ✦ ✦ ✦ ✦

xii

✦ ✦ ✦ ✦ ✦ ✦ ✦ ✦

Although I have never met James Strauss, I have met his students—and in the lives of one's disciples the character of their teacher is reflected. In my [former] capacity as a professor of Philosophy of Religion at Trinity Evangelical Divinity School, I enjoyed the privilege of having graduates of Lincoln Christian College in my classes. I was amazed as one after another distinguished himself as among my brightest and most capable students. What was it about this little Christian school in mid-state Illinois, I thought, that it should be such an academic powerhouse generating good philosophers?

The answer was always the same: "Dr. Strauss!" The name was always said with enthusiasm and admiration. I, too, came to admire this unknown colleague, a humble and dedicated teacher, zealous to train a younger generation with the best skills he could impart and to send them out to think rigorously as Christians and so to change the secular intellectual milieu which shapes American society. His impact can only be truly measured in future generations through the lives he has helped to shape.

William Lane Craig
Philosopher and Christian Apologist
Research Professor, Talbot School of Theology

✦ ✦ ✦ ✦ ✦ ✦ ✦ ✦

Chapter 1:

The Christian Mind—
A Straussian Theme With No Variation:
A Biography of James D. Strauss
by
Dr. Keith Ray

Dr. Keith Ray is the president of Dallas Christian College and is also Jim Strauss's son-in-law. His insight into the life of Dr. Strauss, therefore, comes not only as a former student, but as a family member.

President Ray has a B.A. in church growth and world mission from Lincoln Christian College, an M.Div. in theology and philosophy from Lincoln Christian Seminary, and a D.Min. from Trinity Evangelical Divinity School. His doctoral project was entitled, "Developing a Leadership Model for Examining the Impact of Cultural Trends on the Local Church."

He has served in preaching ministries in Raymond, Lake Fork, and Toluca, Illinois. From 1990-1994, Dr. Ray was the Director of Christian Service at Dallas Christian College and became her president in 1994.

He has published three articles in the *Journal for Christian Studies*: "Evolution and Scientific Models in Biology," "The Relevance of Intentionality for Restoration Hermeneutics," and "Sifting through the Shifting Sands of Philosophical Hermeneutics as Evidenced in the New Hermeneutics." He also wrote a chapter on "Christian Living in a Secular Culture" in *Essentials for Christian Living* published by College Press.

Dr. Ray has developed a number of seminar offerings for local churches which deal with church mission, leadership, baby-boomers, worldview studies, team ministry, grace, reconciliation, the book of Joshua, higher education, how to study the Bible, and the church and culture.

THE CHRISTIAN MIND—A STRAUSSIAN THEME WITH NO VARIATION:

A BIOGRAPHY OF JAMES D. STRAUSS

Ⓔ very student, colleague, or friend of James Strauss knows the ever familiar theological rhapsody of the "Lordship of Jesus Christ." For more than twenty years that theological theme has played a central role in his classroom instruction, published works, preaching, and even in his casual conversation. Those who have studied with James Strauss have heard that incessant phrase: "Jesus is Lord over every category of reality." His is a life devoted to the task of informing, transforming, and challenging the minds of men and women who have come under his influence for the Lordship of Christ.

The remarks that follow are but a feeble attempt to portray the man, his mind, and his ministry. From start to finish, his life is a long journey in the same direction. It has been a tireless effort to encourage, mentor, and lead all who would hear the call to complete submission to Jesus Christ in mind, body, and soul.

James D. Strauss: "A Mind in the Making"

On July 3, 1929, Earnest and Cleo Strauss gave birth to their second son, James Dean. The small town of Herrin in southern Illinois was unaware that into her humble surroundings would come one with a world vision. He was born during the depression in bloody Williamson County, a place that held more promise for a hanging on a Sunday afternoon than the prospect of a modern day prophet.

As a nurse in a nearby hospital and a decorations' designer for a department store, his mother was unaware of the creativity and nurturing spirit being instilled in young James. On the other hand, his father had experienced the trauma of World War I, and later became a coal miner and bookkeeper for Peabody Coal Company. Personally and professionally his father lived on the edge. One moment he would be mining, and the next moment he would be gambling. As far as young James was concerned, his father was the smartest man he knew, with a gambling reputation to prove it. With the mind of his German father and the creativity of his French mother, James grew to love and enjoy his close-knit family.

The family moved north to Catlin, Illinois when James was in second grade. The fond memories of his childhood include a long list of close friends who enjoyed swimming, biking, and softball. Many nights the softball games went until dark, and win or lose, James managed to stay out of the scuffles with the neighborhood boys.

During the winter months sledding and sleigh riding with a friend's father were highlights. With myriads of memories like these, he remembers the family's first refrigerator and washing machine. Many nights he and the family sat around listening to the radio. He was a regular fan of such radio programs as "The Shadow" and "The Lone Ranger." No doubt those early experiences played an important role in the development of his personality and outlook on life.[1]

His high school athletic career led him to letter in both football and basketball. His early academic career included courses like home economics, typing, chemistry, biology, algebra, geometry, and trigonometry. Anticipating a career in engineering, James was very conscientious about his school work. Graduating as

---

[1][Editors: Rumor has it that, as a doctoral student in philosophy at Indiana University, Jim Strauss loved to unwind by watching the Three Stooges!]

salutatorian in his class was an indication that he was moving in the right direction. In addition to that honor, he was voted "most likely to succeed" by his peers. His career aspirations and academic preparation were the early stages in the making of a mind destined for use in the Kingdom of God.

High school life was not restricted to athletics and academics. During his sophomore year he worked at Herschel Dickerson's Grocery Store. He delivered groceries and learned the "meat cutting" trade, touting his ability to distinguish a mediocre cut of meat from a fine one. The second flare in his early work days came from clerking in two men's clothing stores. His fine taste in clothing was born at Deutsch Brothers in Danville, Illinois. That "GQ" look is a trademark to this day rivaled only by his teaching style.

"A Mind in Transformation"

James had all the ingredients for a successful future—a fine, loving home, a strong work ethic, and an enviable academic record. It seemed that he had everything except a faith in Jesus Christ. His father belonged to the Christian Church (Disciples of Christ) and his mother was raised as a Baptist, but neither attended church while James was a young boy. Not until Ed Smith came to the Catlin Church of Christ did things begin to change. Ed visited Dickerson's Grocery Store and extended him an invitation to attend church services. James did so and invited his buddy Bobby Lee Pate to accompany him. A few months later while attending a revival led by Roy Blackmore, James was baptized into Christ. His conversion was all it took for his parents to return to church. This later resulted in his father abandoning gambling and other reckless habits.

Donald Doggett and Elmo Johnson were the first mentors for James. As elders of the Catlin Church, they felt obligated to provide spiritual direction for James's young and eager mind. As coal miners they had little formal education, but had long since exchanged nightly visits to the tavern for home Bible studies. They introduced Jim to the Bible and gave him his first lesson in the fundamentals of Greek. This early discipling laid the foundation for an up and coming theologian.

After high school and his conversion Jim set out for college. He had chosen the field of electrical engineering at the University of Illinois. But something in young James sparked Ed Smith, the preacher at Catlin, to encourage him to attend Bible College. When the spring semester came around, James was off to Cincinnati Bible College. Professors like R. C. Foster, Lewis Foster, and Grayson Ensign made significant impact on the formation of his thinking. At the same time, he had begun preaching on weekends, studying into the wee hours of the night, and only hiking home and back to do laundry.

Already experiencing the rigors of the Christian life and the cost of discipleship, James began to formulate his vision for Kingdom service. The late Grayson Ensign was an early influence in raising philosophical and theological questions that sparked an even greater vision of what would some day become the legacy of the Straussian mindset.

James's life had taken a turn for the best. A keen mind, a sincere heart, and all the ambition of a new convert fueled a career that was unforeseen in the simple life at Catlin. He completed his studies at Cincinnati and then moved on to Christian Theological Seminary where he came under the tutelage of Dr. Walter Sykes. Each new educational venture added to his theological system. From that time forward there was no turning back. He began the long journey toward academic excellence that crystallized his well-known worldview thinking.

"A Mind that Captivates for Christ"

After more than twenty years of service and stewardship with Lincoln Christian Seminary, Dr. Strauss has discipled a generation of influential leaders for Kingdom work. The facets of that discipleship have come in a variety of forms.

The Classroom

While somewhat unorthodox in his pedagogy, his students often leave his classes with their heads spinning. Lectures that spew forth information, questions, and insights all reflect a volcanic teaching style that mesmerizes both the "rookie" student along with the seasoned seminarian. With high expectations, uproarious laughter, and brilliant insight, his classroom becomes an incubator for ideas and issues that are later hammered out in the realities of everyday ministry.

His reputation is not that of an answer man, but of one who raises questions that spur the student on to a lifelong search for the truth. He is a master of describing the broad sweeping movements in the history of thought. One minute he is lecturing on Hegel's *Phenomenology*, next quantum leaping to Barth's *Word of God*, and finally culminating with remarks concerning Kuhnian paradigms. With lectures that integrate human thought with theological truth, the classroom experience reveals the integrative powers of a unique mind that can climb the slopes of a polished pedagogy and descend into the plains of side-splitting laughter.[2]

Donut Shop Discipleship

Luther had his Table Talks; Dr. Strauss has his "donut discussions." Many students knew that when

---

[2][Editors: Dr. Strauss always had a gift for producing the memorable "one liner" that fused humor and insight, often with a sarcastic bent. Some of these are included in this chapter's Appendix.]

classroom instruction was completed, the afterglow continued at Comstock's Bakery. Here Danny always had a delightful dozen waiting for the coffee-clutching theologians. Many classes have reconvened at mid-morning or late afternoon to probe further the reaches of the Straussian mind. At times it was a critique of Kant's *Critique of Pure Reason*, reflections on Strauss's "theology of promise," or simple suggestions for ministry in the local church. In any case, the spiritual and emotional dynamics precipitated by these discussions went far beyond the academic. They were the building blocks for theological syntheses, and they provided a discipleship bond that has planted a sentiment kept by those who to this day long for the good old days at Lincoln Christian Seminary.

Sidewalk Theologian

Most theologians are noted for their "arm chair" posture. This is not so for Dr. Strauss. Every Strauss student has two basic images of their mentor. One is the classroom image during a high powered lecture accompanied by the all too familiar chalk insertion in his ear. The second image is that of Professor Strauss hyper-walking along the sidewalks of the college and seminary campus. Even with an ominous load of books under both arms, he can outpace even the most athletic of students. The inquiring student is required to keep a fast pace with a forty-inch stride to hear the insights of the mobile theologian. Some saw it as humorous, while others understood that his busy schedule did not accommodate special times of exercise and that Dr. Strauss wisely pummeled his body while he discussed theology.

If in a rare moment he was sitting still, it was behind a three-sided wall of books and papers that shrouded his table in the study section of the Jessie Eury Library. No matter where he was or where he was headed, there was always time for a curious student, even if it meant matching the stride of the sidewalk theologian.

The Pulpit

With a style all his own, Dr. Strauss has traveled the globe to preach and teach the good news of Jesus Christ. The pulpit for him is a dramatic platform where the Word of God is expressed and a life ignites with the flame of God's truth. Dynamic, riveting, and insightful— all describe his preaching style. From revivals to camp meetings to campus retreats, he has the unique ability to communicate with all ages, intellects, and dispositions. As one colleague put it, "He can walk and talk with both princes and paupers, peasants and kings." His pulpiteering has always drawn a welcome crowd, sometimes concluding with a standing ovation, only to find him crouched on bended knee behind the pulpit humbly seeking God's blessing on the spoken Word. Whether pulpit or lectern, the supremacy of Christ remains the central theme of his oratory.

Up Close and Personal

For forty years as husband and father, Dr. Strauss has modeled a deep love for his wife Jewel and his two daughters, Joye Lu and Jeaneen Kaye. While often away from home pursuing a Kingdom agenda, his heart is never far away from home. He is always eager to return with an outburst of laughter and joy at the sight of his family. With a home that is truly his castle, his hobbies go beyond reading and writing. His interests gravitate toward the aesthetic. Some days a landscaping project is paramount, and on others another layer of wallpaper is added to the interior design. His affinity toward the beautiful is apparent to all who visit his home. When the household tasks are all finished, a favorite pastime is to view an old classic movie on video, with a special liking for Laurel and Hardy. The "Big

Band" sound is for him the height of musical ecstasy. Benny Goodman or Pete Fountain can set his feet to toe tapping and his hands to knee clapping. He truly is a man of rhythm—in music, the seasons of nature, and for the issues of the Christian community.

Above all else, James Strauss has a heart for the church. As a member of the Jefferson Street Christian Church for the last twenty years, he has embedded in his family a zeal for unconditional commitment to the local church. Over the years, many long weekends ended in a Sunday evening worship service with his family. No matter how tiring or long the journey, worship and fellowship with Christ's body have been of utmost importance to him.

Most men with his intellectual stature live in emotional isolation. Dr. Strauss is an anomaly in that sense. He would prefer a hug to a lecture. While his mind runs deeply, so do his emotions. His sensitivity to students, family, and preaching audience goes without saying. He always has time to listen to fears, frustrations, and questions. Many a spontaneous encounter ends with an equally spontaneous prayer, a verbal affirmation, and is automatically sealed with the all familiar "Straussian" bear hug.

"A Mind at Peace in the Lordship of Christ"

In the twilight years, the legacy continues. James Strauss is a man who has run the race, fought the fight, and continues to wage the battle for tomorrow. In retrospect, there are few, if any, changes Dr. Strauss would make in his life. He has always struggled with the demands of Kingdom service and family priorities. The dedicatory statement from his commentary on Revelation reflects this:

> There is no way I can express, in mortal language, my gratefulness to my wife Jewel and our two little Godsends, Joye Lu and Jeaneen Kay....

There is only one vindication of things they have never received, and the time which was theirs that I have taken from them, because of my prolonged schooling, and that is that it may bring much glory to our Lord and Savior, Jesus Christ.[3]

In the academic arena, if he could make retroactive changes in his life, Dr. Strauss might have implemented much sooner the influence of Thomas Kuhn and Stanley Jaki, both of whom speak about the role of paradigms and worldviews and make viable the discussion of biblical theology in relation to the history of science.

He views himself as another pilgrim in the long journey to the Holy City, attempting at every step to avoid the "castle of doubt." That journey has left many a student, church, and colleague indebted to his vision. Many of his former students are now missionaries around the world, fill pulpits nationwide, and serve as faculty members and administrators in many Bible Colleges.

Never wanting to be caught in a defensive posture, Dr. Strauss speaks more often of "eristics" (rather than "apologetics"), because it suggests a more "positive" initiative-taking approach to positions incompatible with the Christian faith. Utilizing both an evidentialist and presuppositionalist methodology, his life is a tireless devotion to articulating the Christian worldview. From philosophy to science, aesthetics to theology, his is an effort to unify all disciplines under the Lordship of Jesus Christ. In doing so, it has been his career ambition to confront constructively the forces opposing the Kingdom of God and to engage with intellectual integrity our now post-Christian, post-modern culture. The tools for that pilgrimage are in his words nothing less than "Jesus' blood and His

---

[3]James D. Strauss, *The Seer, the Saviour, and the Saved: The Lord of the Future* (Joplin, MO: College Press, 1963, 1972), p. v.

righteousness," the Word of God, the collective Christian mind, and a life marked by servanthood.

For more than ten years, professor Strauss's legacy continued through Lincoln Christian Seminary's Chi Lambda Fellowship—a fellowship which he founded and sponsored which was devoted to integrating all disciplines under the sovereignty of Christ. While Chi Lambda's publication, *A Journal for Christian Studies*, has been discontinued, the annual lectureship continues and, in 1995, it was renamed as "The James D. Strauss Lectureship."

His numerous publications attest to his uncompromising commitment to biblical authority, cultural awareness, and philosophical prowess. His published works and extensive monographs include missiological studies, commentaries on Job, Acts, and Revelation, and studies in the history of science and the great philosophical thinkers of Western civilization.

A Concluding Appreciation

Dr. Strauss has never been intimidated by new ideas. He has searched for new ways to challenge modern thought, while maintaining the integrity of sound doctrine. He has an uncanny ability to discern the non-essentials from the essentials. His intense thinking ability and integrative approach to theology and philosophy provide a foundation for seeing the "big picture." Above all, he is devoted to clear, effective, and comprehensive thinking about the totality of the Christian world and life view. It is that central thrust that has provided the impetus for a lifetime of research, writing, preaching, and teaching.

Those who serve as colleagues at Lincoln Christian Seminary and the numerous students who have sat under his tutelage appreciate his vision in redirecting and empowering both the Restoration Movement and the evangelical community at large. His sense for the imperative of kingdom theology and worldview thinking colors every facet of his ministry. All of this is done with a persuasiveness that fosters an almost contagious vision to confront our materialistic, pluralistic, and humanistic society.

In summary, James D. Strauss is truly a man of God with many gifts and talents. While his primary calling is to that of scholarship and academics, secluded living has never satisfied his zeal for people. He is a man of God, with a heart for mankind. His life exhibits the constant pursuit of a Christian frame of reference, with a passion to "demolish arguments and every pretension that sets itself up against the knowledge of God" and "take captive every thought to make it obedient to Christ" (2 Cor 10:5 NIV).

The years have produced a fruitful harvest. Many are the admirers who have joined and continue to join the ranks of ministry. In the good providence of God, his investment for the Kingdom has only begun to reach its potential as his students take leadership roles in ministry around the globe. The years to come will only pay dividends to a life invested in the eternal nature of Christ's kingdom.

This volume is lovingly dedicated to him by those who have stood on his shoulders, seen a little further, thought a little clearer, and dreamed a little more vividly. A servant among servants, Dr. James Dean Strauss has made the Kingdom of God a better place to serve and one step closer to what God intended for those who affirm that "Jesus Christ is Lord, to the glory of God the Father" (Phil 2:11 NIV).

APPENDIX: SELECT QUOTATIONS
FROM JAMES D. STRAUSS[1]

Many students of Jim Strauss found themselves jotting down his one-liners almost as prolifically as his lectures. His classroom quotes generally mixed humor with insight and sarcasm. Some students could not always interpret the intent of this sarcasm. On the surface, it appeared very negative and cynical. Yet most students understood that professor Strauss claimed, and intended, to be a "theological gadfly"—someone who stings with a purpose. His objective was to awaken Christians and churches to the biblical task of being the kingdom of God in the world.

In expressing his points, Dr. Strauss frequently cited the mythical "Maudie Frickett"—a contrived caricature of ultra we've-always-done-it-that-way church mentality. He repeatedly claimed that "a truck driver on route 10" is more able (and willing) to understand critical kingdom issues than many church people.

The following Strauss quotes may not all be original with him, but they certainly manifest a portion of his personality. The immediate context for these statements is not always clear, but they can be enlightening in a variety of settings.

"Jesus often says, 'Are you sure you want to follow me?' We often say, 'Get 'em into the baptistry and they will grow.' Have you ever seen anything dead grow?"

"We have the theology of 'yeabut'. 'Yeah, I know that's what's in the Bible, but ...'"

"My worry is whether you've had sixteen years of experience or one year of experience sixteen times."

[professing skeptic]: "If God had wanted everybody to go to church, why would he have made the Sunday Times 300 pages long?"

---

[1]Quotations have been compiled from class notes by Paul Clark and Rich Knopp.

"*Sometimes, that's what church is: The* National Inquirer *with candles*"

"'*Does Satan attend your church regularly?*' *In many [churches] he doesn't have to; he's already won the battle.*"

"*At the rate some churches are going down the drain, we'll have to get bigger drains.*"

"*Where was the church? Polishing buckles on the Bible belt.*"

"*He's a 'usetogo'. He used to go, but they had a fight down there and he hasn't been back since.*"

"*If you said, 'Are you alive?' he's say "No" just to get an argument going.*"

"*Don't be average in the name of Jesus. If everyone tried to be average, it would just bring the level down.*"

"*Premeditated mediocrity.*"

"*In the Bible, Christ made preachers out of witnesses, not witnesses out of preachers.*"

"*We've got more pathetic preaching than prophetic preaching.*"

"*All kinds of people are being called who clearly need supernatural help every time they speak.*"

"*Know the Word and know the world; that's all you have to preach.*"

"*Pray for the day we have brain surgeons preaching.*"

"*The cross — the fortunate tragedy.*"

[Regarding Ananias and Sapphira]: "*They were 'provocateurs of fallacious heterodoxy' — they lied.*"

"*Two 'weakies' put together just make one 'big weakie.'*"

"*A penny for your thoughts — and that's overpaying you.*"

"*Almost any except those participating in it would be aware of its smallness.*"

"*Almost everyone is born a baby; some stay that way for a lifetime.*"

"*Arthur Conan Doyle was a medium ... or an extra-large, I don't know which.*"

"*Even a truck driver out on Highway 10 could tell you that.*"

"*There are no immediate answers to ultimate issues.*"

"*Even when you don't have the answer, you may know all there is to know.*"

"I can conceive of things more ridiculous,
but it puts my mind to the test."

"I've talked to people in the loony bin who made
better statements than that."

"I don't know about that, but of course I don't know most things."

"I don't mind working in concrete;
I just don't like to work it after it's set."

[With reference to theological systems]: "I'm not opposed to models;
I know two in New York."

"Like the cow's tail, you're always behind."

"If you want something to die, tell it to the wrong people."

"Is there a possibility that there be a generation that knows what's
going on when it's going on?"

"It is best to know that when things are not in human hands,
they are not out of hand."

"'It is out of the Bible' — Yeah, a long way out of the Bible."

"It's like changing the deck chairs on the Titanic."

"It's like being a long-distance swimmer on the Titanic —
it won't do you any good."

"Man is not any less primitive than he has ever been —
just more tailored."

"No room for grace except at the organ."

"Scopes trial — used to be a trial, now it's a mouthwash."

"The place was so bad that even the cockroaches were
searching for a better building."

"There are desert regions with soil so poor
you can't even raise umbrellas."

"Some people are so deaf that when you write them a letter
they say 'What?'"

"Some furniture goes back to Louis the XIV;
mine goes back to Sears the VIII."

"Some people get exercise from jumping to conclusions."

"Some people wouldn't lose a thing if they lost their mind."

"Stop assuming and start thinking."

"Thank you brethren and cistern, it is an extinct pleasure to be here."

"'That's just my bag' — well, then, get another bag."

"The main weakness is it isn't true."

"The French word for that is 'le bunk'."

"The only place some people carry any weight is on the scales."

"The only taste some people have is in their mouth."

"Many people have diarrhea of the mouth."

*"The sin of silence — sometimes silence is gold,
sometimes it is yellow."*

"The universe is becoming a cosmic cuckoo's nest."

"This is a case of terminal weirdness."

*"There's no point in saying something badly
if it's already been said well."*

*"They don't need to come to school if they're going to turn around, go
home, and do what they could without coming."*

*"We have so many students who qualify for the "Gong" show
that there is a two year backlog."*

*"I don't know, and I don't even want to make up something
to see if you'd believe it."*

"We'll get to evil — and some of you will get there ahead of us."

"Come on in, lay down in front so it'll look like a lot's here."

"We'll not have a break tonight, except maybe in your arm."

"They have the cream — it just hasn't been separated yet."

"Truth should be practical but not all that is practical is the truth."

"We're hoping to thin out our ranks because we're rank as can be."

"We can survive with as few as one, but that's a bedrock minimum."

*"We can't both be committed to the Bible and say
we don't want to hear that."*

"Most people kick dead horses because they don't respond."

"We've got to create dissatisfaction."

"You can't have dead churches that are plugged into God."

"You're always in trouble when only trivia brings excitement."

*"You're going to change the world and you can't even
change the bulletin."*

"The world changes by the molders, not the molded."

"If you put it in your head, you'll have it in a nutshell."

*"He looked like a nerd sitting on the fourth floor
of a two story library."*

*[Regarding the establishment of a new Bible College]: "... another
unaccredited angel factory."*

"Birds flew before men did, but that didn't make them scientists."

"Could you counsel me? My bunion hurts."

"You can't stay home often enough not to hear that."

"I can hear 43 miles in the fog and I never heard that!"

"I don't want a health report — how you feel — I want a book report."

[God]: "If I can create the universe, I can keep you informed."

*"It is not whether these things are relevant to the world, but whether
you are relevant to the world."*

*"When you don't know what you're doing,
take a vote."*

*"When you run out of anything to do,
you have seminars in possibilities."*

"Just have a group grope."

*"Some of you spend more time driving to school than
we have to spend in Acts."*

"If you don't know Acts, you should get the ax."

"Someone has to be healthy enough to help others."

"Not all the redactors are at Harvard Divinity School."

"You can redact by ear filters."

"You can understand it if you're completely irrational."

"You can't change the times just thinking."

"It's like a frog in a beaker ..."

"Like cheap clothes, it was bound to come apart."

"One cannot guard what one cannot understand."

"Maybe God isn't even sick, let alone dead."

"Knowing the Bible is not enough, but you must know the Bible."

Chapter 2:

The Value of Books in a Media Age
or
The Value of Media in an Age of Books
by
Dr. Thomas Tanner

Having served as Library Director at Lincoln Christian College and Seminary in Lincoln, Illinois, Dr. Tanner is currently the Academic Dean and Director of Strategic Planning at Lincoln Christian College. He has a Master of Divinity degree in New Testament from Lincoln Christian Seminary, and three degrees from the University of Illinois at Urbana-Champaign: an M.A. in Classical Literature, an M.S. in Library Science, and a Ph.D. in Information Science.

He has published articles in the *Journal of Library History*, the *Christian Standard*, and the *Journal of Religious and Theological Information*. His *Manual of Style for Bible College and Seminary Students* (published by LCC Press) is now in its fourth edition. Dean Tanner's doctoral dissertation, entitled "The Pastor as Information Professional: An Exploratory Study of How the Ministers of One Midwestern Community Gather and Disseminate Information," was awarded the Berner-Nash Award for Outstanding Doctoral Dissertation by the Graduate School of Library and Information Science at the University of Illinois. It was published in 1994 by Scarecrow Press with the title, *What Ministers Know*.

Dr. Tanner has served as a library consultant for colleges in Missouri, Texas, and Tennessee. He also functions as an evaluator for the North Central Association of Colleges and Schools.

He resides in Lincoln with his wife Debby and daughter Melissa.

THE VALUE OF BOOKS IN A MEDIA AGE
OR
THE VALUE OF MEDIA IN AN AGE OF BOOKS

Introduction

I am delighted to write this essay in honor of Dr. James Strauss, whom I consider one of the most influential people in my professional life. As a librarian, I am especially pleased that the topic noted in the title above was assigned to me by the editors. In fact, my first memory of Dr. Strauss was of him and a book.

I was a fledgling freshman coming to Lincoln Christian College for the very first time. I was riding in a car with my sister, who was a senior at the college. As we turned the corner toward campus, I saw a man out mowing his lawn. He was pushing the mower with one hand and holding a book with the other, scanning it as he mowed. As I turned to my sister in utter disbelief, she calmly said, "Oh, that's Dr. Strauss, one of the professors at school. You'll get used to that. He's always reading." Over the years I have discovered again and again just how right she was. Dr. Strauss was "always reading," but I have never "gotten used to it." As a trained professional in book-based pursuits, I am constantly astonished at the amazing bibliographic prowess of this brilliant and humble man of God.

Yet, I believe even Dr. Strauss would not want to elevate the container over the content. What I mean is that "books" as a format is not the critical issue in the Christian enterprise. The issue is what is in the books, or in any medium. While I have learned much from books, even that medium is not the message. The issue is information, or better yet, knowledge/wisdom. As the poet, T. S. Eliot so aptly observes in "The Rock":

The endless cycle of idea and action,
Endless invention, endless experiment,
Brings knowledge of motion, but not of stillness;
Knowledge of speech, but not of silence;
Knowledge of words, and ignorance of the Word.

Where is the Life we have lost in living?
Where is the wisdom we have lost in knowledge?
Where is the knowledge we have lost in information?

Silence! and preserve respectful distance.
For I perceive approaching
The Rock. Who will perhaps answer our doubtings.
The Rock. The Watcher. The Stranger.
He who has seen what has happened.
And who sees what is to happen.
The Witness. The Critic. The Stranger.
The God-shaken, in whom is the truth inborn.[1]

The Intent of This Essay

My point is that even as a librarian (literally, "person of books") I do not want to elevate any medium of information or knowledge to sacred status. I reserve that for "the Rock." Remember that the Apostle Paul stressed in the book of Romans the value of oral preaching (Rom 10:14-15). As valuable as the book is in a media age or in any age, God chose to begin, not with the printed medium, but with the oral. Continuously, the oral medium is highlighted in the "print" medium of the biblical books. (A concordance study on words for "write" and "speak" make this fairly clear.) I contend that God did not consecrate either medium over the other in the biblical period. I further argue that He has sanctioned neither medium over the other today.

-----

[1]T. S. Eliot, *The Complete Poems and Plays: 1909-1950* (New York: Harcourt, Brace, 1952).

In other words, I would rather talk about the value of media in an age of books, provided I am allowed to define media as information-bearers of any sort, including books. I am not the first to stress the value of all legitimate media in the communication of Christian truth. In his 1964 Terry Lectures at Yale University on the role of religion in science and philosophy, Walter Ong did the same.[2] He discussed, in fact, three major communications media, each of which, he argued, has had a significant impact upon the way Christianity promulgates its message. These three are oral, print, and electronic media.

The intent of this essay is to examine the value of all three of these media—print, electronic, and oral. My goal is not to list "ten good books" or my "five favorite movies." Rather, I want to concentrate on the communication process inherent in each of these media. The scope to which I will limit this essay is communication among Christian leaders, particularly the pastoral ministry. Though I could have cast my net more broadly, I follow Dr. Strauss's lead in concentrating my efforts on ministry. It is no accident that Dr. Strauss chose to let his light shine in a seminary, not a university—to the benefit of a generation of preachers. My methodology is to use a ministerial case study to illustrate the varying values of these various media. The case study involves a research project I conducted among the preaching ministers of a midwestern city of about 100,000 people.[3] In this study I interviewed nearly seventy full-time pastors serving in some twenty different denominations, both Protestant and Catholic. In addition to the interviews, which were often conducted in multiples over a several-week period, I also listened to

---

[2]See Walter Ong, *The Presence of the Word: Some Prolegomena for Cultural and Religious History* (New Haven: Yale University Press, 1967).
[3]Thomas Tanner, *What Preachers Know* (Metuchen, NJ: Scarecrow Press, 1994.

and analyzed nearly fifty sermons from these preachers over the span of ten months.

My major purpose was to find out how these ministers acquired and disseminated information, especially in preaching and counseling—the two professional tasks that they listed as their most predominant. What I learned was that pastors valued all three of these media in communicating the Messiah's message. I also learned, as others have demonstrated before,[4] that these media are not value neutral. Each medium, including print media, exerts both a positive and a negative influence on the communication process and, ultimately, on the message itself. This was seen not only in the case study, but in the literature.

A Review of the Literature on the Value of Media

In the heyday of media-minded McLuhan, the Jesuit scholar Ong asserted strongly the natural bias of historic Christianity for the spoken word—"Faith comes by hearing" (Rom 10:17). However, he also noted the natural affinity of the ministry to electronic media. He included among these media the communication technologies of the telephone, the radio, the television, the cinema, and the computer.[5] This affinity is a consequence, Ong argued, of the re-involvement of the senses in electronically-based communications, particularly that of hearing, which was lost in print media.

Ellul, on the other hand, argued that only the oral is ultimately compatible with the Christian message and that the Church and the clergy "humiliate the

---

[4]For instance, see Ong, *The Presence of the Word;* Jacques Ellul, *The Humiliation of the Word*, trans. by J. M. Hanks (Grand Rapids: Eerdmans, 1985); Neil Postman, *Amusing Ourselves to Death: Public Discourse in the Age of Show Business* (New York: Viking, 1985); and Clyde Fant, "Out of the Gutenberg Galaxy," in his *Preaching for Today*, pp. 159-173 (San Francisco: Harper and Row, 1987).

[5]Ong, *The Presence of the Word*, pp. 87-88.

spoken word" (small and capital "w") when they utilize image-based electronic media. His rationale was that visual media present only distorted "reality," whereas oral media create a universal "truth" that is not limited to what the eye sees.[6] For Ellul, seeing is not believing in that media such as television not only often present a distorted view of reality, they elevate the image over the real or true. (He suggested that one consider the irony of the phrase "pretty as a picture.")

Postman differed from both Ong and Ellul in that he elevated print media over both oral and electronic ones. Though he wrote of the power of, and the rekindled need for, oral discourse in the public life of America, his focus was upon print. In reviewing certain features of American history, Postman (1985) observed that this country "was dominated by a public discourse which took its form from the products of the printing press. For two centuries America declared its intentions, expressed its ideology, designed its laws, sold its products, created its literature and addressed its deities with black squiggles on white paper."[7]

In a chapter on the ministry's use of electronic media, Postman denied that religious information could be conveyed correctly by electronic media, especially television, because of the inability of that medium to be "sacralized." (Television has no "sanctuary" in which the sacred may be separated from the secular. A televised sermon, for example, may often be sandwiched between a fishing show and a rerun of a Sherlock Holmes movie.)

Innis was one of the first to highlight the futility of any of these arguments for or against one set of media over another.[8] His contention is that historically each of these three media has exercised, in turn, a certain

---

[6]Ellul, *The Humiliation of the Word*, p. 22.

[7]Postman, *Amusing Ourselves to Death*, p. 63.

[8]See Harold Innis, *The Bias of Communication* (Toronto: University of Toronto Press, 1951).

monopoly. For anyone to argue against, for example, the use of electronic media is to fight an historically losing battle. James Carey correctly cautioned that monopoly, however, does not mean exclusivity, and he cited the example of the rise of print in the sixteenth century and its subsequent failure, obviously, to displace oral media.[9] In Carey's words, the rise of electronic media in the late twentieth century will only cause print and oral media to become "residual," not absent. The point I wish to make in this essay is that each medium has value and each medium harbingers danger. Both the literature and my case study make this point clear.

A Case Study in the Value of Media

My interviews with the pastors in this case study indicated that although all these ministers used all three media, many ministers often exhibited a marked preference for one of these forms over the other two. The tension over which medium was to be predominant appeared to be based on three basic realities of these pastors' professional lives.

First, most of these pastors were trained in seminary in a very print-oriented culture. As seminarians they read books, conducted library research, and wrote papers as part of their professional degree programs. Even the field-based Doctor of Ministry program that many of these ministers had either finished or were pursuing, consisted primarily of print-based assignments—reading books and writing papers, as these pastors noted during the course of the interviews.

Second, these clergy ministered to congregations that were very electronically-oriented, especially in the relatively affluent community in this study. Many of their parishioners watched television, viewed videos, or used computers almost every day. Most of the pastors in

---

[9]James Carey, "Marshall McLuhan and Harold Adams Innis," *Antioch Review* 27 (1967): 5-39.

this study used computers regularly to research and prepare sermons. Videos were a frequent part of their teaching and even counseling pedagogy. Not one minister denied owning and watching television.

Third, these pastors functioned professionally with communication patterns that were decidedly oral-oriented. Nearly every pastor in this study delivered a weekly oral address, counseled people face-to-face, attended professional conferences to hear speakers and talk to colleagues, and otherwise engaged in oral modes of information dissemination. By contrast, print media were used primarily for information gathering, with very few pastors engaged in regular writing (except for preparation of sermon "notes" for oral dissemination). Electronic media were used less apparently, but the uses discovered were quite creative and considerably varied. The next section will examine more closely how the pastors in this study interacted with these three media.

The Value of Print Media

Eisenstein has demonstrated the profound influences that print media have had upon the way people gather and disseminate information. Among the influential trends she noted were the rise of the library researcher, the spread of the solitary writer, and the popularity of the published author whose works could be read and critiqued.[10]

These print-based influences are also present in contemporary seminary education. Ministerial candidates are trained to use the library (the use of which, for instance, is stressed in one of the thirteen criteria for accreditation by the Association of Theological Schools). Seminarians are also expected to write research and position papers, which are critiqued by peers and professors. While such oral modes of address as

---

[10]See Elizabeth Eisenstein, *The Printing Press as an Agent of Change*, 2 vols. (Oxford: Oxford University Press, 1979).

preaching are part of "skills" courses, there appears to be a print-bias in seminary education. One pastor in this case study noted somewhat negatively this print emphasis when he criticized the "book knowledge" that many seminary-educated pastors brought to the ministry.

Another fundamental factor in examining the print media utilized by pastors is the historical description of the Christian church as a people "of the book." In this study, for example, frequent reference to the printed text of Scripture in the sermons of these pastors was the most visible manifestation of this phenomenon. Of the nearly fifty sermons I heard during the course of this project, the most-frequently cited source during preaching was the Bible (33% of the 552 sources cited). It was often the case that pastors would begin their sermons by reading from the Bible ("our text for today is ...").

Theologically conservative ministers were especially prone not only to read long· sections of Scripture during their sermons, but also to have the congregation follow along in their Bibles. One such pastor observed that his goal in preaching was to "stimulate people to do what the Bereans did and search the Scriptures" (a reference to Acts 17:11). On numerous occasions at these churches, I observed members of the congregation "following along" in their Bibles, whether the pastor had requested them to do so or not. These examples suggest that the prominence enjoyed by the "Written Word" was sufficient to overcome the otherwise oral bias of the sermon.

The one noteworthy exception to this oral bias was the pastor whose sermon manuscripts, which were distributed at every service, read like published articles. The print media features he utilized included such devices as homophones (e.g. a play on the words "I'll" and "aisle" which made little sense orally), frequent citations of other sources, the consistent use of quotation marks which were not noted orally, and the use of complete citations for quoted materials, including publisher, date, and page number. Journal and book titles were even underlined. While two other pastors in this case study distributed printed manuscripts of their sermons, none was as print-oriented as this pastor.

Several reasons were given by the pastors in this study for this lack of preference for print media in information dissemination. For some, the solitary nature of this form of media was not amenable to the people-oriented profession of ministry. Even the necessary "writing" of sermon preparation was a professional conundrum for this pastor:

> I'm too much of a people person to like the time I have to spend by myself working on the sermon. I'd much rather be out there with the people than by myself reading and searching and studying. So, I still struggle with that aspect of ministry.

For others a professional preference for non-print media sometimes combined with a personal proclivity that was often ambivalent. For example, one pastor loved to read, but hated to write. For him preparation, not publication, was a driving force in his use of print media, unless the "publication" was oral.

> Writing is very difficult for me, because part of my personality temperament is that I can never get it well enough prepared and get it done well enough. So you constantly postpone or procrastinate or you read more to get ready. My writing is geared more toward research projects and not books. I can head up research teams [for my denomination], create documents, and do the research kind of stuff, but just the idea of writing the product doesn't appeal to me. It's not my gift. And preaching is no different. Now once my sermon is prepared and I'm in the pulpit, I thoroughly enjoy it, but that is a blood-sweat-and-tears process.

As with many pastors, print media were used by this minister to gather information, but not to disseminate it. Several pastors noted a preference for print media in gathering information. As one observed when asked if he would rather read a book or attend a conference on the same topic:

> I'd rather read a book. You can skim a book to get only what you need. You can scan the table of contents and read the first sentence of each paragraph without reading the whole thing and still get a good feel for the information in it. I like to write notes in the margin too and photocopy sections for my sermon file.

Another commented that he would rather "flip the pages" than "hit the F10 key" on his computer to search for the information he needed. Yet such comments were quite rare among the pastors in this study. Any preference for print media exhibited by these ministers was limited primarily to the acquisition, not the communication, of information. And even this proclivity to print was tempered by a strong reliance upon more personal, informal sources of information.

My observation of these ministers suggests that printed forms of information dissemination were not highly used for at least three reasons. First, there were few professional incentives for using print media to disseminate information. For these ministers, it was "preach or perish," not "publish or perish." There were no local church boards nor denominational judicatories demanding that the pastor write as part of his or her job description, which was not true of oral forms of communication.

Second, disseminating information in printed form was perceived as requiring more time than doing so in oral form. Such print practices as multiple source citations, precise verbatim quotations, and peer review demand a schedule that is rarely possible in ministry, given that oral dissemination is required on an almost daily basis.

Third, writing was a solitary discipline that did not fit the temperament of most pastors.[11] Even given the preference for print that some of these pastors displayed in their information-gathering habits, they still preferred to disseminate that information through non-print media. The need for "eye contact" and "audience participation" that was noted by these pastors in communicating what they found were features that simply were not possible using print media. For example, one pastor noted the considerable "research" he did to prepare his sermons, using a number of books in his own library. Yet, he brought only a few written notes to the pulpit so that he could be "free to hear" the responses of his listeners and adjust his "written" sermon accordingly as he went. Without these oral reactions, he said, he could not "preach at all."

The Value of Electronic Media

Another form of media used by some of the pastors in this study was electronic. By this term is meant those media that utilize such modern communication technologies as the television, the cinema, and the computer.[12] A distinguishing characteristic of these media for this study is their visual orientation, combined with an emphasis on audio in the case of the former two especially.[13]

The focus here is primarily upon television, not so much the computer, as an example of electronic media.

---

[11]Note Roy Oswald and Otto Kroeger, *Personality Type and Religious Leadership* (Washington, DC: The Alban Institute, 1988). Their research indicates that nearly two-thirds of pastors in America are extraverted.

[12]Cf. Ong, *The Presence of the Word*, pp. 87-88.

[13]Also note this distinction in the Fall 1982 issue of *Daedalus: Journal of the American Academy of Arts and Sciences* that was devoted to "Print Culture and Video Culture."

The body of literature on the influences that electronic media, especially television, exercise in the communication of information is quite large, beginning with McLuhan's *Gutenberg Galaxy* in 1962. The following discussion is limited to those influences seen among the pastors I interviewed.

For some of the pastors in this case study the preference for electronic media was limited to information gathering, not communication. A number of pastors noted their need to watch television and movies, for example, because their parishioners were doing so, and, therefore, they needed to be able to "speak the same language." Some preferred televised news to news magazines because of "the time factor." Another pastor refused to use libraries that were not "computerized."

However, for some of the pastors displaying a preference for electronic media, their use of such media was prominent in their role as information disseminators as well. In particular, there were four churches in this community that utilized electronic media rather extensively in communicating Christian truth.

For one large church, the use of electronic media, particularly television as a medium, was quite indirect. The pastor's message was not televised nor disseminated in other electronic media, though he and every other pastor on staff used computers extensively in researching and preparing their weekly messages. Instead, the electronic "bias" of this congregation was felt most clearly in the overall ambiance that characterized the communication methods of the Sunday worship service.

For instance, the newly-constructed sanctuary of this church was decidedly non-traditional in architecture, built "to attract the baby boomer generation" who grew up on television. Not only were there no stained glass windows, no pipe organ, and no large wooden pulpit, there were no hymn books, no pew Bibles, and no printed programs (save for a brief outline). The focus was clearly upon something other than print media. In the place of print media were mood lighting, a sophisticated sound system, and a fifty foot screen onto which were projected the words of various hymns. The church library had been replaced by a bookstore featuring audiocassettes of the preacher's sermons and contemporary Christian video programs. Dramatic presentations, both live and on videotape, were featured in the worship service, and they were used not only as "entertainment," but to introduce the content of the morning message by touching on the same themes.

The one-hour service was divided into several short sections, much like a television program segmented by commercials. The sermons themselves were delivered in a style reminiscent of television news anchors—clearly enunciated, softly spoken, minimally gestured, read from a computer-generated script placed on a Lucite lectern lit by high-powered spots.

For this pastor, the use of electronic media was quite indirect but nonetheless real in his manner of disseminating information. One of the phrases he kept repeating in describing his preaching style was "economy of words," as if to reinforce the time-sensitive nature of television. In fact, a distinguishing feature was this church's appeal to an audience raised on television. Five of the fifteen references to television in the fifty some sermons observed in this study were by this one pastor, whose age marked him as a member of the "television generation." The information in the music, the drama, and the sermons was couched in electronic terms and in a framework congenial to the "baby-boomer television generation" that came by the hundreds to this church's services.

At another church, also rather large, the use of visually-oriented electronic media was even more pronounced. This congregation, though a part of a traditional Protestant denomination, had begun to experiment with newer forms of communication since the arrival several years earlier of a new senior pastor. Part of the transition was felt to be in keeping with the "high church liturgy" that characterized the congregation, since they were already "very visually oriented—vestments, banners, candles, live manger scenes in the sanctuary."

This church featured a musical nightclub for teenagers in the community, complete with a large screen television for showing musical videos. Average attendance was running 600 young people per week, each of whom paid a fee to enter. The youth minister's office looked like an electronic showroom, complete with television, stereo, compact disc player, video cassette recorder, and computer. Several hundred videos used in various programs in the church sat on his shelf.

The pastors' offices were all equipped with computers which were on a local area network, and pastors were not hired unless they were computer literate. The computer program, InfoSearch, was used extensively by these pastors in sermon preparation. A new addition to the church building was being built, and part of the remodeling was to include video monitors at every entrance so that information about church events and programs could be conveyed in electronic format.

The senior pastor of this church talked at length about the "electronic bias" of the modern church member ("we have people with Master's degrees who can't read simple instructions") as a reason for his use of electronic media in disseminating information. The following interchange with this pastor indicates that the key issues that these pastors were wrestling with in the use of electronic media, especially television, were such things as the "bias" and "monopoly" of this form of media in American culture and the ways to use and not to use these media, primarily television, in the church.[14] The discussion of electronic media began with this question about preaching:

---

[14]Note Carey's discussion of "bias" and "monopoly" in his article, "Marshall McLuhan and Harold Adams Innis."

Interviewer: Let me ask you how your preaching differs now from what it did twenty-five years ago?

Pastor: Well, in many ways. For example, the old code language of preaching [which he further describes below] is out of date and doesn't work anymore. It doesn't connect with our culture and our people. I think we're in an incredible time of transition with how language is used. It's images now. We just invested again in more video editing equipment because we believe that's the only way we can do announcements in church anymore. In the new building that we're beginning, when you come in here in eighteen months, at every entrance there will be a monitor on, an information monitor. It will list the activities for the week in the parish as well as video snippets of what we've planned, showing you what these things look like. Okay? For Sunday morning, we are going to be heading very quickly to, instead of the pastor giving three or four minutes of announcements, having two to three minutes of quick video clips showing people what's going on... Just look at MTV. They're the ones that are doing the really creative things with television, with images. That's where we are headed and if you want to reach this younger generation, you have to do it through images, to speak their language.

Interviewer: How has this affected your preaching?

Pastor: I prepare my sermons in images. How can I describe it? I'm highly visual, but I'm very right-brained. What I do is when I prepare to preach a sermon, I literally see the sequence of images, and then I visualize the sermon and I preach the images I see. Now when I preach, it comes across as very logical because people can follow the images.... I honestly believe that preaching as we now know it is a dying art form. TV is the problem, and I believe that it is a problem. Now, problems are things for me that you work with. It doesn't necessarily mean it's a negative, but it takes a tremendous amount of energy to make the transition. I experience younger people who are increasingly value-programmed in terms not only of their values, but even in terms of the media itself in terms of how they learn. I believe, I'm convinced that the attention span is down to twelve seconds. Unless you can create images in your storytelling, you lose people. I probably lose people a lot.

Interviewer: Do your plans regarding the increased use of video mean you will begin to televise your services for those in the community?

Pastor: No, we are convinced that we are a community of worshipping Christians, the body visible. We won't televise because I don't want people to think they can watch church on TV and believe they can get the same experience. We would rather people in the community hear that incredibly neat things are happening here and then be invited by someone to check it out for themselves, than for us to put it out there and have people make a judgement based on what they see on the tube. Plus, I'm convinced that when people turn on the television set they are so accustomed to professional editing and good quality, that when they turn on a cable channel [in any community] to see a church service what they see is an arcane embarrassment.

The "bias" of television was evidenced by this pastor in his comments about how young people learn ("to reach the younger generation, you have to do it through images"). The "monopoly" of television was reflected in his remarks about "preaching as we now know it is a dying art form" because of its non-image base.[15]

---

[15]In contrast, see Ellul's *The Humiliation of the Word.* However, also note the increasing use of the image in various homiletical textbooks: David Buttrick, *Homiletic: Moves and*

This pastor had chosen to deal with these twin issues of bias and monopoly by deciding to use television in limited ways. For example, it would be used as an information delivery channel within the building and as a mental model for preaching (two very different uses), but it would not be used as a public relations device or as a substitute for corporeal, corporate worship. However, the last limit was tempered somewhat by this pastor's criteria concerning the quality of televised church services.

Two other churches in this community had decided to use electronic media in precisely the manner that the first two churches did not, namely by televising their worship services. Both churches were relatively affluent, downtown congregations who owned their own video camera and editing equipment and had lay volunteers in the church who had some professional experience in video production. Both services were televised over local cable television on a weekly basis.

Interviews with the ministers of these two congregations, coupled with extensive observations over a six-week period, revealed two impacts that such use of electronic media had on their information dissemination. First, information was dispensed in a more carefully planned and rehearsed manner than would have been the case with oral media. Second, information was delivered in an electronic media-sensitive manner (i.e., the style of delivery reflected a cognizance of the camera). They appeared, like the pastor of the first church mentioned above, to present themselves as television news anchors, reading or reciting their "scripts" for the camera in measured, professional tones.

However, I was not able to detect any impact of the electronic media upon the topics they chose or the

Structures (Philadelphia: Fortress Press, 1987); Thomas G. Long, *The Witness of Preaching* (Louisville: Westminster Press, 1989); and Thomas Troeger, *Imagining a Sermon* (Nashville: Abingdon Press, 1990).

sources they used. The ministers in both congregations used religious "jargon" that the non-churched person might have difficulty understanding. Somewhat surprisingly, even the topics were not "toned down" for the "user friendly confines" which Postman argued were characteristic of television and that made the use of such media by ministers problematic.[16] For example, one televised sermon featured a message on God as a consuming fire, a topic not likely to attract high viewer ratings.

Perhaps part of the reason electronic media, especially television, were so little used by other pastors to disseminate information may have to do with the "moral baggage" that this medium carried in many of their minds. These pastors, like Postman (1985), may not have believed that television could be sufficiently "sacralized" to be a "worthy" medium for such an "other worldly" message. One pastor, for example, noted how his viewing of a video produced by a nationally-known preacher had convinced him how "television is selling us a worldview that is un-Christian."

According to the literature, some modern ministers view electronic media as having a negative effect upon preaching. Willimon, for example, argued against the image-based orientation of many contemporary sermons because of their tendency to entertain rather than to inform and their preference for storytelling over theological discourse.[17] William Shepherd correctly critiqued this view by noting that neither has to be the case and that storytelling can be both entertaining and informative, as Jesus demonstrated in his use of parables.[18]

---

[16]See Postman, *Amusing Ourselves to Death.*

[17]William Willimon, "Preaching: Entertainment or Exposition?" *Christian Century* 107 (February 28, 1990): 204-206.

[18]William Shepherd, "A Second Look at Inductive Preaching," *Christian Century* 107 (September 19-26, 1990): 822-823.

What this case study did reveal was a strong trend among many pastors to use storytelling in their preaching. This trend may be due to the dominance of electronic media, particularly television, in American society, where the storytelling form appears to predominate.

The Value of Oral Media

By far the most commonly used forms of media to disseminate information by the ministers in this study were oral. Carey noted this natural "bias" that oral media have toward religion and sacred traditions in their conserving, communal, and celebrative aspects.[19] Oral media include dialogue, group discussion, public address, and other forms of verbal interactions between people.

The case study demonstrated how prevalent oral media were not only in gathering information, but also in disseminating or communicating this information. The study indicates that there were two major oral means of communication among these pastors regarding their roles as information disseminators: private conversations in a counseling context and public preaching in the pulpit. The pastor's propensity for oral media is not surprising. Several studies of orality and ministry have confirmed this relationship.[20]

---

[19]See Carey's article, "Marshall McLuhan and Harold Adams Innis." This is also noted by Jack Goody, *The Domestication of the Savage Mind* (Cambridge: Cambridge University Press, 1977); Marshall McLuhan, *Understanding Media* (New York: McGraw-Hill, 1964); D. R. Olsen, "From Utterance to Text: The Bias of Language in Speech and Writing," *Harvard Educational Review* 47 (1977): 257-281; and Walter Ong, *The Presence of the Word* and his *Orality and Literacy: The Technologizing of the Word* (London: Methuen, 1982).

[20]Elaine Lawless studied the oral aspects of the chanted sermons of Southern women preachers in "Oral 'Character' and 'Literary' Art," *Western Folklore* 44 (April 1985): 77-96; and Lyndrey Niles examined the oral addresses of black religious leaders in "Rhetorical Characterizations of Traditional Black Preaching," *Journal of Black Studies* 15 (September 1984): 41-52.

The witness of the Bible is also relevant. From such Scriptural sentiments as "Faith comes by hearing" and "In the beginning was the Word," the church and its leaders have recognized the centrality of the spoken word. The "Written Word" itself displays oral characteristics: Psalm 119 is an acrostic, the Beatitudes are mnemonically structured, Paul asked for his epistles to be "read aloud" to the church recipients, and prophetic visions were spoken by God to the prophets. The emphasis upon preaching, especially in Protestantism, has served to underscore this emphasis.[21] As one pastor observed about communicating Scripture to his congregation, "I want people to have a new hearing of this ancient text." He did not say "a new reading."

In the study of these pastors, the oral bias of their profession became clear in several instances. For example, the interview process itself suggested that these pastors were quite at ease with the oral nature of the interviews. Most of the interviews lasted at least an hour, with twelve extending to more than ninety minutes. One pastor even generalized that "pastors can't give short answers." Long pauses and "I-have-no-idea" answers were relatively rare. These ministers seemed orally facile and ready to respond.

On a number of occasions pastors noted how they often "ad libbed" when preaching by inserting illustrations or citing quotations that came to them extemporaneously. Observations of these pastors' preaching, coupled with follow-up interviews, indicated that quoting Scripture from memory during the sermon was quite prevalent. This reliance upon memory is further evidence of these pastors' orality. In fact, the

---

[21]Note Harry Stout's thesis that the "aural sermon" was the dominant medium even in the literary culture of Puritan New England in his *The New England Soul: Preaching and Religious Culture in Colonial New England* (New York: Oxford University Press, 1986).

publicly preached sermon was the most prominent evidence of how orally oriented these pastors were. For example, only six of the nearly seventy pastors interviewed prepared a full manuscript for their sermons, and of those only three brought the written text to the pulpit. As one explained, "I prepare a complete manuscript so I know what I want to say, but I don't take it to the pulpit because that is too confining. It's too tempting to just read it." Two of the three ministers who did bring a manuscript to the pulpit usually did not read from it—they had it memorized, but they brought it only as "a security blanket"—a rare deference to a book bias.

Most of these pastors preferred an outline to a complete manuscript because they were freer to adapt their message to the need of the moment, an extemporaneous style characteristic of orality. A few pastors used no written notes at all in their preaching. One particular example of this practice of using no written aids in the pulpit was found among the pastors of the church that used electronic media so extensively in their ministry. They used only "visual word pictures" in their heads from which to preach.

The sole exception was a sermon by the senior pastor of this church on the need for the congregation to accept his authority as senior pastor. On this one occasion the pastor read his sermon from a full manuscript because "I wanted to make sure that the sermon was exactly the same at each service and that I not delete any points that I had carefully thought through about the present and hidden congregation." His comment on "the present and hidden congregation" referred to the rhetorical device he employed in this message of talking about a previous, similar congregation he had served while, in fact, making it quite clear that he was really referring to the current congregation. This rhetorical device, however, was displayed with a heavy concession to print media—the sermon manuscript. This concept of a standardized, canonical text is central to print media. However, the concept of a canon is problematic, not only for oral media, but also for electronic forms of communication, particularly those that are computer based.[22]

Even the pastor of the electronically-oriented "baby boomer church" who "read his script" actually used only an extensive outline which he color coded to indicate different kinds of material (e.g. illustration, Scriptural quotation, Greek word). In listening to his sermon at earlier and later services on the same day, it became apparent that he often altered his message, in response to audience reaction, even though the printed outline remained the same.

The sermon was too much of "an auditory event," as one minister observed, to be susceptible to the standardization prevalent in print media. This difference between orality and literacy was evidenced in this pastor's comments about how he used sources in his preaching:

> I need to be very careful with this, but I'm going to go ahead and say it [a possible reference to his perception of my role as a print-oriented researcher and librarian]. If I go through one of these [sermon illustration books] and I find an illustration that doesn't quite fit, but if I could change certain words in it or rewrite it, I'll do it. Now, if it's a quote from somebody, I won't do that. I won't do anything like that. But if it's just a fictitious story, I might be able to change it with a different sentence or two or update some of the really old stories.

This tendency to "change certain words" is entirely in keeping with oral media, but is not usually associated with print, though such lack of a canonical

---

[22]See, for example, Ithiel De Sola Pool, "The Culture of Electronic Print," *Daedalus* 111 (Fall 1982): 17-32.

text is becoming increasingly prominent in electronic media (e.g. hypertext). It is a telling example of how these pastors often reshaped information during the process of disseminating it. Another pastor, who was very print-oriented in his information-gathering role, said that he often "made up stories like Jesus did in the parables" because he did not need to worry about citing sources or quoting them accurately when he preached.

The preference for oral media was noted as well in the counseling role of these pastors. Representative of this oral approach was the comment of the pastor who no longer gave people printed resources when they came for counseling. His rationale stressed a pastoral preference for "people over paper," a theme that was echoed over and over by these pastors. Notice the vocabulary in this pastor's comments that emphasize the communal ("care"), the personal ("their pain"), and the oral ("hear" and "talk about it"):

> That is not what [people] want.... They are more interested in having somebody else hear their pain and at least talk about it and care, than read about it.

This conversational nature of oral media was particularly well suited to the role that many of these pastors played in their counseling. Though printed instruments (such as the Taylor-Johnson Temperament Analysis) were used in counseling, the pastors were much more likely to describe their counselor role with orally-biased phrases. Content analysis of the recorded interviews, for example, revealed these relevant phrases spoken by the pastors about their marked preference for oral media in counseling: "we pray together," "they want a listening ear," "I try to get them to talk," and "I share with them from my own experience."

Conclusion

In this essay I have attempted to demonstrate that all media have value for the Christian communicator. I also recognize that each form of media exhibits its own bias.

Print media allow for careful research based on a textual canon, but engender a solitary scholar mentality inimical to pastoral ministry. For the preaching minister, the book simply brings too strong a bias toward isolation and impersonality for it to be the predominant medium, though these preachers had and used sizable personal libraries, averaging 750 volumes. Not without irony, however, is the fact that The Book is the medium of choice for these pastors.

Electronic media allow for a re-engagement of the senses, but also elevate the artificial over the "real" and bring a sense of moral (read "Hollywood") baggage. Still, these preachers utilized electronic media on a regular basis. Just as Paul began his Areopagus Address with the visual images of the Greco-Roman culture, so too do many ministers draw from the electronic stimuli of our "technotrend society"[23] to reach twentieth-century audiences with first-century truth.

Oral media allow pastors the face-to-face intimacy of information transfer so endemic to ministry, but tend to emphasize the ephemeral over the permanent. Oral media are not generally susceptible to historical criticism or disciplined research. In Homer's words, "the winged word" takes flight too soon. Yet it is this very energy that enticed these ministers to prefer the oral word to communicate the eternal Word.

In the end, I believe each medium has value in the Christian communication enterprise. Sitting here at my computer, let me conclude with a paraphrase from the book of John: "In the end, there is only the Word."

---

[23]Note Daniel Burris and Roger Gittines, *Technotrends* (New York: Harper Business, 1993).

BIBLIOGRAPHY

Burris, Daniel with Roger Gittines. *Technotrends*. New York: Harper Business, 1993.

Buttrick, David. *Homiletic: Moves and Structures*. Philadelphia: Fortress Press, 1987.

Carey, James. "Marshall McLuhan and Harold Adams Innis." *Antioch Review* 27 (1967): 5-39.

De Sola Pool, Ithiel. "The Culture of Electronic Print." *Daedalus* 111 (Fall 1982): 17-32.

Eisenstein, Elizabeth. *The Printing Press as an Agent of Change*. 2 vols. Oxford: Oxford University Press, 1979.

Eliot, T. S. *The Complete Poems and Plays: 1909-1950*. New York: Harcourt, Brace, 1952.

Ellul, Jacques. *The Humiliation of the Word*. Trans. by J. M. Hanks. Grand Rapids: Eerdmans, 1985.

Fant, Clyde. "Out of the Gutenberg Galaxy." In his *Preaching for Today*, pp. 159-173. San Francisco: Harper and Row, 1987.

Goody, Jack. *The Domestication of the Savage Mind*. Cambridge: Cambridge University Press, 1977.

Innis, Harold. *The Bias of Communication*. Toronto: University of Toronto Press, 1951.

Lawless, Elaine. "Oral 'Character' and 'Literary' Art." *Western Folklore* 44 (April 1985): 77-96.

Long, Thomas G. *The Witness of Preaching*. Louisville: Westminster Press, 1989.

McLuhan, Marshall. *The Gutenberg Galaxy*. New York: New American Library, 1962.

_____. *Understanding Media*. New York: McGraw-Hill, 1964.

Niles, Lyndrey. "Rhetorical Characteristics of Traditional Black Preaching." *Journal of Black Studies* 15 (September 1984): 41-52.

Olson, D. R. "From Utterance to Text: The Bias of Language in Speech and Writing." *Harvard Educational Review* 47 (1977): 257-281.

Ong, Walter. *Orality and Literacy: The Technologizing of the Word*. London: Methuen, 1982.

_____. *The Presence of the Word: Some Prolegomena for Cultural and Religious History*. New Haven: Yale University Press, 1967.

Oswald, Roy and Kroeger, Otto. *Personality Type and Religious Leadership*. Washington, DC: The Alban Institute, 1988.

Postman, Neil. *Amusing Ourselves to Death: Public Discourse in the Age of Show Business*. New York: Viking, 1985.

Shepherd, William, Jr. "A Second Look at Inductive Preaching." *Christian Century* 107 (September 19-26, 1990): 822-823.

Stout, Harry. *The New England Soul: Preaching and Religious Culture in Colonial New England*. New York: Oxford University Press, 1986.

Tanner, Thomas M. *What Ministers Know*. Metuchen, NJ: Scarecrow Press, 1994.

Troeger, Thomas. *Imagining a Sermon*. Nashville: Abingdon Press, 1990.

Willimon, William. "Preaching: Entertainment or Exposition?" *Christian Century* 107 (February 28, 1990): 204-206.

Chapter 3:

Rediscovering Our Message
by
Dr. Wayne Shaw

Since 1974, Wayne Shaw has served as the Academic Dean at Lincoln Christian Seminary. He holds a B.A. degree from Lincoln Christian College, a B.D. from Christian Theological Seminary, an M.S. from Butler University, and a Ph.D. in public address from Indiana University. As a part of his doctoral research, Dr. Shaw spent two months with Professor James S. Stewart at the University of Edinburgh.

Dean Shaw has ministered with churches in Lancaster, Dix, and Louisville, Illinois, as well as in Ellettsville, Indiana. He also served as the first minister in churches in Watseka and Bloomington, Illinois.

For several years, Dr. Shaw served as a member of the Commission on Standards of the Accrediting Association of Bible Colleges and as treasurer of the Academy of Homiletics. In 1990, he was president of the Academy of Homiletics during its silver anniversary year. He has served on the continuation committee of the National Missionary Convention, the steering committee of the North American Christian Convention, and the planning committee of the Open Forum of Christian Churches and Churches of Christ and its Missions Task Force. He is currently commissioner on the Chaplaincy Endorsement Commission of Christian Churches and Churches of Christ and a board member of Asia Pacific Christian Mission International and Team Expansion.

Dr. Shaw has preached at numerous conventions and evangelistic meetings. His passion for world evangelism has led him to preach, teach, and observe missionary work in Zimbabwe, Kenya, Zaire, Rwanda, Zambia, Ghana, Liberia, Ivory Coast in Africa, Mexico, India, Indonesia, Austria, and Eastern Europe.

REDISCOVERING OUR MESSAGE

℄ he pulpit is under attack today, but it has always been under attack.[1] Our era is different, but every era is different; so we must face the challenges of our particular era or we will not preach effectively to our age.[2] Since the day the church was born, however, when the Apostle Peter preached the first gospel sermon on the Pentecost following the death, burial, and resurrection of Christ, there have always been Christian preachers with deep convictions about preaching who proclaimed abiding themes that have informed, ordered, and sustained the church's life. These convictions can be summarized as a theology of preaching and a theology to preach. If we do not have a viable theology of preaching, we have nothing to sustain us as preachers; and if we do not have a theology to preach, we have nothing to sustain our hearers.

The purpose here is to address the second concern: rediscovering a theology to preach. Karl Barth claimed that he wrote his works on theology to answer the question, "What is preaching?"[3] Answer it we must, if

---

[1]Clyde E. Fant. *Preaching For Today* (New York: Harper & Row, 1975). Fant devotes a chapter to tracing numerous predictions of the demise of the pulpit across the centuries from the church's beginning, demonstrating that preaching has always had its critics and has always outlasted them.

[2]John R. W. Stott. *Between Two Worlds: the Art of Preaching in the Twentieth Century* (Grand Rapids: Eerdmans, 1982). In a chapter entitled, "Contemporary Objections to Preaching," Stott discusses three arguments being advanced against preaching today: an anti-authority mood; the cybernetics revolution, including the impact of television; and the church's loss of confidence in the gospel.

[3]In his preface to the book of sermons entitled *Come Holy Spirit*, Joseph Fort Newton stated that if we are to understand Barth's theology, we must "hear it all through the question which the

---

we preach at all. But, unfortunately, our answers have not always been biblical, relevant, or even Christian. "What is preaching" is an important question that deserves our best answer.

I have entitled this essay "Rediscovering Our Message" for two reasons. The first is that preaching the Christian message is a continuing process that requires constant study of the Word of God and a growing maturity in discerning the wisdom which is from God.[4] The second is that the best way to restore passion to the pulpit is for preachers to rediscover the freshness of the biblical message and to pass that discovery on to their hearers. Unless the pulpit is on fire, it is nearly impossible to get the pew to burn.

Rediscovering our message means emphasizing some key themes. I begin deliberately with the one theme that has supreme priority. When we preach, we are to preach CHRIST. Paul wrote in 1 Corinthians 2:2, "I determined to know nothing among you but Christ and him crucified." Count Zinzendorf, the founder of the Moravians, exclaimed, "I have one passion in life. It is he, it is he!" Martin Luther declared, "We preach first Christ and last Christ and always Christ. It may seem

---

preacher puts to his own soul and tries to answer, 'What is preaching?'" (See Karl Barth and Edward Thurneysen, *Come Holy Spirit*, tr. by George W. Richards, Elmer G. Homrighousen, and Karl J. Ernst [New York: Round Table Press, Inc., 1933], p. xiv). Also, in the forword to a recent edition of Barth's *Homiletics*, David Buttrick wrote, "More than any thinker in the century, Barth linked theology and preaching: he proposed that theology should be 'nothing other than sermon preparation.'" (See Karl Barth, *Homiletics*, tr. by Geoffrey W. Bromiley and Donald E. Daniels [Louisville: Westminster/John Knox Press, 1991], p. 8). Bromiley stated that for Barth, theology could not be an end in itself. Rather, it has a secondary ministry acting as servant to proclamation as the church's supreme ministry, keeping it in tune with its function as "testimony to the revealed Word of God according to the norm of the scriptural Word" (Ibid., p. 13).

[4]See 1 Corinthians 1:18-2:16 for Paul's discussion of Christian proclamation as it relates to God's revelation in Christ.

like a monotonous theme but we are never at the end of it." Preaching Christ is essential because we are Christian preachers.

But proclaiming Christ has two sides to it. On the one hand, it is imperative that we know Christ and help people know him. James S. Stewart described it well:

> To be "in Christ" means that Christ is the redeemed man's new environment. The human body, by the acts of eating and drinking and breathing, is continually drawing for its strength upon the resources of its physical environment. So the Christian spirit, by prayer and worship and surrender, makes contact with its spiritual environment, which is Christ: thus the soul draws for its strength upon the supplies of power which in Christ are quite inexhaustible. Our primary need as Christians is to know the risen Christ.[5]

On the other hand, it is imperative that we know as much as possible *about* Christ. New converts may only need to have been introduced to Christ and to what he has required of them to become his followers. Much more is needed, however, for those of us who are going to be Christian leaders and spokespersons for Christ. We often hear people talking about the simple message of Jesus, but the message of Jesus is not simple. It consists of profundity on top of profundity and mystery on top of mystery. When one tries to search out all there is to know about Jesus, one runs up against limitation after limitation, like one who tries to plumb the depths of the ocean. But if we cannot know *all* about Him, we need to know as much as possible. When we encounter a Jehovah's Witness or a Mormon or a Muslim, we had

---

[5]James S. Stewart, *A Man In Christ: The Vital Elements of St. Paul's Religion* (London: Hodder and Stoughton Ltd., 1935), pp. 197-198.

better know something about Christology, and only a biblical Christology can counter the New Age counterfeits and other forms of secularized Christianity so popular in the press today.

An incident in Acts 8 illustrates this point. The evangelist Philip had been invited into the chariot of the Ethiopian eunuch to explain the meaning of the passage that the eunuch was reading in Isaiah 53. The Bible says that Philip began at that same Scripture and preached Jesus to him (8:35). But what did he say about Jesus? What are we to say about Jesus? The answer is that there is a flexibility about the presentation of the basic message about Christ in the New Testament, and scholars vary the ways they give their synopsis of the Kerygma.[6] My summary of the mighty acts of God in Jesus Christ is more inclusive than most. Jesus pre-existed with God the Father before he came to Bethlehem's manger; he was born of the Virgin Mary; he grew up in his foster-father Joseph's carpenter shop; he lived a sinless life; he taught as no one has ever taught before or since; he was tried unjustly and crucified

---

[6]Most are variations of C. H. Dodd's list of kerygmatic elements in the apostolic sermons in Acts. (See *The Apostolic Preaching and Its Developments* [Edinburgh: T. & T. Clarke, 1936], pp. 21-23.) In his Forrest Reed Lectures, published as *Disciple Preaching in the First Generation an Ecological Study* (Nashville: The Disciples of Christ Historical Society, 1969), Dwight E. Stevenson emphasized, nearly a century earlier, that Alexander Campbell distinguished between proclamation to the unconverted and teaching to the saints in the assembly of the church. Sidney Greidanus, in *The Modern Preacher and The Ancient Text: Interpreting and Preaching Biblical Literature* (Grand Rapids: Wm. B. Eerdmans Pub. Co., 1988), states the view commonly held today that the New Testament "does not separate preaching and teaching into such rigid, ironclad categories," that in "the same place, both kinds of activity went on," but that "preaching in a missionary situation must have a different emphasis than preaching in an established church" (pp. 6-7). My own view is that all preaching, to be Christian, must have a kerygmatic core, explicitly stated or implied, whether one is evangelizing unbelievers or teaching the saints.

between two thieves; he was buried in a borrowed tomb; he rose from the dead on the third day; and he ascended to God's right hand in glory and power. He reigns in majesty and he guides and empowers His Church today. One day he will come again in splendor and will preside as judge over the whole universe. As his final act of redemption, he will replace this sinful and evil world with a new heaven and a new earth. This is the Christ we are to proclaim; he is to be at the center of our message.

The second key theme is COVENANT. One of the major contributions of our Restoration movement to the Christian world has been to draw the distinction between the new and old covenants when so many have treated the Bible as a level book. Alexander Campbell made the point clearly in his "Sermon on the Law":

There are not a few professors of Christianity who suppose themselves under equal obligations to obey Moses or any other Prophet, as Christ and His Apostles. They cannot understand why any part of divine revelation should not be obligatory on a Christian to observe; nor can they see any reason why the New Testament should be preferred to the Old; or why they should not be regulated equally by each.... Hence it is that many preachers deceive themselves and their hearers by selecting and applying to themselves and their hearers such portions of sacred truth as belong not to them nor their hearers. Even the apostles could not apply the words of Christ to themselves or their hearers until they were able to answer a previous question, "Lord sayest thou this unto *us* or unto *all?*" Nor could the Ethiopian understand the Prophet until he knew whether he spoke of himself or of some other man. Yet many preachers and hearers trouble not themselves about such inquiries. If their text is in the Bible, it is no matter where; and if their hearers be men and women, it is no matter whether Jews or Christians, believers or unbelievers. Often have I seen a preacher and his hearers undergo three or four metamorphoses in an hour. First, he is a moral philosopher, inculcating heathen morality; next he is a Jewish Rabbi, expounding the law; then, a teacher of some Christian precept; and lastly, an ambassador of Christ, negotiating between God and man. The congregation undergo the correlative revolutions: first they are heathens; next Jews: anon Christians; and lastly, treating with the ambassadors for salvation on what is called the terms of the gospel. Thus, Proteus-like, they are all things in an hour.[7]

The distinction between the covenants is essential. The old covenant, as upheld in the Old Testament, is the first act of a two-act play. If we see only the first act, we do not see the whole story.

A few years ago my wife and I went to hear John R. Rice when he visited our city. He was advanced in years but still a very effective evangelist. His sermon about the thief on the cross was delivered effectively, but his content was, in my judgment, biblically incorrect. He stressed that the thief on the cross never joined anyone's church and was never baptized with anybody's baptism; he was saved by faith and faith alone. His problem in interpreting the text was that he made no distinction between the covenants.

The question is this: under which covenant did the penitent thief on the cross live and die? And under which covenant did Jesus live and die? The Hebrew writer says that it was under the old covenant, the

---

[7]This is selected from Campbell's footnote to the first of his concluding deductions in "The Sermon on the Law" preached in 1816. The footnoted statement in the sermon reads, "From what has been said, it follows that there is an essential difference between law and gospel—the Old Testament and the New" (in *Historical Documents Advocating Christian Unity* [Chicago: The Christian Century Co., 1904], pp. 250-252). (It is particularly fitting that a footnote to a sermon be quoted in an essay written in honor of James D. Strauss, a consummate bibliographer).

covenant of Moses. Without the death of a testator, the text says, a covenant is not in effect (9:16-18). We understand his point. Through the provisions of a will, property is bequeathed to others, but it is not worth the paper it is written on until the person dies. Only then does the will come into effect. How do we know that the thief on the cross died under the old covenant? Jesus looked at him and said, "Today you will be with me in paradise" (Luke 23:43). Since he was still alive when he promised paradise to the thief, it is clear that they were still under the old covenant when He gave him that promise. The promises and requirements of the new covenant initiated by Christ's death were not revealed until Peter proclaimed them the day the church began (Acts 2:13-39). The theme of Hebrews is that the new covenant under Christ is superior to the old covenant under Moses. Jesus and his new covenant are better than anything that we have ever known before. Without distinguishing between the covenants, we cannot rightly interpret the Word of God.

The third major theme we must emphasize is the CHURCH. There are two issues to be addressed here. The first is the current gap between Christ and the Church. There are all kinds of people who are for Jesus and against his Church. James Earl Ladd tells about walking through "Pop Off Square" in Portland, Oregon, a place where anyone could say anything they wanted as long as anyone would listen. A man was speaking to four hundred people. "God is all right and Christ is all right," he said, "but to hell with the Church." Four hundred ignorant people cheered! How do you curse a man's bride and give honor to the man? Countless people today will vote for Jesus but have no time for his Church. Even church leaders sometimes have a lover's quarrel with the church because they have been wounded deeply by attacks against their character and leadership.

Because there is a lack of preaching and teaching about the biblical theology of the Church, many church members see it as a place where they can get their problems solved and their needs met. An effective church does address problems and meet needs, but at more than one level. To win the ear of those seeking a church today, one may have to preach to the surface needs of people to earn the opportunity to preach to their deeper needs; and one of their deeper needs, after they understand sin and salvation, is to grasp the nature of the church. T. W. Manson rightly called ecclesiology a branch of Christology. The Church is the body of the living Christ to be and to do in the world what Christ would be or do if He were here in the flesh. It is not merely a series of programs to attend or a variety of activities from which to choose. It is a life to be lived out corporately because we are his body.

Understanding the nature of the church affects how we evangelize. Our particular religious heritage has taught, for example, that when people come into Christ, they automatically become a part of the Church. People are told that if they are genuine Christians, they will take an active part in the church. Statistics indicate, however, that we have not worked hard enough at assimilating new Christians into the local congregation. Lyle Schaller says that one-third to one-half of church members do not really consider themselves part of their church.[8] Is it not a moral issue to invite people to become members of a congregation and not to attempt to assimilate them into the life and the ministry of that local body?

Another key emphasis in preaching is CHRISTIAN HOPE. Alexander Campbell named his journal *The Millennial Harbinger* because he believed that Jesus is coming again, and that to prepare for his

---

[8]Lyle Schaller, *Assimilating New Members* (Nashville: Abingdon Press, 1978), p. 16.

coming, Christians are to evangelize the world. He pled for the unity of all Christians because a divided Christendom will never win the pagan world to Christ. One does not have to agree with Campbell on his theology of the second coming to believe that our churches lack vitality and power because they do not see their life and ministry in the light of the final coming of Christ.

A biblical eschatology will restore a sense of urgency and clarity to our mission. David Buttrick illustrates this point by relating an incident from his days of growing up as the son of George Buttrick, the well-known preacher. As a prank, the children bought a captivating mystery novel, tore the last chapter out, and put it on the night stand in the guest room. Guests would come down red-eyed the next morning. Some of them would be brave enough to ask about the book. Others would go to a bookstore or a library to find it, because not knowing the contents of the last chapter of a mystery novel makes the parts that remain incomplete and confusing. Because we have the Bible, we already know how its story will end. God is moving toward his pre-ordained goal for creation and for the Church.

Recovering the emphasis on the final coming of Christ will restore a sense of urgency about completing the task to evangelize the world that God has given his Church. We have the resources—if we only had the will. God has never given his people a task to accomplish without giving them extraordinary resources for the task.

Emphasizing Christian hope, however, does not mean escaping the responsibilities of living as a Christian in this world. As Christians, we live very much in this world, but we have already begun to partake of the world to come. Imagine this as two circles that overlap: we live in the overlap. We are human and we carry the baggage of this life, but we also see what others have not seen and we have already begun to experience everlasting life in Christ. We walk with our feet on earth and our heads in heaven.

The next theme is CHRISTIAN CONDUCT. It is a cliché, but true, that we are to live in the world, but not of the world. The media evangelize our culture with their own set of values, and they are quite effective.[9] In reaction, much preaching today attempts to legislate morality. There are those who applaud this approach. But I am convinced that it is futile to preach morality without grounding it in God, his grace, and the kerygma, because keeping the Christian ethic is impossible without the indwelling power of the Spirit of God in the Christian's life. We do people a disservice when we tell them to be good rather than to be godly. That every person is to be judged by his or her Christian morality is not arbitrary; it is grounded in the nature and character of God. He made us to be like him and to live like Him.

Paul addresses a problem in his letter to the Colossians that illustrates this principle. The church there had Gentiles who outdid the Jews in being legalistic because they did not have a high Christology. They believed that Jesus was inadequate as their Savior because he manifested himself in human flesh while he claimed to be divine. Since they held that all flesh is evil, Jesus had to be many emanations down the ladder from God; therefore, they set up an elaborate system of good works in order to merit salvation. These were the legalistic church members on the right.

On the left were the "swingers." They believed that since all flesh is evil, it did not matter what one did with his or her body as long as one's mind and spirit were true. They did not consider the sins of the flesh like fornication and drunkenness wrong. Since we have

---

[9]In their book, *Dancing in the Dark* (Grand Rapids: Eerdmans, 1991), six scholars explored the relationship between T.V. and the youth culture. They concluded that "the electronic media and youth are in a *symbiotic* relationship" and they are "dependent on each other" (p. 11).

both the legalists and the libertarians with us today, Paul's problem is ours also: how do we escape these twin evils and live as free men and women in Christ? The secret is to live a Christ-centered life so that our dynamic relationship with the Lord leads us to produce the high moral fruits of the Spirit instead of the works of the flesh. Only in union with Christ and in his power are the high moral standards of Christ possible.

The great Scottish preacher, Thomas Chalmers, wrote a memorable sermon which he called "The Expulsive Power of a New Affection." His point was that one gets rid of an old affection, not by trying to eradicate it, but by replacing it with a stronger one. One can take most of the oxygen out of a bottle with a vacuum pump, but not completely. A successful way to remove all of the oxygen is to put liquid into the bottle to force out the oxygen. A higher morality must always be governed by a higher affection. It is easier to say "no" to something when one has a higher "yes," and the highest "yes" is the imitation of Christ.

Another key emphasis is the COMMISSION of Christ. Passages scattered throughout the New Testament about the Great Commission include Matthew 28:16-20, Mark 16:15-17,[10] Luke 24:46-48, John 20:21, Acts 1:8, and Romans 16:25-27. Paul cannot even offer a benediction to close his great letter to the Romans without praying for the evangelization of the world. But the missionary task does not depend solely on the Great Commission passages. The entire Bible, from Genesis to Revelation, is the story of a missionary God reaching out patiently and redemptively to the entire fallen human race. "The Lord is not slow about his promise as some count slowness, but is forebearing toward you, not wishing that any should perish, but that all should reach

---

[10]The longer ending of Mark 16 has been hotly debated by scholars, but they agree that the point of 16:15-16 is compatible with the other passages on the subject.

repentance" (2 Pet 3:9). The Commission is not optional. The church needs to practice a Great Commission hermeneutic, to read the Bible with church-growth eyes, and to listen to it with Great Commission ears. To turn to the Acts of the Apostles for what it says about sin and salvation, including what it says to do to become a Christian, for example, and to ignore the mandate to evangelize the world is to pervert its basic message. What they preached and taught is an illustration of their obedience to Christ in carrying out his Commission.

The Great Commission has two sides to it. One is the global task to evangelize and to strengthen churches. It begins at the address where we live and goes all the way to the 10/40 window where Satan has his most powerful stronghold today.[11] But we will never build an effective missions program in our churches if we do not also give attention to evangelism where we live. Evangelism is a global task that begins with the dot on the globe where we reside and goes as far as our influence travels. Thousands of Christians are taking the mission mandate seriously. They are instructing and challenging churches, and many of them are going to mission fields. For example, Christian Churches and Churches of Christ have more members and more churches overseas than we do in North America. We also rank third in the number of missionaries outside North America.[12] The picture is not all bright, however. By the year 2,000, we will need 450 recruits to replace

---

[11]The 10/40 window encompasses the latitudes of that section of the globe that is least evangelized. Both paganism and poverty are strongest there.

[12]For the first time in our history, this information is available. The survey was commissioned by the Task Force on Missions of the Open Forum of Christian Churches and Churches of Christ (an ad hoc committee concerned about preserving and revitalizing our restoration heritage). About one-third of our missionaries have responded to our survey of churches and members outside the United States. As of July 1992, we have 4,632 churches reported overseas and 6,000 in North America with 1,200 overseas missionaries.

the missionaries who will be at retirement age. The global mandate is given to every Christian; the task of church leaders is to plant it in the heart of every believer.

The mission mandate is based on every Christian respecting and partnering with every other Christian to accomplish Christ's first priority. Many North American Christians who are committed to the missionary mandate, however, still have a colonial attitude toward foreign missions. They believe that we must help "those poor benighted pagans" in the third world to know the gospel of Christ in order to come out of their darkness and paganism into the light of Western civilization. Implicit in that attitude is a colonial spirit laced with arrogance, prejudice, and ignorance of the biblical nature of the church. As a part of the world-wide body of Christ, Christians must learn from each other. Christian brothers and sisters in the third world have much to teach us that would make us more effective in assisting them in their churches as well as in increasing our effectiveness in American churches as we confront a rapidly changing ethnic climate. There is much to learn from each other in the global church and so much work to do. We need to pray for harvest eyes and a harvest heart, but most of all, for the sovereign blessing of the God of the harvest.

The last key theme is a COSMIC perspective. According to John Ruskin, the most helpful thing we can do is to see something and tell what we saw in a plain way. How does one do that with God's eternal purpose in Christ throughout the ages? How does one talk about the ultimate victory of God over sin and evil in every shape or form? How do you talk about his total redemptive act of creating a new heaven and a new earth? We are limited by our language; therefore, we stutter and stammer as we try to describe the cosmic victory of Christ. Paul was addressing this theme when he wrote in Romans 8:18-25:

I consider that our present sufferings are not worth comparing with the glory that will be revealed in us. The creation waits in eager expectation for the sons of God to be revealed. For the creation was subjected to frustration, not by its own choice, but by the will of the one who subjected it, in hope that the creation itself will be liberated from its bondage to decay and brought into the glorious freedom of the children of God. We know that the whole creation has been groaning as in the pains of childbirth right up to the present time. Not only so, but we ourselves, who have the firstfruits of the Spirit, groan inwardly as we wait eagerly for our adoption as sons, the redemption of our bodies. For in this hope we were saved. But hope that is seen is no hope at all. Who hopes for what he already has? But if we hope for what we do not yet have, we wait for it patiently.

In Revelation 21 and 22, John gives perhaps the grandest cosmic vision ever when he described in vivid imagery the new heaven, the new earth, and the new Jerusalem. He stands us on our tiptoes and allows us to catch a glimpse of the face and mind and heart of God.

To think in cosmic proportions leads one quite naturally to preach doxologically. This is what happened to Paul. After a lengthy discussion of God's dealings in history with Jews and Gentiles (Romans 9-11), he concludes with a poem of praise to God:

Oh, the depth of the riches of the wisdom and knowledge of God! How unsearchable his judgement, and his paths beyond tracing out! Who has known the mind of the Lord? Or who has been his counselor? Who has ever given to God, that God should repay him? For from him and through him and to him are all things. To him be the glory forever! Amen. (Rom 11:33-36)

A cosmic perspective will lead preachers to praise Him and to offer their sermons as acts of worship to God.

A cosmic perspective will also cause the discerning preacher to stick with the great watershed themes of the Christian faith. Two examples will suffice. The dual greetings, "grace" and "peace," appear often in the letters of Paul. They can either be seen as casual greetings or as the deep theological bases for everything else he intended to write. I opt for the latter. If those who belong to Christ continue to be the daily recipients of his grace and peace, then perseverance and victory as the saints of God are possible for every believer.

After concluding his sermon that gave birth to the Church on Pentecost, Peter and the rest of the apostles were asked, "Brethren, what shall we do?" Peter replied with two imperatives and gave two promises that become the core of everything the Church and her members need in order to live redemptively and victoriously in Christ. He said to them, "Repent and be baptized everyone of you in the name of Jesus Christ for the forgiveness of your sins; and you shall receive the gift of the Holy Spirit. For the promise is to you and to your children and to all that are far off, everyone whom the Lord our God calls to him" (Acts 2:37-39). To have our sins forgiven and our lives energized by the Holy Spirit is to possess the core of Christian experience. When one experiences the forgiveness of Christ, the empowering of the Holy Spirit, and the grace and peace of God, the natural response is thanksgiving and praise to God. The preacher with a cosmic perspective who has experienced God's grace will preach doxologically.

These seven key themes represent vital doctrines of the Christian faith that desperately need to be proclaimed from Christian pulpits today. To put it another way, perhaps it would be better to categorize the themes of Covenant, Church, Christian Hope, Conduct, Commission, and Cosmic Perspective as sub-categories of Christology, because Christ is Lord of all of the categories of Christian doctrine and human existence (Eph 1:22-23). At the close of his series of lectures on preaching entitled, *A Faith to Proclaim*, James S. Stewart offered this counsel:

> We must make a point of returning far oftener than we do to Bethlehem and Nazareth and the Cross and the empty tomb, pondering this Gospel in all its breadth and length and depth and height, its loveliness and majesty, its piercing pity and searching challenge.
>
> We must also make time to company with Jesus in the Gospels, to stand with Peter at Capernaum listening to His voice, to kneel with Mary at His feet, to climb the green hill outside the city wall, to run with two breathless creatures to the empty tomb in the Easter dawn.[13]

During a lecture tour in the United States, a student at Union Theological Seminary in Virginia asked Karl Barth, "What truth has come to mean the most to you over the years?" There was silence as he thought for about three minutes. Slowly he raised his head and said, "Jesus loves me. This I know, for the Bible tells me so."[14]

The Christian faith all comes down to that in the end, and that is worth preaching next Sunday.

---

[13]James S. Stewart, *A Faith to Proclaim* (London: Hodder and Stoughton, 1953), p. 159.

[14]Quoted in a sermon by Billy Graham. *20 Centuries of Great Preaching*, Vol. 12. (Waco, Texas: Word Books Publisher, 1971), p. 311.

RECOMMENDED BIBLIOGRAPHY

Achtemeier, Elizabeth. *Preaching From the Old Testament.* Louisville: Westminster/John Knox Press, 1989.

One of the best texts on the subject of preaching from the Old Testament. The author makes a strong case for the necessity of preaching from the OT for the church to understand and obey God's revelation in Christ. She holds some higher-critical views, but is usually sound and very helpful in how to preach theologically from the OT.

Buttrick, David. *Homiletic: Moves and Structures.* Philadelphia: Fortress Press, 1987.

A helpful homiletic for advanced students who will make the effort to plow through his important work. Rather than discussing the character of the preacher, the delivery of sermons, or congregational psychology, he treats the construction of the sermon with a rhetorical-phenomenological approach (as distinct from phenomenology as a philosophical system). He articulates his theory of how consciousness forms in the mind and attempts to utilize that process for structuring sermons. Buttrick is not a staunch conservative.

Cox, James W. *Preaching: A Comprehensive Approach to the Design and Delivery of Sermons.* San Francisco: Harper & Row Publishers, 1985.

An approach to homiletics in the Broadus tradition without ignoring contemporary approaches. The book is valuable for those who believe one should not stray from fundamentals whether one is a beginner or feels the need for a comprehensive review of basics.

Craddock, Fred B. *As One Without Authority.* Nashville: Abingdon Press, 1971.

Offers an emphasis on inductive preaching. Two other works are also valuable: *Preaching* (Nashville: Abingdon Press, 1985) is his comprehensive text on the subject, and *The Bible in the Pulpit of the Christian Church* (Claremont, CA: Disciples Seminary Foundation, 1982) is a series of lectures on hermeneutics and homiletics in the preaching of the first half of our movement's history. His topics are "The Principle of Clarity," "The Principle of Harmony," and "The Principle of Finality." Audio tapes of the lectures are available in the Media Center of Lincoln Christian College and Seminary.

Eslinger, Richard. *A New Hearing: Living Options in Homiletical Method.* Nashville: Abingdon Press, 1987.
A summary and critique of the writings of seven trend-setting homileticians: Edmund A. Steimle, Morris J. Niedenthal, Charles L. Rice's "Preaching As Story," Henry Mitchell's "Narrative in the Black Tradition," Eugene Lowery's "Narrative and the Sermonic Plot," Fred Craddock's "The Inductive Method in Preaching," and David Buttrick's "A Phenomenological Method." He includes a sermon illustrating each method.

Greidanus, Sidney. *The Modern Preacher and the Ancient Text: Interpreting and Preaching Biblical Literature.* Grand Rapids: William B. Eerdmans Publishing Co., 1988.
A more advanced treatment by a conservative scholar who takes seriously contemporary scholarship, hermeneutics and homiletics, the differences in biblical genres, and the Bible as the Word of God. Every preacher who cares about preaching should read this book carefully. At times he shows traces of his Reformed tradition.

Lowry, Eugene L. *The Homiletical Plot: The Sermon as Narrative Art Form.* Atlanta: John Knox Press, 1980.
Lowry contends that the sermon is not a doctrinal lecture. Because it is an event-in-time, it is akin to a play or novel in form. He proposes that the preacher state the idea of the sermon as a homiletical bind and then work toward resolution.

Markquart, Edward F. *Quest for Better Preaching: Resources for Renewal in the Pulpit.* Minneapolis: Augsburg Publishing House, 1985.
A condensation of 23 books on preaching used by a cross section of seminaries. His book allows the busy preacher to survey much of what is going on in homiletics today without the expense and time of reading 23 volumes.

Mitchell, Henry H. *Black Preaching: The Recovery of a Powerful Art.* Nashville: Abingdon Press, 1990.
This is a valuable resource for learning about black preaching (a style that is difficult to capture in writing), and it addresses a growing interest among preachers about how to make the sermon more participatory.

Steimle, Edmund A., Morris J. Niedenthal, and Charles L. Rice. *Preaching the Story.* Philadelphia: Fortress Press, 1980.
The authors define preaching as telling the story. They see narrative as the best method for exegeting the biblical text, for exegeting our experiences, and for shaping the sermon.

Although their emphasis is one-sided, they highlight a method too often neglected.

Stevenson, Dwight E. *Disciple Preaching in the First Generation: An Ecological Study.* Nashville: The Disciples of Christ Historical Society, 1969.

A discussion of Disciple preaching in the sociological context of the nineteenth century. He issues a valuable warning against absolutizing the historical setting and culture of our beginnings, but the major reason for including it here is to call attention to the appendix, "A Modern Vindication of Alexander Campbell's Preaching." He argues that Campbell preceded C. H. Dodd by almost a century in distinguishing between preaching and teaching—preaching for the world and teaching for the church.

Stewart, James S. *Heralds of God.* London: Hodder & Stoughton Limited, 1946.

The Warrack Lectures on preaching by a foremost Scottish preacher of the twentieth century. Though published in 1946, the book speaks as strongly to the world of today as to the period following World War II. He seeks to wed scholarship and evangelism in the pulpit with a strong emphasis on preaching Christ.

Stott, John R. W. *Between Two Worlds: The Art of Preaching in the Twentieth Century.* Grand Rapids: William B. Eerdmans Publishing Company, 1982.

An important book for biblical conservatives attempting to relate Christ and culture in an increasingly secular environment. Stott "bridges" the exegesis of the text and exegesis of the culture in his theory of expository preaching. He faces up to the contemporary objections to preaching and grounds his convictions in a solid theological foundation.

Chapter 4:

The Christian-in-Community:
The Christian Life Viewed Corporately and Personally in the Book of Revelation
by
Dr. Robert Lowery

Since 1975, Robert Lowery has been professor of New Testament at Lincoln Christian Seminary. He holds an A.B. degree from Lincoln Christian College, an M.Div. from Lincoln Christian Seminary, a Th.M. from Gordon-Conwell Theological Seminary, and a Ph.D. in New Testament from the University of Aberdeen. He has also studied at Princeton Theological Seminary and Harvard Divinity School.

Dr. Lowery has served as a youth minister in Ashland, Illinois and as a preaching minister in Dalton City, Illinois. He also worked in preaching and teaching ministries in Hillsboro, New Hampshire and Bedford, Massachusetts. He is a widely sought speaker for revivals, seminars, and church leadership conferences.

Professor Lowery is a member of the Christian Church and Church of Christ National Task Force on the Role of Women in Ministry and is an Adjunct Professor of New Testament with TCM International in Vienna, Austria.

He has published numerous articles, lessons, and book reviews for the *Christian Standard*, *The Lookout*, and the *Standard Lesson Commentary* and has written chapters in several books. He contributed study notes on the Book of Revelation for *The Quest Study Bible* (by Zondervan) and is the author of *The NIV Commentary on the Book of Revelation* (by College Press).

THE CHRISTIAN-IN-COMMUNITY:
THE CHRISTIAN LIFE VIEWED CORPORATELY AND PERSONALLY IN THE BOOK OF REVELATION

"He who has an ear, let him hear
what the Spirit is saying to the churches"
(Rev 2:7)

"... the Ecclesia was a society in which neither
the community was lost in the individuals, nor
the individuals in the community."[1]

"Each community is responsible as a community for its
individual members and for its leaders; each individual
member and leader remains at the same time fully responsible
for himself and his community. This responsibility includes
especially an obligation to discriminate between the good and
the evil, between the true and the false, between life and death,
in a situation where these are readily confused."[2]

It was James Strauss who first challenged me to do an in-depth study on the life of the Christian as revealed in the last book of the New Testament, a challenge which was answered in my doctoral dissertation.[3] Throughout his own commentary Strauss offered tantalizing suggestions as to just how eloquently John wrote about the Christian life,

---

[1]F. J. A. Hort, *The Christian Ecclesia* (London: Macmillan, 1897), p. 48.
[2]See Paul Minear, *I Saw a New Earth: An Introduction to the Visions of the Apocalypse* (Washington, DC: Corpus Books, 1968), pp. 49-50.
[3]"Holy Living in an Unholy World: The Doctrine of the Christian Life in the Book of Revelation." Unpublished Ph.D. dissertation, University of Aberdeen, Aberdeen, Scotland, 1991.

emphasizing that it "is a pilgrimage to the heavenly city."[4]

Why be concerned about Revelation's presentation of the Christian life as one that involves both corporate and personal dimensions? In the West, individualism so pervades our thinking that even in the church we encounter an unhealthy emphasis on individualism.[5] The teaching of Revelation can help us maintain a balance between the personal and the corporate.

What is the relationship between the individual believer and the community of believers in Revelation? The purpose of this study is to answer the question by examining John's presentation of the Christian life from two perspectives: its personal or individual nature and the corporate nature. It will be argued that the Seer is concerned about both aspects, desiring to help his audience maintain a healthy tension between the corporate and the personal. It will be shown that there is a marbling effect, an intermixture of the corporate and the personal throughout Revelation. The study is divided into four parts. First, a brief summary of the Old Testament perspective concerning the personal and the corporate will be offered. Next, analogous studies concerned with the relationship between the personal and the corporate in the New Testament will be summarized, with special focus on the Gospel of John. Third, a detailed analysis of the personal and the corporate aspects of the Christian life in Revelation will be presented. Finally, conclusions will be given reflecting on how Revelation contributes to our understanding of the Bible's teaching on the relationship between the corporate and the personal. Specifically, the

---

[4]James Strauss, *The Seer, The Savior, and the Saved* (Joplin, MO: College Press Publishing Co., 1971), p. 362.

[5]For introductions to the cultural values of the United States, past and present, see the two volumes edited by R. Bellah et al., *Habits of the Heart* (New York: Harper, 1985) and *Individualism and Commitment in American Life* (New York: Harper, 1987).

focus will be on how the study helps in communicating the book's message to individuals today.

The Old Testament Teaching

In the Old Testament man[6] is never viewed as an isolated unit, cut off from others. He lives in constant reaction toward others. It has been frequently argued that one finds in the Old Testament an oscillation with regard to the social unit, either being thought of as an association of individuals (e.g., servants) or as a corporate personality (e.g., servant).[7]

In recent years two conclusions concerning collectivism and individualism have been generally recognized by Old Testament scholars. First, the importance of the individual and his relationship to the community is found throughout the history of Israel and is not limited to the writings of Jeremiah and Ezekiel.[8] An individual biblical author may emphasize one aspect

---

[6]Throughout the essay words like "man" and "mankind" and masculine pronouns are used only to provide smoother reading. Unfortunately, our language gives gender a greater significance than it should possess and, so far, a suitable and easy solution for writing has not been presented.

[7]For further insight on the personal and corporate elements in the Bible see E. Best, *One Body in Christ* (London: SPCK, 1955); B. J. Malina, *The New Testament World* (Atlanta: John Knox, 1981), esp. pp. 51-70; R. Shedd, *Man in Community: A Study of St. Paul's Application of Old Testament and Early Jewish Conceptions of Human Solidarity* (London: Epworth, 1958); H. W. Robinson *Corporate Personality in Ancient Israel* (Philadelphia: Fortress, 1964); and W. W. Klein, *The New Chosen People: A Corporate View of Election* (Grand Rapids: Zondervan, 1992).

[8]See H. H. Rowley, *The Faith of Israel* (Philadelphia: Westminster, 1956), pp. 104ff. who cites Achan as an example, demonstrating that the individual and community formed a single unit. Individuals like Enoch, Noah, and Abraham are singled out and testify to the recognition of the importance of the worth of individuals and of the reality of an individual relationship to God. Yet even though the individual is to be viewed as an individual, he is never divorced from the community.

and then the other, but "both sides belong to the wholeness of biblical thought in all periods."[9]

Second, it is generally agreed that the Old Testament avoids both extreme collectivism and extreme individualism. Individuals are rewarded and punished according to their piety and sin. There is, however, no suggestion in the Old Testament of a radical individualism in which the person lives outside of community. Rowley reminds us: "Every individual had his share of responsibility for the life of the community. He was not merely a fragment of the corporate whole; he was a responsible individual."[10] Every individual is a member of the community. The nation of Israel was viewed as an organic whole; individual members were knit together as parts of one another without losing their individuality.

Thus, both the corporate and the individual are intricately bound up. Together the community and the individuals within the community strive to do God's will. What the individual does affects the life of the community as well as his own destiny, and what the community does affects the individual members.

The New Testament Teaching with Focus on the Gospel of John

Abraham Malherbe offers the following observation on moral nurture in the New Testament: "Although the impression may be gained that most instruction was of groups, in fact the desirability of personal, individual instruction was widely recognized (cf. Matt 18:15; Acts 20:31; 1 Thess 2:11; 5:11)."[11] It is the dual concern for both the individual and the

---

[9]Ibid., p. 100.
[10]Ibid., p. 105.
[11]See his *Moral Exhortation, A Greco-Roman Sourcebook* (Philadelphia: Westminster Press, 1986), p. 48.

community of believers as presented in the New Testament that we turn to at this point.

To be a Christian means that one lives in community. An individualism which denigrates the importance of community is not sanctioned in the writings of the New Testament. The Christian life is highly personal but never merely individual.

In recent years the Gospel of John has been offered as a paradigm for the New Testament's understanding of the relationship between the corporate and personal aspects of the Christian life.[12] A summary of the conclusions reached by C. F. D. Moule will illustrate conclusions recognized by many scholars as valid. First, Moule has argued that the pendulum has swung too far in emphasizing the corporate while minimizing the individualistic emphasis in the Bible.[13] Consequently, he proposes to reappraise the Johannine outlook with regard to the individualism found in the Gospel. He proposes that "the Fourth Gospel is one of the most strongly individualistic of all the New Testament writings, and the 'realized eschatology'[14] which is so familiar a feature of this Gospel is the result rather of this individualism than of anything more profound or radical in its thought."[15]

---

[12]See C. F. D. Moule's two studies, "The Individualism of the Fourth Gospel," *Novum Testamentum* 5 (1962): 171-190 and "A Neglected Factor in the Interpretation of Johannine Eschatology," *Studies in John Presented to Professor Dr. J. N. Sevenster* (Leiden: E. J. Brill, 1970), pp. 155-160 and S. S. Smalley, *John: Evangelist and Interpreter* (Nashville: Thomas Nelson, 1984), pp. 233f.

[13]I will be using the terms "personalism" and "individualism" (or "personal" and "individual") interchangeably.

[14]In using the phrase "realized eschatology" Dodd argued that for Jesus the Kingdom was present, that Jesus taught the reality of the Kingdom as realized in his own ministry. Moreover, he suggested that in the unprecedented and unrepeatable events of Jesus' life "the powers of the world to come" are present and made real. See *The Parables of Jesus* (London: Nisbet & Co., 1935), p. 50.

[15]See "The Individualism of the Fourth Gospel," p. 172.

Moule avers that the whole story is not to be found in examining only the imagery of the temple of Christ's body, the Shepherd and the one flock, and the vine and the branches. The corporate emphasis of these images is not to be denied, but realized eschatology is present on the level of the individual. For example, he suggests that John himself is a symbol of the individual believer who stands in close relationship to Jesus. Furthermore, he cites a variety of passages which focus on the individual (e.g., 3:18 referring to "the one believing" and 5:24 "the one hearing my word and believing"). The emphasis on individuals is suggested in the relationship between Jesus and two disciples (1:38), Peter (1:42), Philip (1:43), Nathaniel (1:47), Nicodemus (3:1ff), the Samaritan woman (4:1ff), the infirm man (5:1ff), the blind man (9:1ff), and others.[16] Indeed, the raising of Lazarus from the dead anticipates the final resurrection on an individual scale.[17]

To focus on the individualism in the Johannine writings must not lead to an exclusion of the corporate nature of the church.[18] Both are present in the New Testament as a whole and in John's Gospel in particular.

---

[16]Ibid., p. 182f.

[17]Ibid., p. 184.

[18]Note the warning by R. Schnackenburg: "For all the claim he makes on the individual, John does not represent a moral individualism or an existential ethics. With all the early Church he always envisages the individual as a member of the Church which transmits to him Christ's instructions and calls for their realization within the Church.... Without the Church as believing and redeemed community, Christian life for John too is impossible of accomplishment. The Church, by its appearance and position in the midst of the 'world', contributes most strongly to affect and determine the being and action of the individual." See *The Moral Teaching of the New Testament*, Tr. by D. Smith and G. H. Kon (New York: Crossroad, 1987), pp. 330-331.

The Teaching of the Book of Revelation

In turning to Revelation we see the same paradigm offered by Moule and others with regard to the relationship between the personal and the corporate. The Seer is concerned about the individual believer who is bound to the Christian community as well as to the community as a whole. He is in line with the other New Testament writers who do not view the Christian life as one in isolation; Christians live in a state of solidarity with one another.

Aside from general observations made by various scholars over the years,[19] there has been no attempt to offer a synthesis of the Seer's presentation of the corporate and the individual aspects of the Christian life.

In Revelation the church is often presented as a body, a group maintaining solidarity against the evil forces in the world. Indeed, the opening verses reveal

---

[19]Three examples may be cited. First, commentators do note the personal element in their comments on relevant verses. For instance, Swete, *The Apocalypse of St. John* (Grand Rapids: Eerdmans, 1906), p. 29, makes the observation on 2:7 (and the parallel passages in chapters 2 and 3) on the call to hear: "At the end of each of these instructions ... is an individualizing note, calling upon each of the hearers of the book (i.3) to appropriate the warnings and promises addressed to the churches." In analyzing Revelation's contribution to the doctrine of divine election and protection, I. H. Marshall proposes that "the messages are addressed not simply to the churches but also to their individual members; both the praise and the blame and the promises of reward and loss apply to the individual members as well as to the groups represented by their 'angels.' Consequently, these chapters are of importance with regard to the perseverance and destiny of individuals as well as of churches" (*Kept by the Power of God* [Minneapolis: Bethany Fellowship, 1969], p. 173). Finally, Feret discusses the balance between the one and the many in his chapter "The Church in History and the Holy Jerusalem," in his *The Apocalypse of St. John*, Tr. by E. Corathiel (Philadelphia: Westminster, 1952), pp. 137-171. His main emphasis is that the individual's victory over evil depends, in part, upon the faithfulness of the Church as well as the influence of the Church depends upon the individual in his personal life as a member of the Church (see pp. 154-155).

that the contents of the book are directed toward the corporate church (1:4,11; cf. 22:16). Furthermore, it is generally recognized that the book was to be read before the assembled congregations (1:3).

More particularly, through the use of several collective designations the Seer demonstrates his concern for the corporate aspect of the Christian life. Some of the more important designations are kingdom (1:6; 5:10), people (18:4; 21:3), church (1:4; 2:1; 22:16), the two witnesses in chapter 11, the woman of chapter 12, the bride of chapters 19 and 21, and the New Jerusalem of chapters 21-22.[20]

In addition to the designations which have a collective emphasis, the corporate aspect is observed in many of the pericopes in which exhortation takes place. For example, the second person singular imperatives used in the messages to the seven churches emphasize that the Church as a whole is in view. In each of the seven messages the church in a particular geographical setting is addressed: "to the angel of the church in Ephesus ..." (see 2:1,8,12,18; 3:1,7,14).[21] Accordingly, the churches are commanded to repent (2:5,16; 3:3,9), to remember (2:5; 3:5), to do deeds (2:5), not to fear (2:10), to be faithful (2:10), to be watchful (3:2), to strengthen (3:2), to keep (3:3), to hold fast (3:11), and to be zealous (3:19).

Words of commendation and rebuke are spoken to the church as a whole. As with the second person singular imperatives, so the second person singular

---

[20]See D. E. Aune, "St. John's Portrait of the Church in the Apocalypse," *Evangelical Quarterly* 38 (1966): 131-149 and H. Gebbhardt, *The Doctrine of the Apocalypse and Its Relation to the Doctrine of the Gospel and Epistles of John* (Edinburgh: T. & T. Clark, 1878), pp. 184f. for discussions on the corporate emphasis of these images for the church.

[21]Regardless of how one identifies the angel, it is recognized that it is ultimately the church as a whole that is being addressed, and hence the various imperatives, even though they are singular in number, are directed to the Church.

pronouns[22] and the second person singular indicative verbs,[23] are used in assessing the life of the whole church. A church may be commended for its work, toil, tirelessness, perseverance, commitment to Jesus, rejection of false teachers and apostles, faithfulness, love, service, and progress in works. On the other hand, a church may be rebuked because of its abandonment of love, failure to do works, tolerating false teachers and a false prophetess which led to idolatry and immorality, self-satisfaction, and lukewarmness.

Yet we must not emphasize the corporate aspect and neglect the individual or the personal. Not only was the corporate church expected to respond to the revelation, individual members are addressed as well. The intensely personal character of the Christian life complements the corporate aspect.

For example, several terms which are not collective in emphasis are used to describe one or more Christians, namely, priests (1:6, 5:10; 20:6), saints (5:8; 13:7; 14:12), servants (1:1; 7:3; 22:3) and fellow-servants (6:11), apostles (18:20; 21:14) and brothers, the 144,000 (7:4f,; 14:1f.) and the great multitude (7:9f.).

One finds a concern for the individual or individuals in many of the exhortations. The majority of the sixteen third person singular imperatives are used in connection with the Christian. In 22:17 we read: "let the one who is thirsty come" and "let the one who wishes take the water of life without cost." This passage appears to be an invitation addressed ultimately to the person who is not yet a Christian.[24] On the other hand,

---

[22]See the use of "you" and "yours" in 2:2{2},4{2},5{2},9,10,14,15, 16,19{3},20; 3:1,2,3,8{2},9{2},10,11,15,16,17; cf. 22:9{2}. The pronouns are used either in the words of commendation or rebuke.

[23]See the second person verbs in 2:2,3,4,5,6,9,14,15; 3:1,3,4, 8,10,11,15,16,17. The various verbs are used either in the context of rebuke or commendation.

[24]See I. T. Beckwith, *The Apocalypse of John* (Grand Rapids: Baker Book House, 1919), p. 778.

another phrase in 22:17, "and let the one who hears say 'Come,'" is in the context of requesting that the Lord fulfill his promise to come.[25]

In Revelation 22:11 four third person singular imperatives are found in which individuals are to continue in their ways of righteousness and holiness or their ways of wickedness and depravity.[26] In confronting the beasts the Christian is called upon to hear the call to endurance in 13:9 or to determine the identity of the beast out of the earth in 13:18. The remaining imperatives are a call to hear (2:7,11,17,29; 3:6,13,22).

Numerous substantive participles, both singular and plural, are found in Revelation describing a Christian or multi-Christians. The most significant of these is John's reference to the conqueror in 2:7,11,17,26; 3:5,12,21; 15:2; 21:7. Individual Christians are also reminded that they are obeyers (1:3; 2:26; 12:17) and keepers of the testimony of Jesus (14:12; 22:7,9). Furthermore, Christians are called upon to be hearers (2:7,11,17,29; 3:6,13,22; 22:17,18; cf. 1:3), watchers (16:15), those who keep their garments to avoid nakedness and shameful exposure (16:15), fearers (11:18; 19:5) and followers (14:4).

There are individual Christians singled out by name because of their faithfulness, namely John (1:9, etc.) and Antipas (2:13). On the other hand, there is the false prophetess Jezebel who is marked for criticism and judgment (2:20ff.). Certain Christians in Sardis had not defiled themselves (3:4). In other churches there were members who were guilty of either spreading false teaching (e.g., those who falsely claimed to be apostles according to 2:2, those who were described as the Nicolaitans in 2:6 and 15, those who held to the teaching of Balaam in 2:14f.) or following the false teachings (e.g., the so-called "children" of Jezebel in 2:20f.)

---

[25]Swete, *The Apocalypse of St. John*, p. 310.
[26]Ibid., pp. 305f.

Words of judgment are spoken against individuals within the churches of Pergamum (2:16) and Thyatira (2:21f.). Images of judgment of individuals are also found in 14:9-16; 16:15; 20:11-15; 21:8,27; 22:15,18-19.[27] The promises found at the end of each of the seven messages are directed toward the individual who is the conqueror (2:7,10b-11,17a,29; 3:4-5,11-12,21).

Special mention should be made of the use of the word "each" in Revelation. Of the seven occurrences of the term, four are found in the context of some type of reward given to, or judgment of, the individual (2:23; 6:11; 20:13; 21:12).[28]

The phrase "here is" often introduces exhortations to the individual Christians to demonstrate wisdom (13:18; 17:9) or endurance (13:10; 14:12). The uses of the construction "if any" focuses on the individual in 13:9-10; 14:9b-11; 20:15. The Christian is called upon to demonstrate obedience (13:9) and acceptance of his fate (13:10) in confronting the beast. He is warned about the dire consequences of worshipping the beast (14:9b-11). In Rev 20:15 there is a warning that each person will be punished if his name is not found in the book of life.

The individual Christian (16:15; 20:6; 22:7) or the individual Christians (1:3; 14:13; 19:9; 22:14) are pronounced blessed if they remain faithful to God by obeying the words found in the revelation, keeping their garments with them, refusing to worship the beast, etc.

Finally, the various lists found in Revelation (14:4-5; 21:8,27; 22:15) describe those individuals who reflect the particular virtues or vices being praised or condemned. They are not virtues or vices ascribed to the corporate but to the individual.

---

[27]Ibid., pp. 107f.

[28]The exceptions found in 5:8; 21:21; and 22:2 are not concerned with the Christian life.

Implications for Preaching and Teaching

With regard to the Book of Revelation, what general conclusions may be drawn on the basis of the observations made thus far concerning the corporate and personal aspects of the Christian life? Specifically, how may our conclusions help in communicating the book's message to people today? Five observations will be presented.

First, numerous designations are found throughout the book focusing on the individual or multi-individuals. All Christians are priests, saints, servants, fellow-servants, brothers, offspring, the called, the chosen, and the faithful. Christians are depicted as the 144,000 who are sealed as well as the great multitude. On the other hand, some Christians are designated apostles and prophets. To be sure, it has been suggested in this essay that collective terms are used (e.g., church, kingdom, people, etc.), but the majority of the descriptions emphasize the personal aspect of the Christian life.

Second, there are diverse themes closely associated with the individual side of the Christian life. Several of these should be especially noted. Although the corporate images of the holy city (the New Jerusalem) and the bride are found in the last two chapters of the book, the predominant number of passages referring to the promises made and rewards to be given are concerned with the individual believers (2:7b,11b,17b,26-28; 3:4b-5,12,20-21; 6:11; 7:9-17; 14:13; 20:4-6; 21:3-4,7; 22:12).[29] Even though the church as a whole is addressed in the various messages recorded in chapters 2 and 3, each message ends with a reference to the promise made to the overcomer. Related to the theme of promise and reward is the motif of judgment. At the parousia, judgment awaits each individual (7:9-17;

---

[29]Note the crown imagery used to describe reward is connected with two churches, Smyrna in 2:10b and Philadelphia in 3:11.

14:9-12; 20:11-15; 21:8,27; 22:15; cf. 22:18-19). Acts of violence and other forms of opposition are carried out against the members of the church (6:9; 7:14; 13:10,16-17; 17:3b-6; 18:24; 19:2; 20:4).[30] The so-called Beatitudes, emphasizing privilege and responsibility, are directed towards individual Christians and not the church corporate (1:3; 14:13; 16:15; 19:9; 20:6; 22:7,14). The moral characteristics of the Christian are emphasized in 14:3-5 and 22:11.[31] Christians are the recipients of Christ's love (1:5) and his redemptive work (1:5; 5:9; 14:3-4). The prayers of the saints are referred to in 5:8; 8:3-4, and possibly 16:7.[32] Finally, the Christian beseeches the Lord to come in 22:17.

In considering the above themes with the view to determining whether the corporate or the personal is being stressed, the concepts of overcoming and keeping the word of God and the testimony of Jesus always have the individual dimension in focus. The themes of witness (2:13; 6:9; 12:11,17; 17:6; 19:10; 20:4) and obedience (1:9; 6:9; 12:17; 19:10; 20:4) are generally identified with the individual or individuals. Both the work (2:6,22; 14:13; 20:12; 22:12) and labor (14:13) of Christians are highlighted.[33] Three out of seven occurrences of the term "endurance" appear in the context of describing a characteristic of Christians (1:9; 13:10; 14:12), while the remaining four refer to the endurance of a church in general (2:2,3,19; 3:10).

Third, with regard to the structure of the book as a whole and the structure of the parts, a concern for the corporate and the personal aspects may be discerned.

---

[30]At various points the hostile acts are carried out against the church corporate (2:9; 3:9; 11:1f.; 12:13f.; 20:9).

[31]See also the warnings to Christians in 21:8,27; 22:15.

[32]So G. B. Caird, *A Commentary on the Revelation of St. John the Divine*, Harper's New Testament Commentary (New York: Harper and Row, 1966), p. 245.

[33]The work and labor of the church is stressed in 2;2,5,19,23; 3:1,2,8,15 and 2:2,3, respectively.

For example, the book begins with a focus on both the collective (1:4,11 referring to the "church") and the personal (1:3 referring to those who obey),[34] and it ends in a similar manner (22:16 referring to the churches and 22:7,9,11,12 referring to individuals). Furthermore, while seven churches are addressed in chapters 2 and 3, each message ends with a call to the individual member to hear, overcome, and anticipate a reward. In addition to the ones referred to above, numerous other paragraphs throughout the book are concerned about the personal dimensions of the Christian.[35]

Fourth, individuals, both good and evil, are often singled out in the messages to the seven churches and in the lists of vices. Antipas and those in Sardis who have not soiled their garments are praised (2:13; 3:4). On the other hand, wicked individuals within the church are mentioned, namely, the false apostles (2:2), the Nicolaitans (2:6,15), those accepting the teaching of Balaam (2:14,16), and Jezebel and her followers (2:20-23). Of course, the lists of vices serve as a warning to Christians concerning their behavior (21:8,27; 22:15).

Fifth, the church is to be held accountable for what the individual members believe and how they behave. It is responsible for rebuking and disciplining false apostles (2:2), a false prophetess and her children (2:20ff.), and false teachers (2:6,15). Moreover, the judgment of any one church will not affect those individuals who respond to the message and remain faithful. Those who have remained faithful in Sardis (3:4) and those who renew their fellowship with Christ in Laodicea (3:20) shall be found acceptable. Yet, the faithfulness of the church does not necessarily guarantee

---

[34]As noted previously the corporate aspect is also found in the reference to the kingdom in 1:6, and the individual dimension is stressed in referring to Christians as priests in the same verse.

[35]For examples: 5:8-10; 6:9-11; 7:1-3; 7:4-8; 7:9-12; 7:13-17; 8:1-5; 12:7-12; 12:13-17; 13:9-10, 13:18; 14:1-5; 14:9-12; 14:13; 15:2-4; 16:12-15; 17:3b-6; 17:7-14; 18:21-24; 19:9-10; 20:4-5a; 20:11-15.

the salvation of individual members. For example, the church in Thyatira is praised for its deeds, love, faith, service, and perseverance (2:19), but judgment awaits Jezebel and her followers (2:22-23).

Conclusion

It is clear that the Seer thinks of the church as an association of individuals and as a corporate personality. Indeed, our survey reveals that there is an oscillation between the individual and the corporate. The two are intertwined. One must be careful, however, in making a clear distinction between the individual and the corporate aspects of the Christian life. For example, does the church conquer as a body or as individuals who make up the body? Does the Christian stand alone in confronting tribulations and seductive powers by remaining faithful? Or does the individual stand with the support and protection of the community as a whole? Essentially, the book teaches that only the church corporate can be designated as "eternally secure," while the individual believers who make up the church maintain their position only as they remain faithful to their original commitment.

Revelation does not teach a radical individualism in which the importance of the community is diminished or denigrated. The individual Christian is always the individual-in-community. The uniqueness of the person is never lost sight of, including his responsibilities and privileges, but it is never the uniqueness of the individual at the expense of the community. There is the call for the Christian to live out his or her faith in a community of believers. Hence, the book's teaching of the person-in-community helps the Christian avoid two extremes: radical individualism where the person lives unto himself and radical collectivism where individual responsibility is minimized.

Biblical individualism always means that the individual is ever under Christ's Lordship and involved in the church. The idea of the autonomous Christian is to be rejected. As individual Christians fulfill their obligations, they do so not in an individualistic manner but as members of the community. Revelation complements the other New Testament writings. In light of the book's historical setting in which Christians were facing (or going to face) hostile and seductive forces, there is the overwhelming sense of solidarity of the Christian community as it confronts the solidarity of the pagan community. On the other hand, there is the emphasis on individual responsibility of the members of the Christian community as they attempt to live victoriously. The believer lives, endures, triumphs, and witnesses in association with other believers. He does so with others who profess a common allegiance to, and dependence upon, Christ the Lord. Communal and individual interests are intertwined. In Revelation the believer would have every right to apply the message to himself, but he must never forget that the words of the prophecy are heard by him as a member of the Christian community. All the passages addressed to the individual are addressed not to an isolated person, but to a person who is a member of the community.

Thus, our study reveals that we cannot keep individual and corporate aspects in watertight compartments. There is interaction and overlapping. Yet one must not overlook the fact that at times one or the other is being stressed. There is the call to responsible individualism always within the framework of the community of believers. A faithful community is the context for the life of faith. No Christian life can develop and remain healthy apart from a community of faith. Revelation offers a challenge to privatism and radical individualism by reminding us that the Christian life is to be nurtured in the context of community. As a hostile and seductive world is confronted, the Christian life is a life lived out in close relationship with Christ within the Christian community.

RECOMMENDED BIBLIOGRAPHY

Aune, D. E. "St. John's Portrait of the Church in the Apocalypse." *Evangelical Quarterly* 38 (1966): 131-149. [I]
A helpful discussion of the images of the church in light of Revelation's historical setting. [Intermediate]

Boer, H. R. *The Book of Revelation*. Grand Rapids: William B. Eerdmans, 1979.
An excellent exposition highlighting the book's meaning for today. [Beginning]

Fiorenza, E. S. *The Book of Revelation: Justice and Judgment*. Philadelphia: Fortress Press, 1988.
A challenging set of essays focusing on the literary character, historical setting, and theological themes. [Advanced]

Minear, P. S. *I Saw a New Earth: An Introduction to the Visions of the Apocalypse*. Washington, DC: Corpus Books, 1968.
A model of sound biblical scholarship, emphasizing the relevance of the Seer's message. [Intermediate]

Peterson, E. H. *Reversed Thunder: The Revelation of John and the Praying Imagination*. San Francisco: Harper, 1988.
This is the finest effort in print which seeks to reveal the book's powerful message to today's Christians. [Intermediate]

Chapter 5:

The Unity of Scripture:
The Theology of Promise
by
Dr. Robert Kurka

Since 1992, Robert Kurka has been an Associate Professor of Bible and Theology at Lincoln Christian College. For seven years prior, he taught Bible and Theology at St. Louis Christian College.

Professor Kurka holds a B.A. degree from Minnesota Bible College, an M.Div. from Lincoln Christian Seminary, and a D.Min. from Trinity Evangelical Divinity School.

He has had seventeen years of preaching experience and a wide variety of ministries, including new church work, an inter-denominational ministry, university campus ministry, and inner city congregational leadership. Dr. Kurka is a regular lecturer for the popular course, "Perspectives on the World Christian Movement," which is taught throughout the Midwest and through Trinity Evangelical Divinity School.

Intensely interested in cross-cultural missions, Dr. Kurka has worked with churches in the Republic of South Africa and led short-term mission trips to a Navaho Indian reservation and to Haiti. He serves on the supervisory boards of the Central Illinois Evangelistic Association, the Christian Student Fellowship in St. Louis, and the Gateway Region of the U.S. Center for World Mission.

Dr. Kurka's published works include articles on "Salvation" in *Essentials of Christian Faith* (College Press, 1992), and "God's Purpose and Plan" and "The Church and the Covenant" in *Completing the Task* (College Press, 1995). Various articles and book reviews have also appeared in *The Christian Standard.*

THE UNITY OF SCRIPTURE:
THE "THEOLOGY OF PROMISE"

"For in him every one of God's promises is a 'yes'"
(2 Cor 1:20 NRSV)

erhaps no passage of Scripture better captures the quintessence of James Strauss's understanding of the Bible than Paul's pithy statement in the second Corinthian correspondence.[1] This terse declaration has provided Dr. Strauss and others (namely Willis Beecher and Walter Kaiser) with a hermeneutical paradigm that not only unites the Old Testament to the New, but provides a perceived exegetical "center" that consciously drives the biblical authors from Genesis to Revelation. It is the purpose of this essay to describe the "promise theology" approach; discuss some of the recent evaluations of "promise" theology; and suggest, as an admitted admirer of this methodology, a modification of the Kaiser-Strauss proposal that attempts to avoid the Kaiser's premillenial tendencies with an appropriate degree of exegetical integrity.

"Promise": A Unifying Center

Traditionally, the study of the Bible has been conducted largely in the domain of the systematic theologian who uses a *deductive* approach that catalogs Scripture under doctrinal headings: God, humanity, sin, salvation, etc. This "topical" approach has an impressive theological history: from the Nicene Creed to Peter Lombard, from Calvin to Hodge to Erickson, many Christians have come to an "orderly understanding" of their faith and the Bible that proclaims it. While this

---

[1] 2 Corinthians 1:20 has prominently appeared in many of Dr. Strauss's syllabi and lectures on biblical theology.

form of systematic organization brings with it many merits, it also frequently becomes a servant to dogmatic or confessional theology by buttressing presumed beliefs that may wholly ignore the intended purposes of Scripture's context. Consequently, systematic theologies may offer less insight into the mind of the biblical author than into the Calvinistic, Arminian, or Pentecostal convictions of the theologians, as they "conveniently" select or omit verses and passages that "comply" with their doctrinal agenda.

Not only does this approach tend to force Scripture into a "confessional conformity," it also tends to create a "trickle-down" effect in which the New Testament *controls* the Old Testament text, thus further distancing the contemporary reader from its authorial intent.[2] This is certainly not about contesting the legitimacy of the systematic task; indeed, theological communication (at least in the West) is impossible without it. What is being challenged, however, is the sequence in which the systematic enterprise is employed. Rather than being, as it often is, the *a priori* "map" that determines what roads we will discover on our journey, systematics should be in the realm of the "discovered"— the *conclusions* rather than the presuppositions of the exegetical task.

The above observations mirror the suspicions as well as the theological contentions of Kaiser and Strauss as they both believe they have come across an approach that starts first with the biblical text itself; that preserves a real unity and balance to Scripture (instead of relegating the Old Testament to a mere supporting role for the New); and that places systematic theology in the final step of the hermeneutical process rather than

---

[2]Walter C. Kaiser, Jr., *Toward an Old Testament Theology* (Grand Rapids: Zondervan, 1978), pp. 10-11; also see Robert Kurka, "The Doctrine of Salvation," in *Essentials of Christian Faith*, ed. S. Burris (Joplin: College Press, 1992).

in the initial ones.[3] Their solution, therefore, is to provide an historical, chronological, and essentially inductive march beginning in the Old and *consummated* in the New Testament, keyed by one theme identified as "Promise."

In Kaiser's classic seminal work, *Toward an Old Testament Theology*, the Gordon-Conwell scholar "swims against the current" by suggesting a center that both integrates the OT canon and explicates the NT's relationship to it. Above all, this theme can be exegetically derived, a definite improvement over such forced "centers" as Eichrodt's "covenant" or Bright's "Kingdom of God." Kaiser believes he has found it in the NT Greek word, *epangelia*, which refers to the idea of "promise."[4]

Kaiser notes that *epangelia* is found in about forty NT passages in which the writers reflect upon the essence of the Old. There is only *one* promise, for there is only one plan of God, although it is made up of many specifications. Such variant features of the promise include:

> ... the word of blessing for Gentiles (Gal. 3:8,14,29; Eph. 1:13; 2:12; 3:6-7); the doctrine of the resurrection of the dead (Acts 26:6-8; 2 Tim. 1:1; Heb. 9:15; 10:36; 2 Pet. 3:4,9; 1 John 2:24-25); the promise of the Holy Spirit in a new fullness (Luke 24:49; Acts 2:33-39; Gal. 3:14); the doctrine of the redemption from sin and its consequences (Rom. 4:2-5, 9-10; James 2:21-23); and the greatest of all, the promise of

---

[3]See G. R. Osborne, *The Hermeneutical Spiral* (Downers Grove: InterVarsity Press, 1991), pp. 263-85. (Some of Strauss's students might even contend that systematics should be virtually jettisoned!)

[4]Kaiser, *Toward an Old Testament Theology*, pp. 33-35. Kaiser readily admits the bulk of OT scholarship has dismissed the location of a canonical center, including such "heavyweights" as G. E. Wright and Gerhard von Rad (pp. 23-24).

Jesus the Messiah (Luke 1:69-70,72-73; Acts 2:38-39; 3:25-26; 7:2,17-18; 13:23,32-33; Gal. 3:12).[5]

With this impressive *epangeliastic* witness as his exegetical guide, Kaiser proceeds to the OT text to defend the NT writers' hermeneutical integrity. The rigid lexicographer will, no doubt, be chagrined to find that the OT does not directly employ the word "promise" as its own key term, but this is a fact Kaiser readily admits; he argues that it is simply the apostle's way of *summarizing* a "constellation of themes" rather than one specific Old Testament word.[6]

The earliest such "promise" expression is evidenced in the creation narrative as God "blesses" both the fish and fowl (Gen 1:22) and then His supreme creation—humankind (Gen 1:28).[7] This term (Hebrew *barak*) serves to integrate the pre-patriarchal narrative of Genesis 1-11, recurring at significant junctures (5:2; 9:1,26) and culminating in God's call to Abraham (12:2-3) not only to be a recipient of His "blessing" but also its missionary. Therefore, "blessing" identifies God's created

---

[5]Ibid., p. 265.

[6]Ibid., pp. 29-34.

[7]Ibid., p. 33. Kaiser also sees "promise vocabulary" evidenced in the repeated use of the verb *dibber* ("to speak") in some *thirty* promising contexts (e.g., Exod 12:25; Deut 9:28; 12:20; 19:8; 27:3; Josh 23:5,10; 1 Kings 8:56; 2 Sam 7:28). Furthermore, several "formulae" are repeatedly found which succinctly summarize the central action of God, notably: "I will ... be your God and the God of your descendants after you" (Gen 17:7; cf. 28:21 NIV); "I will take you as my own people" (Exod 6:7); and "I will dwell among the Israelites and be their God" (Exod 29:45-46). In its most comprehensive version, it read, "I will be your God; you shall be my people; and I will dwell in the midst of you"—a tripartite promise which is echoed throughout Leviticus (11:45; 22:33; 25:38; 26:12,44,45), Deuteronomy, Jeremiah, Ezekiel, and in the NT books of 2 Corinthians and Revelation. Another formula is enunciated in Genesis 15:7: 'I am the LORD, who brought you out of Ur of the Chaldeans." It is succeeded by the even more salvific declaration, "I am the Lord your God who brought you out of the Land of Egypt" (repeated nearly 125 times in the OT).

purposes for humanity and constitutes a "promise" that, in spite of the intrusion of fellowship-breaking sin (cf. Gen 3:1-8; 4:8; 6:5-8; 11:1-4), God will still enjoy a relationship with His most valued creation. The cost of rescuing this blessing will not come without considerable expense to God, as He "promises" to Satan, Adam, and Eve that such payment will be made by the "seed of the woman" (Gen 3:15) through an act of suffering ("bruised heel"). Kaiser is also quick to note the unusual Hebrew (and later, Greek/LXX) grammatical construction in which an individual "he" (Hebrew *hu*) emerges out of the woman's corporate seed and crushes Satan's head—a linguistic idiosyncrasy that obviously points to the singular work of Jesus yet to come, *and* to the future corporate beneficiaries of that salvific act.[8] Christ's death-blow to sin and to the serpent means life for the rest of the woman's seed—men and women of faith.

The second key promise passage in the blessing's ("pre-history") prologomena is found in Genesis 9. James Strauss and others see the promise element residing in the "rainbow oath" that God makes to Noah (9:13-17), a pledge which follows a restatement of blessing (9:1).[9] Kaiser, however, takes his promise theology in a slightly different direction, locating the *epangeliastic* emphasis in Noah's declaration (9:27) that *Elohim* (not Japheth) will live in the tents of Shem.[10] If Kaiser's rendering of this verse is correct, the ninth chapter of Genesis is primarily concerned with identifying the particular people in which God will make Himself known (the Shemites), thereby

---

[8]Ibid., pp. 36-37; see also R. A. Martin, "The Earliest Messianic Interpretation of Genesis 3:15," *Journal of Biblical Literature* 84 (1965): 427.

[9]James Strauss, syllabus: "The Fusion of Horizons: Two Testaments/One Bible" (Lincoln, IL: LCS, 1994) as well as "God's Promise and Universal History: The Theology of Romans 9" in *Grace Unlimited*, ed. C. H. Pinnock (Minneapolis: Bethany House, 1975), pp. 190-208.

[10]See Kaiser, *Towards and Old Testament Theology*, pp. 37-39, 80-81.

preparing the reader for God's call of a descendent of Shem, Abraham (Gen 12), as well as allegedly providing the "tent pitching" motif used in John 1:14 ("the Word became flesh and 'tabernacled' among us").

The keynote and programmatic "promise" passage for Strauss, Kaiser, and most others is unquestionably Genesis 12:1-3. In God's call to Abraham, the theme of "blessing" is once again repeated as well as expanded. Yahweh, in this case, has singled out the Shemite Abraham to receive both this blessing and the blessing of other people (12:3a; cf. 14:19 where Melchizedek "blesses" Abraham). Furthermore, Abraham is not simply to hoard this divine favor but rather is *commanded* to "be a blessing" (12:2 relates an imperative with consequential force) and, finally, to extend this blessing to every "family" (*mishpachah*) on the earth. This global mandate of "blessing-bearing" is seen by both Strauss and Kaiser as the initial "great commission" in Scripture, antedating Jesus' better known disciple-making call (Matt 28:18-20) by 2,000 years.[11] Not surprisingly, then, these two promise theologians have been noted for their strong missions concern and zeal, a passion inherent in their biblical theology.[12]

God's commission to Abraham also recounts and further clarifies a previous "promise element" in both Genesis 3 and 9—namely the theme of the "seed." Genesis 12 interprets the seed of "the woman" in terms

---

[11]Ibid., p. 87. Also note many of Dr. Strauss's handouts, including "Promise and Pilgrims and Journey of Resident Aliens"; "Resident Aliens Racing Toward the Twenty-first Century" (Lincoln, IL: LCS, 1994); and "Promise in Galatians and Romans" (Lincoln, IL: LCS, 1993). See also his Job commentary, *The Shattering of Silence* (Joplin: College Press, 1976), pp. 581-82.

[12]Kaiser has established himself as perhaps the "key" theologian in the U.S. Center for World Missions' "Perspectives" courses, and Strauss has been a frequent speaker at Christian Church/Churches of Christ missionary conventions, "faith-promise" meetings, etc. A current LCC missions professor attributes his own world mission vision and subsequent field service to Dr. Strauss's *theology* courses.

of a "great nation" (keeping intact the individual aspect of *zera* as well as developing its corporate side) and also locates the specific "tent of Shem" (9:27) in which Yahweh will dwell. The Messianic line is now clearly established, and the source of universal blessing (corporate as well as individual) is now clearly articulated. Kaiser further notes that there is one other constituent part of the Abrahamic promise: a "new" element which will "drive" subsequent Scripture in the same manner as the seed and blessing themes—the divine gift of *land*.[13] From this passage forward, Kaiser sees this promise of the land of Canaan as an inseparable component in the flow of *epangeliastic* history, a conviction which he adamantly refuses to negotiate away.[14]

It is here that both James Strauss and I depart from Kaiser. We find his "land" literalism unnecessary, due in large part to the subsequent "spiritualizing" of "the land," notably in Psalms and Isaiah, and to the absence, if not outright "denunciation," of such physical concerns in NT promise reflections.

For example, in Psalm 95:11 the psalmist restates Yahweh's stern warning to the disobedient Exodus-era Israelites: "They shall never enter my rest" (cf. Num 14:11). This "rest" (*menuchah*) suggests more than merely a physical safety in the promised land; a spiritual tranquillity or peace with Yahweh seems to be the focus. Certainly this latter sense is understood by the writer of Hebrews as he appropriates this admonition in both chapters three and four when he invokes the readers of his epistle to "make every effort to enter that [spiritual, eschatological] rest" (Heb 4:11). This same spiritual and eternity-oriented concept of "rest" is likewise seen in Psalms 116:7 and 132:8,14.

---

[13]Kaiser, *Towards an Old Testament Theology*, pp. 89-91.
[14]See Walter C. Kaiser, Jr., *Toward Rediscovering the Old Testament* (Grand Rapids: Zondervan, 1987), pp. 46-58.

Isaiah utilizes *menuchah* vocabulary in reference to both Israel's forfeited "place of rest" (28:12) (which contextually is more of a spiritual repose) and the Lord's "resting place" (66:1) which cannot be localized. Yahweh's "rest" is spiritual and available to all His people no matter where they might reside. One could also think of the same non-spatial notion of land or rest in Ezekiel 11, where the "Sovereign Lord" through his prophet reassures His exiled people that His "sanctuary" [*miggedash*] has not been left behind in Judah but is rather with them "in the countries where they have gone" (v. 16).[15]

In a somewhat different vein, a most convincing case for a "spiritualized" land is ably argued by Christopher J. H. Wright in a fine work, *God's People in God's Land*. Wright contends that in the well-accepted eschatological development of later Israelite prophecy, there is "a 'loosening' of—almost a dispensing with—the ancient family land basis in the future 'constitution' of the relationship between God and His people."[16] This is seen, according to this capable British scholar, in descriptions of the land's *inclusiveness* (e.g., Isa 56:37 where the "foreigner" (who has no stake in the land) and the "eunuch" (who has no family or posterity) are

---

[15]John Castelein has suggested that the "sanctuary" or "temple" theme is also an important aspect of a "spiritualized land" development in the "promise." Jesus becomes *the true Temple* (John 1:14 ("tabernacle"), John 2; Acts 7; 1 Cor 3,6; Eph 2; 1 Pet 2; and Rev 21:22) in much the same way that He becomes the "individual fulfillment" of the other two Abrahamic promises (i.e., seed and blessing). This interpretation certainly has merit and gives real specificity to Paul's claim that Christ answers "yes" to every promise of God.

[Editors: Indeed, Christ was not only a servant to the circumcision "to confirm the promises given to the fathers" (Rom 15:8 NASV), he was crucified "in order that in Christ Jesus the blessing of Abraham might come to the Gentiles, so that we might receive the promise of the Spirit through faith" (Gal 3:14 NASV; cf. Rom 4:16).]

[16]Christopher J. H. Wright. *God's People in God's Land* (Grand Rapids: Eerdmans, 1990), p. 110.

promised a permanent acceptance and inclusion in Israel's covenant.[17]   The "barren" woman (Isa 54:1), another excluded citizen, is also told to rejoice in her new-found inheritance, as well as is the "alien" (Ezek 47:22) who is given a stake in whatever tribe he chooses to settle (v. 23) in the eschatological restored land.

It is this "spiritualized" land, then, that Paul has in mind in Ephesians 2:11-3:6 when he describes God's new household as comprised of Gentile people who are "no longer foreigners or aliens" (2:19) but rather "joint heirs," a "joint body," and "joint sharers" with Israel through the work of Christ, by the Holy Spirit. Wright notes:

> So then, by incorporation into the Messiah, all nations are enabled to enter upon the privileges and responsibilities of God's people. Christ himself takes over the significance and function of the land kinship qualification "in Christ" answering to "in the land," denotes a status and a relationship, a position of inclusion and security, a privilege with attendant responsibilities.[18]

Furthermore, this Gentile incorporation into the covenant promises of Israel is more than a spiritual *abstraction*, however; for like its geographical *type*, the present oneness in Christ involves *social* and *economic* dimensions. Wright carefully argues that the New Testament *koinon* or "fellowship" vocabulary is analogous to the ancient Israelite economic system: both are shared experiences; both express concern for the poor and needy (1 John 3:17); both are concerned with equality among God's people (2 Cor 8:13-15; cf. Exod 16:18); and both convey a prophetic indignation at those who deprive or

---

[17]Ibid.
[18]Ibid., p. 111.

defraud fellow members of God's family of their rightful divine bequest.[19]

Consequently, Wright comments that

> Christ and all that flows from Christ "fulfills" the Old Testament, taking up and transforming it into something that can be the experience of everyman— everyman in Christ. There is thus great perception in a passing remark of the Jewish scholar Raphael Loewe: "the sociological basis on which Christianity rests is not the tie of kinship, as in the case of Judaism, but that of fellowship—fellowship in Christ."[20]

In summation, then, for the promise theologian, Genesis 12:1-3 codifies the seminal promise ideas of the first eleven chapters, and it sets forth a three-pronged schematic which the rest of the OT will consciously develop and eventually see fulfilled in the person and work of Jesus Christ (2 Cor 1:20). Consequently, from Genesis 12:4 to Revelation 22:21, the Scriptures are seen to present a unified theology rotating around a promise involving three *broad* elements (blessing, seed, and land) which, in turn, is ratified in the ministry, death, and resurrection of the "woman's seed"—Jesus.

Upon establishing the "promise parameters," Walter Kaiser proceeds to trace the successive eras of the OT in terms of how each period, respectively, interprets and contributes to the themes of blessing ("heritage" is his term), seed, and land. In words that echo the promise to Abraham almost verbatim, Yahweh "appears" first to Isaac, and then Jacob, reaffirming that

> I will give you and your descendants the land on which you are lying. Your descendants will be like the dust of the earth, and you will spread out to the

---

[19]Ibid., pp. 111-112.
[20]Ibid., p. 114.

west and to the east, to the north and to the south. All peoples on earth will be blessed through you and your offspring (Gen 28:13:14 NIV; cf. Gen 26:34).

All three elements appear in these early patriarchal episodes, underscoring the comprehensive nature of the promise. However, as we near the end of Genesis, we see that the Mosaic author focuses in a special way on the "seed" theme. So, for instance, in Jacob's farewell address, we catch a further glimpse of the future ruler who was promised in 3:15: "Judah, your brothers will praise you .... The scepter will not depart from Judah, nor the ruler's staff from between his feet, until he comes to whom it belongs and the obedience of the nations is his" (Gen 49:8,10).

Likewise, the final chapters of Genesis present the corporate nuance of "seed," as the sole son of Abraham has now grown into the twelve sons of Jacob—a nation in the making—setting the stage for the community theme in Exodus. Thus, Genesis concludes with a picture of both the Savior and the saved.

This complex and multi-faceted development of this one promise element ("seed") illustrates how the Kaiser-Strauss theology differs from Eichrodt's "covenant" approach which somewhat artificially fits the OT contents into a fairly well-defined and static idea. While promise theology sees the unfolding plan of God revolve around three key themes, these themes are of such a broad nature that the theologian is encouraged to "let them take their course" instead of feeling obligated to ignore data that does not "fit" into an already prescribed motif. Thus, one is not constrained to restrict the "seed" to either Christ or the *people* of God, nor is one compelled to define the one conqueror of Satan (Gen 3:15) in such a tight manner that the powerful ruler of Genesis 49 cannot be clarified by subsequent portraits of the Prophet (Deut 18) or the Suffering Servant (Isa 53). The promise theologian, at least in Kaiser and Strauss's view, has the advantage of working with an integrated

OT, identified by the NT's *epangelia* vocabulary, which in turn sets forth a three-fold "agenda" that is broad-based, non-prescriptive and inductively-constructed. Kaiser offers this comment:

> More often than not the [thematic] growth was slow, delayed or even dormant, only to burst forth after a long period in a new shoot off the main trunk. But such growth as the writers of Scripture tell it, was always connected to the main trunk: an epigenetic growth; i.e. there was a growth of the record of events, meanings, and teachings as time went on around a fixed core that contributed life to the whole emerging mass.[21]

The imagery of the tree is most helpful for understanding the "Theology of Promise," for it helps us picture the Bible as an interrelated organism: a "seedling" (Genesis) will grow into a sizable trunk with many limbs, branches, and leaves—all clearly distinguishable parts, but still parts of one tree. Thus, at each stage of its biological development, the revelation tree was "complete" and adequate to communicate God's truth to that generation, though subsequent centuries would undoubtedly illumine things further, if not even supersede prior "patterns" (cf. Heb 9:9-14). Consequently, this *epigenetic* (organic) model breathes considerable life and vitality into one's study of Scripture, while "promise" allows the reader to enjoy the sometimes surprising development of the biblical organism and yet always to have a reference point by which to connect one's discoveries.

Having noted, then, the flexibility of "promise" and its three main constituent elements, we can now better appreciate the Kaiser/Strauss OT chronology which attempts to give an *epangeliastic* summary of each successive historical era. This is as follows:

---

[21]Kaiser, *Toward an Old Testament Theology*, p. 8.

1. Patriarchal Era: *Provisions* of the Promise (blessing, seed, and land).
2. Mosaic Era: *People* of the Promise (seed).
3. Pre-Monarchial Era: *Place* of the Promise (land).
4. Davidic Era: *King* of the Promise (seed).
5. Sapiential Era: *Life* in the Promise (reflection on the meaning of Promise).
6. Ninth-Century Prophets: *Day* of the Promise (anticipation of universal blessing).
7. Eighth-Century Prophets: *Servant* of the Promise (seed—especially the Messiah).
8. Seventh-Century Prophets: *Renewal* of the Promise (blessing).
9. Exilic Times: *Kingdom* of the Promise (seed—both individual and corporate).
10. Postexilic Times: *Triumph* of the Promise (seed and blessing).[22]

It must be noted that the key "promise" themes enumerated for each era merely highlight the most dominant element in the respective period and are not meant to suggest that the other themes (or variations of them) are absent. For instance, although Deuteronomy is heavily oriented around "possessing the land" promised to Abraham, Isaac, and Jacob (e.g. Deut 1:8; 6:10,18), this final Pentateuchal book provides one of the most important portraits of the coming "seed of redemption" as the Mosaic author predicts that the Lord "will raise up for you a prophet like me" (Deut 18:15). Likewise, the Davidic era's obsession with David and his ultimate royal successor (Jesus) cannot be understood apart from the theme of "universal blessing," for indeed the promise given to the Davidic house was a "charter for humanity" (2 Sam 7:19, Kaiser's translation).

By the same token, however, important OT concepts such as Law (or covenants, for that matter) are

---

[22]Ibid., pp. 52-54.

not seen as autonomous, disconnected innovations that are periodically "imposed" into the life situations of God's people but rather as "instruments of God's promise" to have (and redeem) a people for Himself and thereby bring world-wide blessing. The same thing may be noted about Daniel's anticipation of the eschatological resurrection of the dead (Dan 12:2): rather than appearing "out of the blue" as a doctrinal novelty, this Judeo-Christian "hope" also finds its orb in the larger galaxy of the "seed" as well as "universal blessing."

Thus, it is not surprising that the NT writers (not only Paul), speak of a *single* promise of God that has been unfolding since its first announcement in the OT: "And now it is because of my hope in what God has promised our fathers that I am on trial today. This is the promise our twelve tribes are hoping to see fulfilled ..." (Acts 26:6-7 NIV). Yet they also refer to "the *promises* that God made to the patriarchs" (Rom 15:8) due to the multi-faceted and all-inclusive nature of that singular promise. This observation has not escaped the notice of the esteemed OT scholar, Claus Westermann, who saw in the OT an "*unbroken line* of transmission of the promises."[23]

Our discussion of "promise theology" would not be complete, however, if we failed at least briefly to discuss Dr. Strauss's "special contribution" to the *epangeliastic* motif—namely, the NT's role as (promise) "fulfillment."[24] The latter testament justifies its canonical status by proclaiming the "glad tidings" that the promises of God

---

[23]Claus Westermann, "The Way of the Promise Through the Old Testament," in *The Old Testament and Christian Faith: A Theological Discussion*, ed. Bernhard W. Anderson (New York: Harper & Row, 1963), p. 214 (emphasis added).

[24]"Promise-Fulfillment" is identified as the theme of the Bible in James Strauss's massive 1969 "New Testament Theology" syllabus which was intended to structure a book on biblical theology which, God willing, may yet be written.

have been brought to *fulfillment* in Jesus Christ. Two key NT texts come immediately to mind in this regard:

(1) "Do not think that I have come to abolish the Law or the Prophets. I have not come to abolish them but *fulfill* them" (Matt 5:17 NIV).

(2) "We tell you the good news: What God *promised* our fathers, he has *fulfilled* for us, their children, by raising up Jesus" (Acts 13:32-33 NIV).

The verb *pleróo* is used in both passages (as an aorist infinitive in Matthew and as a perfect active in Acts), and conveys the imagery of filling up "a cup or bowl to the brim."[25] In both instances, Jesus is seen as the person who is the "mediator" or guarantor of the OT promise, a conclusion that Paul echoes in the "yes passage" (2 Cor 1:20) which James Strauss dearly loves. Because of the Christ, then, the NT can confidently testify that its message is no less than the gospel *promised* beforehand through his prophets (Rom 1:2), that its Spirit is "the *promised* Holy Spirit" (Acts 2:33), and that its resurrection is what "God has *promised* our fathers" (Acts 26:6-8). In fact, its central figure, Jesus, is the *promised* descendant of Sarah (Rom 9:9), Abraham (Gal 3:16), and David (Acts 13:23). In his classic defense of the gospel before King Agrippa, Paul captured the essence of the "promise-fulfillment" relationship between the testaments as he boldly declared that "I am saying *nothing* beyond what the prophets and Moses said would happen" (Acts 26:22 emphasis added).

In summation, the NT declares that all the promises of the OT have met their "fulfillment" through Christ, although some *epangeliastic* features await His *second* coming for their completion (e.g., the general resurrection of the dead, the new heavens and new

---

[25]R. Schippers, "Fullness" (Pleroo), in *New International Dictionary of New Testament Theology* (Grand Rapids: Zondervan, 1975-78), vol. 1, pp. 733-41.

earth). This faithfulness to the paradigmatic Abrahamic promise was guaranteed because of God's character which he demonstrated in the giving of His word and oath (Heb 6:13-18; cf. Gen 12:2-3, 22:16-18). Furthermore, this Christ-centered promise can never be "annulled," even by the law, for the law is "subordinate" to promise (Gal 3:17-18). Thus from Genesis to Revelation, we have one story—a story of "promise"— with only one notable difference: namely, any uncertainty about God's ability to deliver on His pledge has been once and for all removed in the person and work of Christ (the "fulfilling" message of the NT).[26]

Some Recent Evaluations of Promise Theology

Promise theology has not been without its critics. In his recent work, *Old Testament Theology: Its History, Method, and Message*, Southern Baptist scholar Ralph Smith candidly remarks that "most OT theologians have not been convinced by Kaiser's claims."[27] One problem is that the Kaiser-Strauss approach demands that the OT (and NT) be viewed as a canonical *whole* rather than as a collection of somewhat disconnected narratives and

---

[26]In an outline entitled "Promise in Galatians and Romans," Strauss contrasts Paul's use of "promise" between his Galatian and Roman epistles. In Galatians 3, the apostle connects the "promise" with the giving of the Spirit (3:14; cf. 4,6) as well as with Abrahamic inheritance—which was granted not through Law but promise (3:18). In Romans, on the other hand, the Pauline "promise theology" is less apologetic and more directly tied to the apostle's missionary efforts (Rom 1:1-5; 15:8-9) which are oriented towards both the Jew and Greek.

[27]Ralph L. Smith, *Old Testament Theology: Its History, Method, and Message* (Nashville: Broadman & Holman, 1993), p. 81. See, however, Robert Hubbard's "surprising" admission that "most Christian scholars incorporate some form of this promise/fulfillment approach in their O.T. theologies." "Doing Old Testament Theology Today," in *Studies in Old Testament Theology*, ed. R. Hubbard, R. Johnston, and R. Meye (Dallas: Word, 1992), p. 33.

didactic material—something which is a "given" in many scholarly OT circles. Obviously, contemporary biblical criticisms (source, tradition, and form) are essentially dismissed, if not ignored, if one adopts the organic, *epangeliastic* approach of Kaiser-Strauss. Smith, again, tersely comments: "They [OT scholars] are not ready to abandon the use of source, form, history of tradition, or canonical criticism in doing OT theology."[28]

Kaiser responds by calling his critics (those who are proponents of the afore-mentioned discipline) to "listen to the canon as a canonical witness to itself."[29] He further cautions that

> a text should be innocent of all charges of artificiality until they are [*sic*] proven guilty by clear external witnesses. The text should first be dealt with on its own terms. All editorial impositions designated by modernity (... deduced from broad philosophical and sociological impositions over the text) which can be credited with atomizing the text and deleting the connectors allegedly assigned to pious or misguided redactors must be excluded from the discipline until validated by evidence.[30]

Kaiser concludes his plea for objectivity with this rather pessimistic, if not "angry" dictum: "Biblical theology will always remain an endangered species until the heavy-handed methodology of imaginary source criticism, history of tradition, and certain types of form criticism are arrested."[31]

Promise theology critics are not only limited to the ranks of practitioners of literary criticism, but are well in evidence in Kaiser's (and Strauss's) own conservative evangelical camp. Kaiser's former Trinity

---

[28]Ibid., p. 81.
[29]Kaiser, *Toward an Old Testament Theology*, p. 7.
[30]Ibid.
[31]Ibid.

Evangelical Divinity School colleague, Grant Osborne, is perhaps one of his most charitable evaluators when he affirms the promise theme's ability to unite both the Testaments as well as other biblical themes such as covenant, the Godhead, communion, etc.[32] On the other hand, Osborne speaks for many who are reticent about "promise" as he notes: "Several portions of Scripture (such as wisdom or the Johannine corpus) have no emphasis upon this, and in many ways, it is one aspect rather than the whole of the redemptive plan."[33]

James Strauss, likewise, has failed to win a significant following for his "promise-fulfillment" theology for many of the same reasons that Osborne enumerates. John Castelein, for one, has noted a lack of a genuinely identifiable "promise" theme in the Wisdom books (a general recurring criticism) and has also expressed discomfort with the premillenial notions that seem to follow Kaiser's emphasis upon the promise of a literal "land."[34] It may well be that I am in the minority among current Lincoln faculty regarding this methodological disposition toward *epangeliastic* theology.

In Osborne's widely-acclaimed hermeneutics tome, *The Hermeneutical Spiral*, the author sets forth six indispensable criteria which any "central motif" approach should meet:

1. The motif must express the nature/character of the Godhead.
2. The theme(s) should account for the people of God as they relate to God, their world, and one another.
3. The concept(s) must include the world of humankind as the object of God's redemptive love.
4. The motif must explain the dialectical relationship between the testaments.

---

[32]Osborne, *The Hermeneutical Spiral*, p. 283.
[33]Ibid.
[34]In informal discussion, Dr. John Castelein has expressed these reservations about biblical theology several times.

5. The motif must contain and sum up the individual emphases of the diverse parts of Scripture, such as wisdom, as well as apocalyptic or epistolary portions.
6. The theme(s) should account for other potential unifying themes and must truly unite them under a single rubric. It should explain and balance the others and not merely be imposed upon them.[35]

How well does "promise theology" meet Osborne's criteria? In my somewhat biased view, it seems to score quite highly. Granted, the "Wisdom critique" has been leveled before and admittedly appears to be the most obvious defect of the promise motif. However, I am not yet persuaded by this criticism, for it appears that such a charge may still be the product of a too-rigid lexicography. Perhaps Ralph Smith's comment would provide an appropriate conclusion to our evaluation section. While chiding Kaiser for "almost totally ignore[ing] such topics as creation, cult and wisdom," he nonetheless has to admit that "Kaiser's claims have not yet been disproved."[36] My suspicion is that James Strauss, the Popperian falsificationist, might very well concur with Smith's assessment and invite his skeptics to refute his argument. After all, Strauss would seem to say, "'Promise' is suggested by the New Testament writers, not me."

"Toward" a Modified "Promise" Approach

In formulating my own version of the Kaiser-Strauss promise theology, I am more concerned about the "inherent" premillenial nuance in regard to the "land" element than the oft-noted Wisdom weakness. As noted earlier in this essay, Dr. Kaiser places great weight upon the "*land* of Israel" as an "everlasting quality" of the

---

[35]Osborne, *The Hermeneutical Spiral*, p. 283.
[36]Smith, *Old Testament Theology*, p. 81.

Abrahamic covenant (promise).[37] Thus, the present day Christian is "obligated" to include a physical, Palestine-based Israel (albeit a Christ-worshipping one) in his or her theology. I would beg to differ with Kaiser on three grounds (two of which are included in his own "defense" of the multi-faceted nature of *epangelia*).

First, as discussed earlier, I would acknowledge a "revision" of the land theme from one of geography to a more spiritual theme of "rest" (*menuchah*). Summarily speaking, the Scriptural text itself does not restrict the land theme to geography but rather progressively chooses to "spiritualize it."

Secondly, in Kaiser's own "Promise Outline" of the OT (enumerated earlier in this essay), the element of land significantly fades from center stage following the conquest of Canaan. While the exile (c. 586 B.C.) does promise a literal return to the Palestinian land, it is important to note that only 42,000 Jews returned to Judah (Ezek 2:64), whereas most remained scattered throughout the world, which is not accidental in light of God's promise to "bless all the families of the earth" (Gen 12:3). Furthermore, while His people were in *Babylon*, the Lord made it clear that His "sanctuary" was in their midst (Ezek 11:16). Even Ezekiel's "restoration" chapters (40-48) seem to present a land concept which far transcends the small Palestinian borders—a "new city" which John of the Apocalypse readily uses in his portrait of heaven (Rev 21-22).

---

[37]Kaiser, *Toward Rediscovering the Old Testament*, pp. 49-53. Kaiser contends that Genesis 17:8 ("The whole land of Canaan, where you are now an alien, I will give as an everlasting ['oLam] possession to you and your descendants after you; and I will be their God") makes the land an irrevocable part of the promise. Many scholars contend that this "forever" possession of "Canaan" is more temporal in nature, and reached its fulfillment in OT Israel. For example, see Philip E. Hughes, "The Olive Tree of Romans 11," *Evangelical Quarterly* 20 (1948): 26. The New Testament does little to support Kaiser's permanent land promise.

Thirdly, my own study has yielded an impressive "silence" about the land element from the pages of the *New* Testament (the "fulfillment" of promise). In both Jesus' and Paul's summary of the contents of the OT scriptures, we find the explicit mention of "land" conspicuously absent:

> Then he opened their minds so they could understand the Scriptures. He told them, "This is what is written: The Christ will suffer and rise from the dead on the third day, and repentance and forgiveness of sins will be preached in his name to all nations, beginning at Jerusalem" (Luke 24:45-47 NIV).

> But I have had God's help to this very day, and so I stand here and testify to small and great alike. I am saying nothing beyond what the prophets and Moses said would happen—that the Christ would suffer and, as the first to rise from the dead, would proclaim light to his own people and to the Gentiles (Acts 26:22-23 NIV).

Two biblical themes, however, are noted by both the Lord and his apostle: the suffering and death of the Messiah for sin (the "seed" element in Gen 3:15), and the proclamation of salvation to all the nations (the "universal blessing" in Gen 12:3). Nothing is said about restoring the land to Israel, although when such an idea is addressed to Jesus just prior to His ascension, He essentially "brushes off" this concern and instead utters a command to take the gospel "to the ends of the earth" (Acts 1:6-8). The literal "land" component of the Abrahamic promise appears to have had a built-in "obsolescence"; in fact, the risen Jesus saw this concern as more of a hindrance to *world* evangelization than anything else.

Thus, I have emerged from the "canonical witness" with a *two-pronged* promise motif, as wide and inclusive as Kaiser's, though without the land as an "everlasting element"—an element that appears to be more temporary than this brilliant theologian would care to admit. I do not pretend that my version of *epangeliastic* theology is without flaws or does not suffer from its own form of exegetical myopia. But until someone can more adequately explain why the NT encapsulates the OT with a "promise" cloth, I must stand with James Strauss and make the Pauline confession "in him every one of God's promises is '*yes*'" (2 Cor 1:20).

RECOMMENDED BIBLIOGRAPHY

Baker, David. *Two Testaments, One Bible.* Downers Grove, IL: InterVarsity, 1992.
> Originally published in 1977, Baker does an admirable job in demonstrating the essential unity of Scripture while preserving the individual contribution of each testament.

Childs, Brevard S. *Introduction to the Old Testament as Scripture.* Philadelphia: Fortress, 1979.
> In one of the most discussed (and debated) books of the 1980s, Childs spends less time on the typical matters of introduction and a great deal on theology. His "canonical approach" asks what function the individual books, in their final form, serve within their present context of Scripture. This brings a new "holism" to the study of Scripture (versus the traditional liberal "atomization" of the text), although Childs has not necessarily given up some of the "old" historical critical assumptions.

Dodd, C. H. *According to the Scriptures: The Substructure of New Testament Theology.* London: Nisbet, 1952.
> A comparatively small volume, but one which, nevertheless, provides a valuable discussion of major Old Testament themes in the New, as well on how the Old Testament is used in New Testament theology. It is a stimulating treatise, although it is marked by Dodd's tendency to overstate his evidence.

Eichrodt, Walter. *Theology of the Old Testament.* Translated by J. A. Baker. 2 Vols. Philadelphia: Westminster, 1961, 1967.
> This is the classic statement of a "synchronic" approach to OT theology (and its relationship to the New), as the author proposes a centering theme of "covenant." This is one of the "Landmark" OT theologies to appear in the twentieth century (Von Rad is the other) and often reflects the neo-orthodoxy of Barth as much as the text of Scripture.

Fuller, Daniel P. *The Unity of the Bible.* Grand Rapids: Zondervan, 1992.
> This long-time professor at Fuller Seminary has brought together over thirty years of his classroom notes and previous writings in this one volume. Through an inductive, chronological approach (allegedly established in Peter's Pentecost sermon), Fuller attempts to demonstrate that the "plan of God" integrates the pages of Scripture from Genesis to Revelation. Fuller

displays a profound insight into the missiological character of God's special revelation.

Goppelt, Leonard. *A Theology of the New Testament.* 2 vols. Grand Rapids: Eerdmans, 1981-82.

Goppelt's volumes give an immense amount of data and insight into the discipline of biblical theology, especially in its understanding of "salvation" as a dynamic, historically developing concept. Somewhat marked by German historical critical assumptions, Goppelt's work, nonetheless, is a carefully written and generally balanced paradigm of the methodology Dr. Strauss would propose in studying Scripture.

Hasel, Gerhard F. *Old Testament Theology: Basic Issues in the Current Debate.* 3rd ed. Grand Rapids: Eerdmans, 1982.

This volume gives a rather comprehensive survey of the major approaches that are currently "in vogue" in OT theology. He offers fair and insightful critiques of Eichrodt, Von Rad, and Childs although I am disappointed in Hasel's denial of an unifying center in the OT, and his advocacy of a multiplex of (seemingly disconnected) themes.

Kaiser, Walter C., Jr. *Toward an Old Testament Theology.* Grand Rapids: Zondervan, 1978.

Kaiser contends that an exegetically-derived canonical center to Scripture can be found in *epangelia* ("promise"). While the author's thesis has not received as wide an acceptance as I anticipated, there have been very few definitive rejoinders to "promise" and even fewer genuine alternatives.

Osborne, Grant R. *The Hermeneutical Spiral.* Downers Grove, IL: InterVarsity, 1991.

Although this volume is primarily a hermeneutics text, not a biblical theology, it is nonetheless one of the finest works in print in analyzing the components of that discipline and how one moves from a biblical to systematic theology. This book should be read prior to attempting an evaluation of "promise," "covenant," or any other biblical theology approach.

Rad, Gerhard von. *Old Testament Theology.* 2 vols. New York: Harper & Row, 1962-65.

The second of the "Landmark" OT theologies produced in this century, Von Rad proposes a *diachronic* method (in contrast to Eichrodt) to studying the developments of Scripture; he offers an analysis of traditions as they are constructed and applied from generation to generation. This book, also, is the product of a neó-orthodox epistemology, and it reduces the study of the biblical text to a "history of religions" (evolutionary) program.

Strauss, James D. "God's Promise and Universal History." In *Grace Unlimited*. Edited by Clark H. Pinnock. Minneapolis: Bethany House, 1975.

In searching for a representative piece of Dr. Strauss's employment of "promise theology," the reader would perhaps be best served by reading this *Grace Unlimited* presentation. Although this chapter is not a thorough-going treatment of the *epangeliastic* theme, it does, nonetheless, well illustrate the author's biblical theology approach. Paul's treatment of Israel's place in God's redemptive history is summarized (at least for Strauss) by the word "promise."

Terrien, Samuel. *The Elusive Presence: Toward a New Biblical Theology*. San Francisco: Harper & Row, 1978.

In contrast to Eichrodt's scriptural "center" in "covenant," Terrien suggests the theme of "God's elusive presence." While God's presence brings comprehension to our human existence, it is a presence that is also "concealed" (in the Old Testament) so that He will not be "reduced" by his creatures. An interesting, though somewhat "bizarre" thesis, especially for a canonical center.

A "Promise" Time-Line

Gen 3:15 Promised seed of woman	**Gen 9** Rainbow Promise	**Gen 2:1ff** Promise to Abraham 2000 B.C.	**Gen 26:2-5** Promise to Isaac 1900 B.C.
Gen 35:9-10 Promise to Jacob 1750 B.C.	**Ex 6:2-8; 19:3-8** Promise to the nation of Israel 1440 B.C.	**Num 14:10-12** God about to destroy Israelites and make a nation thru Moses 1440 B.C.	**Deut 25:1-15** Promise given to next generation of Israel 1440 B.C.
2 Sam 7 Promise to David 1000 B.C.	**Joel 2:28-32** Promise of the Spirit and salvation 800 B.C.?	**Micah 5:2-5** Promise of a ruler who is ancient and will bring peace 750 B.C.	**Isa 9:6-7** A promised child: Almighty God and Prince of Peace 725 B.C.
Isa 37-66 Promise of Messiah; Israel to serve as light to nations 722 B.C.	**Ezek 34:20-31** Promise of one Shepherd and a covenant of peace 537 B.C.	**Dan 2:44-45; 7:27** Promise of an eternal kingdom 520 B.C.	**Dan 12:1** Promise of a Resurrection 520 B.C.
Lk 2:6-7,10-14 Jesus is born and praised c. 6 B.C.	**Matt, Mk, Lk, John** Jesus' ministry, death, resurrection, ascension, pentecost A.D. 29-33	**Acts 2:14-39** Joel's promise is fulfilled at Pentecost; the promise is for all who are called A.D. 33	**Gal 3** Christ Jesus is the seed promised by God; by faith is one a child of Abraham A.D. 49
2 Cor 1:20 All promises fulfilled in Christ A.D. 56	**Rom 4, 9-11** Faith in Christ realizes the promise; faith makes one a part of true Israel	**Phlm. 2:9-1** Christ is the cosmic ruler A.D. 62	**2 Pet 3:4-13** Rainbow promise holds, but Christ's return is promised A.D. 65

Chapter 6:

Speaking to Other Worlds:
Multicultural America
by
Dr. Roger Edrington

Roger Edrington is the Executive Vice President and Director of Multi-Cultural Education at San Jose Christian College, San Jose, California. The multi-cultural training program seeks to educate emerging church leaders of many ethnic groups. His cross-cultural emphasis has helped the college student body move from being predominantly European-American to one of fifty percent ethnic groups other than European-American.

For twelve years, Dr. Edrington labored as a missionary in England and helped in establishing Springdale College, a theological college for ministers and lay persons in Birmingham, England.

As a consultant for Food for the Hungry International, Dr. Edrington worked on a research project to ensure "no more Ethiopian famines." The work involved interacting with the directors of many governmental, non-governmental, and inter-governmental relief agencies in Ethiopia, Sudan, Kenya, and Europe.

Dr. Edrington received his B.A. and M.Div. degrees from Lincoln Christian College and Seminary respectively and his Ph.D. in theology from the University of Birmingham in England. His doctoral thesis was published as *Everyday Men: Living in a Climate of Unbelief*, which examines unbelief within the English working class and how they might be reached for Christ.

His published articles have appeared in *The Lookout, The Christian Standard, Purpose,* and *The San Jose Mercury News.*

SPEAKING TO OTHER WORLDS: MULTICULTURAL AMERICA

"If you're not thinking ethnically in America, you're not thinking at all."

Jesus, of course, already told us to think ethnically when he commissioned his disciples for service to all the ethnic groups, but these words have been forgotten and remembered numerous times in church history. Even in the middle of his mission, Peter forgot this commission a few times, but God always brought him back to that great truth that the good news is for *all* people and that absolutizing customs and cultural patterns is not a mark of Christian discipleship (Acts 10; Gal 2:11-21).

> Christ commanded the church to make disciples of *panta ta ethne*, all the peoples. Not to Anglo-Americanize them or make them behave like white middle-class Protestants, but rather to disciple them within their cultures, transformationally, until all areas of their lives have been leavened by the gospel.[1]

While American Christians have often been leaders in sending the gospel to lands beyond, they have been strangely reluctant to deal with the peoples of varied cultural heritages on their own shores. Mission was clear in those early days when white American Christians sent missionaries off to dark-skinned natives of other lands. The problems have come when those same dark-skinned natives along with olive-toned Orientals and bronzed-colored Latinos have joined the

---

[1]Roger S. Greenway and Timothy M. Monsma, *Cities, Missions' New Frontier* (Grand Rapids: Baker, 1989), p. 81.

white-skinned Europeans as partners in the American dream.

America is no longer the same as it was in 1908 when Israel Zangwill wrote:

> America is God's Crucible, the great Melting-Pot where all the races of Europe are melting and re-forming.... Germans and Frenchmen, Irishmen and Englishmen, Jews and Russians—into the Crucible with you all! God is making the American![2]

If God was at work firing up His steel melting pot at the turn of this century, the end of this century is signaling a new recipe for making Americans. What is God at work doing? Could he be stirring up a new multi-cultural nation, a country which looks more like the apocalyptic heavenly goal—"a great multitude that no one could count, from every nation, tribe, people and language" (Rev 7:9 NIV)—than a mono-cultural one could ever be?

One American in four already describes himself or herself as Hispanic or non-white. By the end of this century, if all the ethnic groups continue growing at their current rate, there will be 22% more Asians and 21% more Hispanics in the USA. African-Americans will have increased by about 12% while European-Americans, today's dominant culture, will increase by only 2%.[3] Our world and our home mission field are changing.

America: A Microcosm of the World

"Once America was a microcosm of European nationalities. Today America is a microcosm of the world."[4] America speaks 636 languages and dialects and

---

[2]Tom Morganthau, "America: Still A Melting Pot?" *Newsweek* 122 (August 9, 1993): 16.
[3]William A. Henry III, "Beyond the Melting Pot," *Time* 139 (April 9, 1990): 28.
[4]Henry, "Beyond the Melting Pot," p. 29.

is made up of 500 ethnic groups.[5]   If you do not lump European nationalities together, America has no majority at all.   Even in 1980 statistics:

> The largest single identifiable ethnic strain are people of British ancestry—who make up just 15% of the American population. They barely outnumber German Americans (13%) or blacks (11%). Millions of Americans cannot identify themselves at all ethnically, due to intermixture over the generations.[6]

California leads the way in becoming the *most diverse* and, if you can see it that way, the *most beautiful* blend of peoples and cultures. "By the year 2000, California will have become the world's first 100% minority modern economy."[7]   Since California is already the sixth largest economy in the world,[8] this shift in ethnic groups is vitally significant.

In California during the next decade, four out of five of the new residents will be Hispanic or Asian. The nonwhite and Hispanic students in California already comprise more than half of the students in the school systems.   According to a California Department of Finance study, by 2040 California is expected to be 50% Hispanic, 32% European-American, 6% African-American, and 12% Asians, American Indians, and Pacific Islanders.[9]   This "browning of America" is already obvious in San Jose, California, where I work, with few

---

[5]Oscar Romo, *American Mosaic: Church Planting in Ethnic America* (Nashville: Broadman Press, 1993), p. 44.

[6]Thomas Sowell, *Ethnic America* (New York: Basic Books, 1981), p. 3.

[7]Richard Carlson and Bruce Goldman, *2020 Vision: Long View of a Changing World* (Stanford: Stanford Alumni Association, 1991), p. 64.

[8]Based on 1988-89 statistics in John Clements, *California Facts* (Dallas: Clements Research II, 1989), pp. 1,5.

[9]Marilyn Lewis, "Twice-as-Crowded State is Forecast," *San Jose Mercury News* (April 14, 1993): 1.

cultural groups *un*represented. *Time* magazine announced in 1990 that the San Jose telephone book listed 14 columns of Nguyens (a Vietnamese surname) while only eight columns of Joneses.[10] In 1993 there are 19 columns of Nguyens and only seven columns of Joneses. Los Angeles in the twenty-first century is expected to be "home to more races, religions, cultures, languages, and people than any other city in the world."[11]

Christians may seize the opportunities and gain from the merits of all these peoples and cultures, *or* they may live even in the most diverse areas and be little affected by this new mix of cultures. Churches find it quite easy, just like some of the earliest Jewish churches, to ignore those from other cultural backgrounds. But they do so at great loss to Christ and His church.

The Rise of the Pacific Rim

The rise of the Pacific Rim as the world's trade center is shifting the way America does business. John Naisbitt describes the magnitude of this "economic miracle of Asia":

> Asia's Pacific Rim region is twice as large as Europe and the United States. Today Asia has half of the world's population. By the year 2000 it will have two-thirds, while Europe will have only 6 percent. Asia is a $3 trillion market growing at the rate of $3 billion a week. Any way you measure it, geographically, demographically, or economically, the Pacific Rim is a powerful global presence.[12]

---

[10]Henry, "Beyond the Melting Pot," p. 29.

[11]Zena Pearlstone, *Ethnic Los Angeles* (Beverly Hills, CA: Hillcrest Press, 1990), p. 39; cited in Oscar Romo, *American Mosaic*, p. 56.

[12]John Naisbitt, *Megatrends 2000* (New York: William Morrow Publishers, 1990), p. 178.

Naisbitt further describes the Pacific Rim as "emerging like a dynamic young America but on a much grander scale."[13] This becomes even more interesting when this "dynamic young America" immigrates to America to become Chinese-Americans, Korean-Americans, Cambodian-Americans, Vietnamese-Americans, and other Asian-Americans. The prophecy of John Hay, U.S. Secretary of State at the turn of the last century, has been fulfilled: "The Mediterranean is the ocean of the past, the Atlantic the ocean of the present, the Pacific the ocean of the future."[14] What this means is that the growing prominence of the Pacific Rim should now affect the way Christians carry out their Father's business.

The influential shift toward the Pacific Rim is not only economic, it is cultural. These countries use more than 1,000 languages and have among the most varied religious and cultural traditions in the world.[15] This cultural influence will have an impact on American society and it should affect how Christians involve themselves in cross-cultural evangelism to Asian-Americans and Asians in their own countries.

The fact that the Pacific Rim countries also have a greater commitment to higher education than the USA or Western Europe[16] will impact Christian education. Since many "Asian Americans take advantage of

---

[13]Naisbitt, *Megatrends 2000*, p. 178.
[14]Naisbitt, *Megatrends 2000*, p. 179.
[15]Ibid.
[16]Don Shinn uses statistical measurements to show that educational attainment is more important to well-being in Korea than in America. "People in Korea, like the Chinese and Japanese, whose culture has been dominated by Confucian ethics, still believe strongly that a good quality of life cannot be attained without higher education.... For the same reason, newly arrived Asian-Americans are represented far beyond their population share at virtually every top-ranking university in this country." See Shinn's "Education and the Quality of Life in Korea and the United States: A Cross-Cultural Perspective," *Public Opinion Quarterly* 50 (1986): 368.

America's propensity to redistribute wealth in the form of education—the kind that really counts in an information intensive world"[17]—Christian education may need to be evangelistic *educationally* as well as offer ministry-training. Many of the peoples of Asia come to the USA as adherents of non-Christian religions, but many also come as Christians. Korean-American Christians are influencing Christians of other ethnic groups through their highly-committed prayer patterns, their spiritual view of the world, and their evangelistic fervor. Chinese-American Christians bring a compassionate concern for the evangelization of China and the rest of the Chinese world. Immigrants from Cambodia, Laos, and Vietnam have become Christians in refugee camps with amazing testimonies of God's saving love in the midst of extreme adversity and persecution. It is not merely that Americans have something to give new immigrants, immigrants have something to give to Americans. This mutual giving and receiving is a sign of the new partnership that is developing among Christians from all around the world.

Although some of the projections for change in ethnicity ratios are more conservative than the ones cited here, nonetheless, the trends are the same: a growing diversity of ethnic groups in the USA is undeniable.

Multi-Culturalism

Out of this great convergence of people from many cultural heritages on one location, the term "multi-culturalism" was born. Multi-culturalism promotes heightened respect for people from every cultural background, emphasizing that all cultures have significance and value. This view opposes "cultural

---

[17]Carlson and Goldman, *2020 Vision*, p. 65.

imperialism," which has as its goal a desire to foster a uniform, supreme culture in every aspect of society. Although multi-culturalism has the possibility of creating division as a consequence of political correctness,[18] when seen in a proper context of celebrating unity *and* diversity, it can be embraced by Christians with joy, knowing that people with one particular cultural heritage are not the only people God has created. Although it is God who creates people, it is people who create cultures and societies. If no particular culture is God created or ordained, culture in general is relative, not absolute, even though every culture will have evil and good aspects when judged from a Christian perspective.

Just as in that first multi-cultural Pentecostal experience, the Sovereign God is stirring up our world. He is bringing both a mission field and a rich cultural lesson to our doorstep, a step which we may step over and ignore or step onto and use as a foundation for a new kind of society. Cultural diversity forces followers of Jesus to consider carefully the difference between gospel and context, Christianity and culture. This diversity affords the ordinary American Christian the opportunity to do what only cross-cultural missionaries could do in the past: to find the core truths of Jesus

---

[18]Historian Arthur M. Schlesinger Jr. writes that "the multiethnic dogma belittles *unum* and glorifies *pluribus*" (cited in "America's Immigrant Challenge," *Time* 142 [Special Issue, Fall 1993]: 9). William A. Henry III challenges the dogma of multi-culturalism and its twin, political correctness: "The greatest intellectual danger of political correctness is its assumption that there are some ideas too dangerous to be heard, some words too hurtful to be allowed, some opinions no one is ever again permitted to hold.... Political correctness argues that the price of peace in a racially diverse America may be suppressing ideas that cause such pain. Perhaps that could mean a more civilized nation. Up to now, though, America's genius has not been in its civility, but rather in its raucous barroom brawl in search of truth." See "The Politics of Separation," *Time* 142 (Special Issue, Fall 1993): 75.

around which Christians build their own cultural expressions. Multi-culturalism, without its dogma or militant demands, should be welcomed in the church as a God-given opportunity to love our distant neighbors, our friends, and even our enemies.

Christian colleges and seminaries will need to give serious consideration to culturally appropriate education, bi-cultural education, and even bi-lingual education. Western education patterns may be appropriate for those who have come to the USA to learn in Western schools, but interacting effectively with multi-cultural America will need more careful consideration.[19]

We must take a different view of under-represented minorities in our colleges and seminaries, which means "viewing minorities as an investment rather than a problem."[20] If our churches are not representative of our multi-cultural society, then our colleges are not likely to be either. And if our ministry-training institutions are not multi-cultural, they will send no diversity of leaders to the churches. Both parts of this circular problem must be addressed. Churches must take seriously the challenge to become multi-cultural, but the ministers who preach to them must learn this important lesson in college and seminary.

Beyond the Melting Pot

The interesting point about the past is that Europeans largely melted in the American pot. There are some who today proudly call themselves Italian or Irish, Swedish or Polish, but one can hardly tell the

---

[19]See Arthur Levin and Associates, *Shaping Higher Education's Future: Demographic Realities and Opportunities, 1990-2000* (San Francisco: Jossey-Bass Publishers, 1990) for an analysis of the shift in ethnic groups in higher education.
[20]Arthur Levin, *Shaping Higher Education's Future*, p. 22.

---

difference. Most are simply European-Americans or, more popularly but less accurately, Anglo-Americans.

Still barely the largest USA ethnic minority yet with almost no new immigration, African-American society is still in ferment. Many African-Americans feel that they have joined the mainstream in values and, despite some marked distinctions in cultural background, have *largely* become a part of the dominant culture. Numerous other African-Americans, however, feel that they have been greatly victimized by institutionalized racism. This has left many African-Americans with alienation, disenfranchisement, resentments toward the dominant society, and serious social problems. The nation's largest riots, after the Rodney King verdict in 1992, revealed again the smoldering cauldron below the smooth surface of ethnic and racial relations.[21] And certainly the issues exposed in the 1994-1995 O. J. Simpson trial have fueled the fires even further.

When recent immigrants came as political refugees from Cambodia, Laos, Vietnam, Nicaragua, and El Salvador or came to seek a new life from Korea, Mexico, the Philippines, Hong Kong, India, Russia, and China, seasoned Americans threw them in the melting pot, but they did not dissolve. Assimilation is not the necessary expectation of immigrants today. American society is *beyond* the melting pot.[22]

American society has often been described as more like a vast cultural mosaic,[23] each piece with its

---

[21]See Carlson and Goldman, *2020 Vision*, pp. 66-68 for an interesting perspective of African-Americans as "discriminated-against, rural-to-urban immigrants."

[22]The melting pot is not a popular image now. "Ironically, there was relatively little intermarriage during the era of 'melting pot' theories, but such intermarriage is now much more widespread in the era when the concept is rejected by intellectuals." Thomas Sowell, *Ethnic America* (New York: Basic Books, 1981), p. 286.

[23]Oscar Romo's *American Mosaic* and Deborah Sue Brunsman's *Red & Yellow, Black & White: The Challenge of Evangelizing*

own distinctive colors which make up a beautiful picture when placed together. Others have suggested that America is more like a stew,[24] tossed salad, tapestry, or rainbow. These images, however, may not be sharp enough to show the complexity of a society holding on to many distinct cultures. What is clear is that many American ethnic groups today *want* to maintain at least some of their cultural distinctives and keep their indigenous languages. They are Americans, but they do not feel a need to become like all the rest. While prior generations of immigrants felt that they had to learn English quickly to survive, today many Hispanics, for example, maintain that the Spanish language is inseparable from their ethnic and cultural identity and expect to remain bilingual, if not primarily Spanish speaking, for life.[25] These new immigrants reject the conforming and confining melting pot stereotype. They can be good Americans without dissolving their cultural distinctiveness into one giant vat.[26] American indi-

---

America's Ethnic Mosaic (Joplin: College Press, 1991) are two recent examples.

[24]C. Peter Wagner prefers the stewpot, in which "each ingredient is changed and flavored by the other ingredients. The changes are for the better. The carrots, the potatoes, the meat, and the onions all taste better after they come in contact with each other in the stewpot. While they enrich each other, each ingredient nevertheless maintains its own identity and integrity. If the stew is overcooked the ingredients lose their identity and it becomes mush, not nearly as palatable a dish." See "A Vision for Evangelizing the Real America," *International Bulletin* X (April 1986): 60.

[25]Henry, "Beyond the Melting Pot," p. 29.

[26]Criticizing the melting pot is not new, but in earlier books it was still primarily dealing with European-American ethnic issues. Novak, for instance, defines "ethnics" as mainly "the descendants of the immigrants of Southern and Eastern Europe." See F. Michael Novak, *The Rise of the Unmeltable Ethnic* (New York: MacMillan, 1972), p. 46. Novak continues (p. 49) by quoting Leonard Dinnerstein and Frederic Cople Jaher in *The Aliens* (New York: Appleton-Century-Crofts, 1970): "Although popular rhetoric glorified the country as a melting pot of different peoples, in actuality this has meant melting diversity into conformity with Anglo-Saxon characteristics. Those

vidualism, pluralism,[27] and relativism have given philosophical backbone to these instinctive beliefs of the new immigrants. Who is to say that things must always stay the same in America? America has always been a changing place. Ellis Island processed refugees and seekers of a new world by the hundreds of thousands. America is truly a place for a mixture of new people. Its culture, fueled by the electronic media, changes more rapidly than perhaps any place on earth.

Carlson and Goldman end their excellent description of "The Changing American" with these comments:

> The United States is the first country that has tried to blend Europe, Africa, and Asia[28] into a single egalitarian nation. For the foreseeable future—the next 100 years—immigration pressures will be overwhelming. More than ever, the solutions to this country's problems reside not in divisiveness, but in reaffirmation of a pluralistic ideal within a vibrant economy. How are we going to treat our growing elderly population? How are we going to take care of our kids? How are we going to work within our minorities to accelerate them into the mainstream? These are tough questions to answer, and all the answers will be costly—but answer them we must, or lose our leadership role in the 21st century.[29]

---

unable or unwilling to accomplish the transformation have suffered varying degrees of abuse and ostracism because middle-class America demands conformity before it gives acceptance." Note also Nathan Glazer and Daniel Patrick Moynihan, *Beyond the Melting Pot* (Cambridge: M.I.T. Press, 1963).

[27]"American pluralism was not an ideal with which people started but an accommodation to which they were driven by the destructive toll of mutual intolerance in a country too large and diverse for effective dominance by any one segment of the population." Thomas Sowell, *Ethnic America* (New York: Basic Books, 1981), p. 3.

[28]Latin America should be included as well.

[29]Carlson and Goldman, *2020 Vision*, p. 69.

Immigration

Besides higher birth rates among many non-European groups, immigration is the obvious explanation for a multi-cultural America. An often forgotten fact is that *all* Americans, except those natives improperly named Indians, are from immigrant stock. The issue for many, however, is still what kind of stock you are: European stock has been considered the progenitor of the true American, while those immigrants from the rest of the world are foreigners all their lives. Until 1965, immigration law was clearly biased toward immigration from Europe. The moral awakening of the 1960s and the civil rights movement made it possible for immigrants of different races and colors to enter the United States.[30] Now only 10 to 15 percent of America's immigrants come from Europe. Many immigrants have also entered illegally and Immigration and Naturalization Services agents apprehended almost one million illegals at the borders in 1988,[31] further intensifying the immigration debate.

The world has become interested in American success and opportunities, and America has also become interested in the world. Carlson and Goldman write that America is lucky that people want to come to this country where immigrants can be successfully absorbed and assimilated, unlike Japan, for example, which never fully accepts immigrants.[32] Tom Morganthau explains America's immigration policy as a mixture of altruism and self-interest:

> Current U.S. policy contains elements of both—but it is a blurry, heavily brokered policy that has been cobbled together over the decades to reflect the changing fads and competing interests of domestic

---

[30]Morganthau, "America: Still A Melting Pot?" p. 20.
[31]Carlson and Goldman, *2020 Vision*, pp. 62-63.
[32]Carlson and Goldman, *2020 Vision*, pp. 63-64.

politics. A purely selfish policy would accept only immigrants who could contribute to economic or social progress. But this idea—awarding visas on the basis of talent or skill—has always been opposed by organized labor and other groups, and it is a minor feature of today's law, totalling about 140,000 out of 810,000 visas annually. Conversely, providing a haven for refugees is in the best tradition of the American conscience, and the United States has taken a lot of refugees since 1970—1.5 million Vietnamese, Laotians, Cambodians, Cubans, Russians, and other oppressed nationalities.

But the vast majority of those who get here are ordinary folks pursuing a better life—and ... this, too, is part of the American tradition.[33]

Although the public mood toward immigration is turning sour again,[34] the fact is that, even economically, America needs immigrants. With native-born Americans taking skilled technological and office jobs, there is a need for labor intensive, low-skilled, low-wage, service jobs which often only immigrants are willing to perform. Many Americans decry the social service money spent on immigrants, but some estimates show that immigrants actually put more in the government's coffers than they take out. Illegal immigrants are not eligible for services (although there is, of course, fraud), so they can only give to the economy in work, spending power, and paying sales taxes.

In 1991, the United States government granted 1.8 million people legal permanent residence. Seventy-nine percent of these legal immigrants chose just seven states as their new homes, the largest and border states predominating, as the following table indicates:[35]

---

[33]Morganthau, "America: Still A Melting Pot?" p. 22.

[34]See "America's Immigrant Challenge," *Time* 142 [Special Issue, Fall 1993]: 10-12.

[35]See Morganthau, "America: Still A Melting Pot?" pp. 22-23.

California	40%	Illinois	4%
Texas	12%	New Jersey	3%
New York	10%	Arizona	2%
Florida	8%		

This immigration trend will most likely continue with California's hospitable weather, shared border with Mexico, and Pacific Rim gateway giving continued reasons for immigrants to position themselves in the nation's most populous state.

Illegal immigration, whether over a Tijuana fence at night or in a *Golden Venture*-type ship, continues despite attempts to beef up the border patrols. Political asylum laws, enacted on the presumption that travelling communist artists would be the recipients, are now invoked by those from war-torn countries of the left and the right. Some churches, once considered only sanctuaries for retreat to God, have declared themselves political sanctuaries and whole cities have followed this trend of harboring those in political peril.

The government finds itself in the unenviable task of deciding which immigrants have come for true political reasons (acceptable) and which have come for mere economic gain (unacceptable), the latter being the very reason which brought most European immigrants to America in the first place. In the past, this was often determined by which political regime the USA supported, but recently more impartiality has been maintained in the policy.

The immigration issue is not an easy one to settle, even for Christians. However, the fluctuation between the poles of altruism and self-interest keeps American Christians ineffective and paralyzed in their mission to people from cultural heritages so different from their own. This ambivalence and sometimes resentment toward new immigrants may be a factor in the eagerness to spend cross-cultural mission money outside the USA but not inside.

Eyes and Ears on God

Sensitive and sensible Christians, of course, will not be blind or deaf to these facts of our world. They will have one eye on God and another eye on people. They will have one ear listening to the word of God while the other ear eavesdrops and actively listens to the world of God. Just as the changes in society suggest which particular point of the gospel is demanded, the changes in peoples reveal which particular people the gospel should focus on (see Acts 11:44-48). A careful demographic analysis cannot be ignored by the church who listens to God's sending Spirit. Through his vast sovereignty and ability to create opportunities out of tragedy, he has brought people of many cultures to our doors.

The gospel brings great hope for the newer involuntary immigrants, for example. Many lost everything—home, bank accounts, family, country—and are now forced to adapt to a new culture. They did not choose to be in the USA. They are not people with a mission going to another culture but often people who have lost their mission and perhaps the freedom to return to their homeland. Others have chosen to come to this country out of a desire for greater opportunities themselves, buying into an American dream from afar, just like those first dreamers who landed on these shores.

Many immigrants have found in the gospel a great treat. They have discovered that Jesus has a message for them that they had not heard and may have never heard in their own country. Forgiveness of past sins, healing of wounds, salvation of spirit, and new LIFE in Jesus are some of what Christ can give these involuntary immigrants through the church of Jesus Christ. They find that the church also meets a social need in helping them regain lost self-worth, as parts of their own cultures and identities have been shattered.

The church has helped them sink new roots into unfamiliar soil.

With newer immigrants, there is usually only a small window of time through which they can be reached. If they have not seen and accepted Jesus in those first few years, they will likely return to the religious heritage from which they came, if it has become established here, or they will turn to the "other gospel"—the gospel of secular materialism, which is preached so effectively in American media, at shopping centers, and through the lives of those around them.

What Kind of Churches Will Serve New Immigrants?

Some churches will simply insist that newcomers express only those needs which the churches already know how to fill and require that newcomers worship with existing cultural styles or not at all. These churches will relate the gospel neither to the views of unbelievers nor to the culture of believers from different cultural heritages. While perhaps giving great sums to missions, these churches are not mission-minded if they cannot or will not let the gospel have its power to work in a cultural heritage other than their own.

On the other hand, churches which will serve new immigrants will have most, if not all, of the following characteristics:

(1) Serving churches will *value people of all cultural heritages* and the customs and practices of all people. These churches realize that America no longer reflects a single cultural heritage and must make way for people to retain their distinctive cultures while embracing a new God.

(2) Serving churches will *treat all people with dignity.* These Christians do not condescend to or patronize people. They allow people to give what they can, and to receive the help they need.

3) Serving churches will promote *maximum flexibility*. (a) Worship styles will be various and those differences will be respected. (b) They will need to overcome controversy over cultural behavior. Simple issues, like what food is cooked or eaten in a church building or how one uses the toilet, have caused churches to part company with their brothers and sisters from another ethnic group. (c) They will realize that methods of conflict resolution are different. European-American Christians may accuse Asians of not dealing with problems honestly, when the reality is that Asians deal with problems indirectly rather than directly. Cross-cultural churches will have to work at their relationships just as Christians do their marriages. At times they may need outside cross-cultural counselors to help them.

(4) Serving churches will *minimize denominational and party line loyalties* and treat all Christians as brothers and sisters. These loyalties are both foreign to the gospel and foreign to these individuals. We must look for the issues which unite and be willing to let our cultural religious background be subordinate to biblical Christianity.

(5) Serving churches will *relate the gospel to the whole person*, not just the soul. Social issues are significant. Many immigrants will need help with immigration issues, welfare, social services, learning English, getting jobs, paying bills, starting businesses, and more. Many African-American churches routinely have social workers on their church staffs or have ready access to other caring agencies.

(6) Serving churches will *want people to be involved with their church for the people's own sake, not the church's growth*. Among some churches, there is a new problem of vying for "serving" ethnic churches, a kind of reverse status for those who help the needy. Churches whose motivation is simply to capitalize on

numbers or diversity statistics are not serving people but only serving themselves.

Planting Churches

Starting a church among immigrants is not a typical "new church venture" where one discovers a new housing development, rents a school and some office space, and plants a church. The newest, often poorest immigrants will not normally be in the areas where European-Americans begin new churches. They are in the older areas which have been deserted by others who are moving up the ladder. The latest immigrants usually push the poorest people out—and perhaps up. This is true for many Southeast Asians and Hispanics, for example.

Other groups may not be found in the poorer areas but are scattered around the cities. Chinese, often well-heeled businesspeople, have come to the USA escaping expected economic tyranny in Hong Kong or political troubles in the People's Republic, or they are seeking better economic opportunities than Taiwan or Singapore offer. Koreans and Indians, who have left their Asian homes in search of Western education and a better life, are distributed in pockets across the cities. European-Americans may not know where these immigrants live, but the people from each cultural group know.

"Grandparenting" Churches

Although there are many models for starting churches of various cultural heritages, a desire for utilizing the ethnic group's own resources and empowering its leaders presents a model for birthing churches.

Leaders from the target group's own cultural heritage are best suited to birth their own churches.[36] These churches will largely be single-culture churches, using their own heart languages and following their own cultural patterns, although these patterns will necessarily be modified because of being in the host country. Even with good leadership in ethnic churches, "grandparents" may be needed for these churches to emerge. These are people from the host country who can act as liaisons, encouragers, and empowerers to ethnic ministries. Not only individuals, but churches, Christian colleges, evangelistic associations, and other parachurch groups can act as these "grandparents."

Just as grandparents do not make the best parents, a cross-cultural birthing plan is not at its best if there is a same-culture "parent" who is already an integral part of the immigrant culture. Instead of planting a church themselves, "grandparents" encourage the parent to go ahead and start the church. The "grandparents" will be available when needed, but not to do the daily parenting.

In this model, leaders from a single cultural heritage work from their own framework to reach their own people. There are several benefits of working "first culture to first culture."

(1) Communication is more accurate. Cross-cultural communication is risky communication at best. Missiologists agree that first culture to first culture missions allows the clearest communication. The accents are more authentic and easy to follow and the language use is more complete.

---

[36]Southern Baptists have by far the largest work among various cultural heritages in the USA with 7,000 congregations among 101 ethnic groups and 97 American Indian tribes which study the Bible in 98 languages throughout the United States and its territories. Ninety-eight percent of their new churches are planted by leaders from among the targeted ethnic group. See Oscar Romo, *American Mosaic*, p. 90.

(2) The gospel is more likely to be contextualized.

(3) Leaders are more likely to be effective in their own communities.

(4) There are no costly delays due to preparing cross-cultural missionaries.

This model of "grandparenting," however, does not let seasoned Americans off the hook. It merely means that they do not have the full responsibility. "Grandparents" are generation- and culture-gappers, often better at bridging the gap than the parents themselves. These hosts will help the leaders serve in this new land and gain the bi-cultural skills which are necessary. They are missionaries who are truly cross-cultural in their desire to communicate and their willingness to serve and love.

Parachurch organizations which work in church planting will have to think of themselves as cross-cultural missionaries. Missionaries in other lands are used to working daily with different cultural expectations. They expect to be shocked. In the USA, seasoned Americans often expect the ethnic leader to conform to USA models of a growing church. They may mistakenly think that in the home mission field the *only* differences are those of race, language, and physical features. Christians must see these cultural groups as different in complex ways, knowing that focusing on the superficial differences often clouds us from recognizing the significant cultural issues. When Christian leaders from a given cultural group work with their own group, these problems are alleviated.

Churches and organizations who wish to be effective "grandparents" will have to be flexible on some of the principles they hold so dearly:

(1) American organizations have just learned a new form of accountability in the wake of so much lack of accountability; yet church planting within a different cultural heritage group may reveal that the leaders have an entirely different concept of accountability and trust.

Those in different cultural groups may believe that the biblical way is to trust in the *person* rather than in written prescriptions and policies. If organizations demand that accountability be demonstrated in European-American terms, the relationship itself may be lost. European-Americans may forget that written reports and audited financial reports are a culturally determined way of demonstrating financial accountability. But *we may have to discover other ways of accountability for people of other cultural heritages* where this is not the norm—*at least* until they can learn these methods.

(2) Grandparent churches may need to see that *new churches may properly begin without a fully developed concept of what they should be and how they should operate.* The people should have the freedom to develop the church as they see fit, just as new Christians did in Jerusalem, Antioch, and Corinth. This *will* cause problems, but why should it be any different than the experience of the earliest churches while they got on their feet? Established churches will also need to be reminded of their own inadequacies in order to keep them from self-righteously judging young churches.

(3) Although American churches may feel that they have the right to demand certain things from ethnic churches whom they support, Paul says that he is *willing to give up his rights for the sake of the gospel* (see 1 Cor 8:13; 9:19-23). In working together as partners in ministry with those of other cultures, there are many so-called "rights" to give up. If we do not give them up, the gospel will not go forward and will not become appropriately contextualized in multi-cultural America.

Not only must "grandparenting" organizations maintain their flexibility, first generation ethnic leaders must also be adaptable, remaining focused on the vision of developing an effective church instead of establishing a cultural citadel. While same-culture churches may be the most effective strategy in reaching first generation immigrants, they may not be so effective with the second and third generations who have no vital connection with the old customs and language. Leith Anderson even offers the following revolutionary consideration:

> Within only a generation they may not even know the language and culture of the old country, which forces the ethnic church to negotiate a new definition of success or die with the old generation.
> This raises an important secondary question. Is there anything wrong with a church serving a single generation and then closing down? It may be that the practical life of most churches is thirty-five to fifty years. After that they become obsolete and ineffective unless they are renewed. A church that intends to serve a specific audience (ethnic, generational, or other) may be highly successful for one generation and then close its doors.[37]

Cross-Cultural Mission

Developing a missionary venture based on the "grandparenting" model does not mean that *cross-cultural* mission is unneeded or inappropriate. Many groups in the USA will not be reached with the gospel unless someone crosses a cultural or linguistic barrier. Some of the circumstances in which cross-cultural mission will have great benefits are the following: (1) when there are few Christian leaders in the given cultural group; (2) when the ethnic leaders are not mature enough or are unable to plant a church; (3) when groups are new to the country; (4) when making a transition to the new country is not being managed well; and (5) when problems among the particular ethnic group are significant (e.g. unemployment, social problems among young people, first and

---

[37]Leith Anderson, *A Church for the 21st Century* (Minneapolis: Bethany House, 1992), p. 83.

second generation issues, people not applying Christianity well to normal life, numbers of people falling away from Christ).

Help from the host culture is often *not* appropriate when groups are at the stage of developing their independence and are establishing a Christian community on their own or when groups already have solid, growing churches.

It is helpful for American Christians to work cross-culturally, but only if they truly have a missionary mindset. It is not a simple task of taking a few people from a given culture and making a church. Veteran missionaries seem to have the best track record in this area, but any who are willing to learn the principles of cross-cultural ministry will be able to offer much. Those who embark on cross-cultural ministry, even in the USA, note that it has changed their lives, just as it did for Peter and Paul and all who have followed in their steps.

Cross-cultural ministers must help each other keep the important issues at the forefront of the mission. We must keep each other on track, because even the most culturally sensitive individuals naturally veer off into their comfortable culture. It is hard enough to keep a foreign missionary from a powerful country from the dangers of cultural imperialism; it is a huge task to keep the American cross-cultural evangelist on target when one's own culture constantly beckons for the return to one's own customary patterns.

Eldin Villafane aptly summarizes this discussion with four priorities to guide churches and organizations in working interculturally: (1) empowerment that values others; (2) evangelism that is holistic; (3) education that is contextual; and (4) ecclesiastical structures that liberate.[38]

---

[38]Eldin Villafane of Gordon Conwell Seminary; cited in Al Hammond, "The Challenge of Multi-Cultural America," *All The People* (Special Edition): 1.

Developing an Urban Theology

It is impossible to speak of multi-cultural ministry without speaking of urban issues. Although there are some exceptions, most immigrants have congregated in urban areas. Even those who come from remote rural areas have clustered themselves in urban areas where services are available and where people can try to reform their lives together. People who are used to interdependent, interconnected lives often move together as closely as possible for mutual support, to preserve their culture, and to maintain their dignity in an alien land. Thus they create almost tribal villages within an urban setting.

Cities have come to dominate the entire world culture today. In 1900, there were 20 cities of over a million in population; now there are 340. By A.D. 2000 there will be over 400 "world class cities" with one million plus people. Today over 2.3 billion people call a city their home and there are 95,000 new *non-Christians* moving to these cities *every day*. With nearly half of the world's population living in towns and cities by the start of the new millennium,[39] Harvey Cox's prediction is almost reality: "Future historians will record the twentieth century as that century in which the whole world became one immense city."[40]

Developing an urban theology is essential for Christ's church to regain its mission to the cities. Ray Bakke,[41] Roger Greenway, Harvie M. Conn, and others have made substantial progress in calling Christians to

---

[39]J. D. Douglas, ed., *Proclaim Christ Until He Comes* (Minneapolis: World Wide Publications, 1990), p. 279.

[40]Quoted in Michael Pabarcus, "Seeking the Peace of the City: Theological Reflection on Urban Mission," (St. Louis Christian College unpublished paper, 1989): 1.

[41]See Ray Bakke, *The Urban Christian: Effective Ministry in Today's Urban World* (Downer's Grove: InterVarsity Press, 1987). International Urban Associates, of which Bakke is executive director, also produces a newsletter dealing with urban issues.

reconsider the city, using the Bible itself as their justification.[42] They call for rethinking what the Bible actually says about the city:

> We cannot expect lives to be changed, city neighbor-hoods improved, and vital churches established if our labors spring from feeble, even distorted, theological roots. The urban missiologists, therefore, must blaze a trail that the missionary practitioner can follow. Workers in the streets will not move forward as they should unless there are urban missiologists ahead of them, behind them, and alongside them, sounding true and prophetic notes.[43]

Yet followers of Jesus, especially those whose churches are located in rural or suburban areas, often fail to be convinced by the above reasoning:

> If the Bible is such an urban book, why do we not see it that way? It is simply because we approach the Bible from an essentially rural theological perspective. When we read the Bible, we are thinking "country"

---

[42]Although there are unappealing aspects, the city is a positive biblical theme. There are over 1,000 references to cities in scripture. Even in the marginally populated lands of the Old Testament, people huddled in cities like Nineveh, Babylon, and Jerusalem. Paul writes his letters to city churches and Jesus reveals his message to seven urban congregations. Jerusalem is an esteemed city and the New Jerusalem is the final resting place for believers. As Ray Bakke proclaims in a video presentation from Lausanne II in Manila, "The Bible may start in a garden but it ends in a city. We couldn't honor him more, I suspect than by loving him and by beginning to love the city. We've got an urban future whether we like it or not." See Douglas, *Proclaim Christ Until He Comes*, p. 279.

[43]Greenway and Monsma, *Cities, Missions' New Frontier*, p. 1. On the other hand, Jacque Ellul in *The Meaning of the City* (Grand Rapids: Eerdmans, 1970) believes that the city symbolizes the supreme work of man and is thus a rejection of God. Yet he sees God as electing the city as an instrument of grace for the believer. His analysis should be balanced with the modern urban theologians previously mentioned.

instead of "city." We see what we read through "rural glasses."[44]

Those few rural people who have developed compassion and perhaps pity on the city and have established churches have rarely succeeded, often because they are unprepared by their churches, their seminaries, and their theology. Greenway and Monsma contend:

> Until there are enough people who have prepared themselves for urban mission by gaining a firm hold on an adequate theology for the city and biblical understanding of ethnicity, evangelistic efforts among urban ethnics will continue to be weak and faltering. Most of America's evangelical schools are located in suburbs and small towns. Many have intentionally relocated their campuses away from ethnic neighborhoods and urban congestion. Is it any wonder, then, that the Bible is read and theology is discussed in ways that filter out the city with its pressing social issues, poverty, suffering, and maze of people? Does it surprise us that we find it difficult to address the city's problems from well-developed theological perspectives?[45]

Urban missionaries in Los Angeles Bill and Carmelita Pile write:

> No Bible College course taught us urban ministry and we were woefully unprepared for it in Los Angeles. We had to reread the whole Bible through urban glasses. We were trapped in white, anglo-saxon, middle-class American mentality. Worse, we didn't know there was any other. Some might learn faster

---

[44]See Robert C. Linthicum, *City of God, City of Satan: A Biblical Theology of the Urban Church* (Grand Rapids: Zondervan Publishing House, 1991), p. 22.

[45]Greenway and Monsma, *Cities, Missions' New Frontier*, p. 79.

than we did, but it took God about ten years to get us where he wanted us.[46]

Developing an urban theology is no more intellectually demanding than developing any other theology. Where it is demanding is on our fleshly self, the very self that resists looking at institutionalized poverty, rampant suffering, and serious societal breakdown. The flesh calls us to preserve ourselves and stay away from the demands of the city, while the Spirit calls us to give ourselves away for the sake of the gospel. The content and methods of theological education must change if we are to minister to the needs of the city. Does the cloistered, affluent, rural environment lend itself to developing city-minded, community-involved Christian leaders? The statistics tell us it does not. Even seminary-developed missionaries to other countries are rarely tackling those teeming third world cities which have problems which could overwhelm any army.

Theological education that trains leaders to minister beyond the traditional white middle-class church and is adaptable to the needs of the ethnic congregations must be developed and expanded. This calls for new approaches to theological education, drawing from the best in the traditions of both the majority and the minority communities without enslavement to any one model.[47]

Roger Greenway lists nine possible agendas for seminaries and Christian colleges that desire to pursue urban relevancy. They are worth repeating here because

---

[46]Bill Pile and Carmelita Pile, "Urban Ministry: Stay A While," *HeartBeat* 52 (January 1994): 1.

[47]Greenway and Monsma, *Cities, Missions' New Frontier*, p. 87.

of the important shaping functions that these institutions play on the church:[48]

(1) Develop a biblical theology that deals adequately with the city, ethnicity, and the many things the Bible says about the poor, the sojourner, the refugee. Mission, after all, springs from theology and biblical understanding.

(2) Encourage students to focus their church-history and biblical-studies assignments on themes relating to the city, urban ministries, the poor, minorities, and the multiracial character of the church.

(3) Invite guest speakers from foreign communities and inner-city ministries on a regular basis, make attendance at their lectures mandatory, and encourage them to speak freely about the matters that affect their people.

(4) Insist that faculty and students become involved with ethnic people, inner-city churches, and the poor. Perhaps suburban churches can develop vital connections with city churches through the seminary.

(5) Expand field-work positions and internships in city churches and urban-mission programs. This will give students practical experience in working with different races and cultures.

(6) Add required courses designed to introduce nonurban men and women to urban issues and ministries.

(7) Establish an urban campus in a multicultural setting where all students will take at least some classes, with the urban atmosphere as part of the learning experience.[49] It is one thing to theorize about contextualization, quite another thing to *do* it. I doubt whether contextualization can be done outside the actual context.

---

[48]See Greenway and Monsma, *Cities, Missions' New Frontier*, pp. 87-88.
[49][Editors: Lincoln Christian Seminary recently established an on-site M.A.-level urban missions program at its Chicago Center for Urban Mission under the direction of Professor Mark Shelley.]

(8) Encourage students to live in interracial communities and to involve themselves as much as they can in neighborhood life.

(9) Incorporate into courses on cults and non-Christian religions actual face-to-face confrontation, dialogue, and evangelism on the street. That can be done easily in the city, where alien cultures and adherents to other faiths are met not in textbooks, but in flesh and blood. There one quickly learns that Buddhists, Muslims, and Jews are real people, and that is exciting. After reading about them and their beliefs, the best education is to meet them personally and engage them in serious conversation.

Barriers To Urban Ethnic Evangelism

Roger Greenway proclaims that he has "never met a Christian who argued against the evangelization of new ethnic populations in American cities."[50] However, Christians still face a number of barriers to reaching urban ethnics for Christ. Some of these barriers include (1) ambivalence toward immigrants; (2) the negative image of the city; (3) a fear of the social gospel; (4) white flight to the suburbs; (5) cultural inflexibility; and (6) an inadequate theology of the city.[51]

Although there are some serious issues involved in these barriers, they are fueled by misconceptions of people, God, and culture. To direct our mission based on these obstacles is to limit mission and concede the city and many ethnic groups to Satan. Christians must be willing to confront these barriers directly and hurdle them or knock them down. Some of the barriers will require that preachers speak prophetically to people who are more concerned with their own comfort than following the disquieting message of a God who calls us

---

[50]Greenway and Monsma, *Cities, Missions' New Frontier*, p. 72.
[51]See Greenway and Monsma, *Cities, Missions' New Frontier*, pp. 73-79.

to leave our seclusion and march in the battlegrounds of Satan.

Conclusion

America *is* multi-cultural and diverse. Americans are different from one another. There is no denying it and little likelihood of changing it.

Those differences gain their impact, however, from the bonds that unite them in one vast and variegated country. They are differences that should not divide or weaken America, but distinguish and strengthen it. They are the reasons to keep the welcome mat, however worn and tattered at times, always ready at the door.[52]

Christians must respond to multi-cultural America with at least the same welcome mat. We are inter-cultural followers of Jesus and cross-cultural missionaries, knowing that our final allegiance does not belong to any nationality or cultural heritage group. Although many European-Americans will lament and some will condemn the changes in America, longing for the good old days when most Americans were European and some were quietly black cannot be the response of Christians. Besides the inherent racism, cultural arrogance, and smug heterogeneity implied, it is simply not the call of God.

God has called us to be a light to the *ethne*—the people of all cultural heritages of the world. This is the very challenge which another nation, inflicted by its own cultural and religious superiority, resisted long ago. The challenge of reaching only our own kind is too insignificant, too provincial, and not motivated by the loving heart of God. "Us only" ministry is powered by a

---

[52]"America's Immigrant Challenge," *Time* 142 (Special Issue, Fall 1993): 9.

God too small. Isaiah's prophecy is also a powerful reminder to the modern church: "It is too small a thing for you to be my servant to restore the tribes of Jacob and bring back those of Israel I have kept. I will also make you a light for the Gentiles, that you may bring my salvation to the ends of the earth" (Isa 49:6 NIV).

When the ends of the earth come to us, we must thank God that he has made the challenge *easier* for those of us who live in the USA. Without having to cross geographic borders, we gain the opportunity to use our heavenly passport to cross cultural borders in order to give Light to people whom God loves. Being involved in *this* mission will change us. It will help us see both people and culture with new illumination. In that context, perhaps we will see Him truly as the Light of the World.

RECOMMENDED BIBLIOGRAPHY

Augsburger, David W. *Pastoral Counseling Across Cultures.* Philadelphia: The Westminster Press, 1986.
> An extremely helpful volume which deals with normal counseling topics like grace and human failure, values, the family, sexuality, but in a cross-cultural context. Most simply stated Augsburger's message is that "to be culturally effective is a gift, a gift received through learning from other cultures, through being teachable in encounterers with those who differ, and through coming to esteem other worldviews equally with one's own."

Bakke, Ray. *The Urban Christian: Effective Ministry in Today's Urban World.* Downer's Grove: InterVarsity Press, 1987.
> A helpful, personal-experience-oriented book about effective ministry in the urban world.

Greenway, Roger S. and Timothy M. Monsma. *Cities, Missions' New Frontier.* Grand Rapids: Baker, 1989.
> An excellent resource that is thoughtful in biblical, demographic, and practical ministry. It begins with a biblical framework for developing a theology of mission to the city and ends with practical issues like raising families, using church buildings, and pastoring in the city. The authors develop what almost becomes a manual for urban ministry.

Linthicum, Robert C. *City of God, City of Satan: A Biblical Theology of the Urban Church.* Grand Rapids: Zondervan, 1991.
> This book reveals a way of looking at the city as a battleground between God and Satan. Linthicum deals with personal and systemic evil, but also includes God's positive viewpoint toward cities and their peoples. Practical spirituality balances activism in tackling the cities' powers.

Mindel, Charles H., Robert W. Habenstein, and Roosevelt Wright, eds. *Ethnic Families in America: Patterns and Variations.* New York: Elsevier, 1988.
> A large volume which includes parts on the following: European, Hispanic, Asian, historically subjugated, and socioreligious ethnic minorities. Within these parts, chapters on specific ethnic minorities typically include descriptions of cultural patterns, demographics, family structures, and changes since the cultural group has been in the USA.

Romo, Oscar. *American Mosaic: Church Planting in Ethnic America.* Nashville: Broadman Press, 1993.

Despite this book's many weaknesses (poorly organized and written, broad generalizations, repetitive themes, and ignoring churches other than Southern Baptist), the strength is in the results of the Southern Baptist churches who have over 7,000 congregations among 101 ethnic groups and 97 American Indian tribes that study the Bible in 98 languages throughout the United States and its territories. Solid principles and thought-provoking ideas can be gleaned from this work, which is one of the few on the subject.

Sowell, Thomas. *Ethnic America.* New York: Basic Books, 1981.

Although not up-to-date and missing important recent ethnic groups, Sowell gives a helpful overall view of "The American Mosaic" and several specific groups: Irish, Germans, Jews, Italians, Chinese, Japanese, Blacks, Puerto Ricans, and Mexicans. His chapter on "Implications" compares the "success" of selected immigrant groups.

Chapter 7:

The Kingdom of God:
A Dynamic Missiology
by
Dr. Paul Clark

Paul Clark and his wife, Rickie, have labored as missionaries in Japan since 1985. Dr. Clark has been the president of Osaka Bible Seminary since 1989. He was born in Oregon but went with his parents to Japan from 1950-1955. After serving three years in the Army Special Forces (Green Beret), Dr. Clark graduated from San Jose Bible College in California. He holds M.A. and M.Div. degrees in theology and philosophy from Lincoln Christian Seminary. His thesis was on "Adams' Art," which was an apologetic critique of the photographer artist, Ansel Adams, whose ideas were often similar to the Japanese mind. While at Lincoln, he was an organizing officer of Chi-Lambda Fellowship and an editor for its *Journal of Christian Studies*.

Dr. Clark completed his Doctor of Missiology (D.Miss.) degree from Trinity Evangelical Divinity School near Chicago. His dissertation topic was "Understanding the Resistance of Japan to Christianity" which involved a critique of "Western" Christianity and a challenge to develop a more biblical theology of missions.

President Clark has functioned as program chairman and keynote speaker for the Hayama Missionary Seminar, an annual all-Japan forum for missionaries, and has held ministries in Oregon, California, and Illinois.

THE KINGDOM OF GOD: A DYNAMIC MISSIOLOGY:

Emptiness, emptiness, all is emptiness ...
without
The ordering sound of the high calling of
God

An Autobiographical Preface

Having been conceived in the parsonage and raised on the mission field, my thoughts arise from a lifetime association with the church and her missionary enterprise. Following my graduation from San Jose Bible College in 1967, I was ordained to the ministry, fulfilling my commitment as a youth to the ministry and missions. The ensuing years of ministry and a summer's visit back in Japan (1975) intensified the sense of need to further equip my life for ministry. As a result, ten years of seminary studies followed. My seminary studies were imbued with a calling and commitment to return to Japan as a missionary and, should it be determined the Lord's will, follow my father as president of Osaka Bible Seminary.

I had come to my intellectual awakening through the L'Abri ministry of Francis and Edith Schaeffer. My study at Lincoln Christian Seminary was a time spent under the discipling guidance of Dr. James D. Strauss. He affirmed and amplified many themes I had either already worked out or begun to formulate; and to these and to what I did not know, he added much.

For many, there seems to be little connection between the difficult work of studying theology and philosophy and doing evangelism. For me, however, theology and philosophy offer the very foundation for one to evangelize. As with Isaiah, *understanding* fills one with the awe of God and the great desire to go.

Commitment derived from such an understanding brings with it a sense of calling, though it may be accompanied by isolation if not suffering. I have labored from the beginning to apply what I learned from Dr. Strauss to the proclamation of the gospel; yet always, in virtually every class hour spent with Doc, I was asked to do just that. As many know, Jim Strauss is an evangelist at heart.

Ever since, my mind has been filled with biblical, theological, philosophical, and missiological reflections on the church (or the kingdom of God) in the world. I have some concern about how my reflections may be taken. I am not anxious over how I might be received, but over whether or not I am understood. Opinions cannot change what is or what has been, but we must try to understand what *is*, if we are to be a part of any helpful change.

There are appeals, and then there are *appeals*. There is the missionary appeal for funds, and there is the appeal that is an *entreaty* or an *earnest plea* to take heed! What follows is the latter. At once, this is an appeal or summons to world evangelism at every level of kingdom concern. This is one missionary's *appeal*.

Confusion Over Missions

Man has "filled the earth" and we have become a global village. The globalization that has occurred at the end of the twentieth century was hardly imaginable at its beginning. It has occurred so swiftly that there are those living who have seen it all happen in their lifetime. Yet, though man has indeed been fruitful, multiplied, and harnessed the universe, he has hardly been faithful. Indeed, the world community exists in an unstable and anxious state. In this so-called time of "peace," world economies are in chaos, and there are over thirty localized "war zones" where man's inhumanity to man is being perpetrated, and in many cases, perpetuated; and the creation groans at the hand of man's abuse. Generally within the church, an indifference and an apathetic attitude exist toward this chaos and man's lostness that bring the haunting words of Cain to mind, "Am I my brother's keeper?" It is evident everywhere under the sun that humanity's greatest need is to be evangelized by the gospel of God.[1] At the same time the world community has imposed itself upon the church's cherished traditions and theologies about how this should be accomplished. Missiologist David J. Hesselgrave says, "We have arrived at a day of great confusion as to the nature and future of the Christian mission. Some say that the day of missions is past. Others say its finest hour is just before us."[2] Considering that evangelism is a *sine qua non* of the church, it may be both. As a matter of fact, it is no longer business as usual in world missions today. It has been suggested that our Western missions enterprise is graying and may even "be recruiting and training missionaries for a world that no longer exists."[3] The so-called "great" missionary churches are on the decrease, and a major missionary executive describes the mission

---

[1]My presence as a missionary in Japan is grounded first in Genesis and not in Matthew. Working through Ephesians and the gospel of Mark led me to understand that the "great commission" loses its meaning unless it is grounded in Genesis. God has wrapped up "all things" in Christ to his purpose and, in Christ, has made it possible for man once again to be a part of His plan. The High Calling! To be with God forever—in this life as he indwells us and in life as it shall be when we dwell with him. This is the gospel that Jesus proclaimed: God's purpose for creation, especially his human creation, has been recovered. To be received, however, it must be proclaimed. When one understands this, one hears as clearly as Isaiah did, "Whom shall I send, who will go for us?" (Isa 6:8; cf. Eph 1:10; Mark 1:14-15; Gen 1:26-28; 3:15; Rom 5:19; 10:14-15).

[2]David J. Hesselgrave, *Today's Choices For Tomorrow's Mission: An Evangelical Perspective On Trends and Issues In Missions* (Grand Rapids: Zondervan Publishing House, 1988), p. 21.

[3]William David Taylor, *Evangelical Missions Quarterly* (July 1993): 243.

community as "a struggling community."[4] This hyper-critical description of missions in the church as we have known it reflects the considerable change that is particularly occurring within the Christian community of the West. That something is awry should be all but apparent. Thus, David Bosch's statement of the obvious becomes a diagnosis: "An inadequate foundation for mission and ambiguous missionary motives and aims are bound to lead to an unsatisfactory missionary practice."[5] Nothing less than a paradigmatic shift has occurred in missions. Waves of criticism have followed from the time of Roland Allen's publications, *Missionary Methods, St. Paul's or Ours?* (1912), *Missionary Principles* (1913), and particularly his *The Spontaneous Expansion of the Church and the Causes Which Hinder It* (1927). Severe criticism against the old mission/missions paradigm has been coming since the 1930s. Some time ago four such books appeared by missions personnel in the same year, 1964: *Missions in a Time of Testing*; *Missionary, Go Home*; *The Unpopular Missionary*; and *The Ugly Missionary*. The controversy has continued unabated into the present.

It is true that "in some Christian circles there is no sign of such a failure or nerve" and "to even suggest that there is a fundamental crisis in missions would be [considered] tantamount to making concessions to 'liberal' theology and to doubting the abiding validity of the faith once handed down to us."[6] Nevertheless,

---

[4]Paul McKaughan, *Evangelical Missions Quarterly* (July 1993): 251. Paul McKaughan is executive director of The Evangelical Fellowship of Mission Agencies.

[5]David J. Bosch, *Transforming Mission: Paradigm Shifts in Theology of Mission*, American Society of Missiology Series, No. 16 (Maryknoll, NY: Orbis Books, 1991), p. 5.

[6]Ibid., p. 7. Both notes are presented in reflection and editorial comments in publications familiar to the Restoration Movement. See Walter Birney, *Christian Standard* (July 11, 1993): 9; and Norman Weaver, *Horizons* (September 1993): 2.

irrespective of opinion and surface appearances, the ongoing success of the missionary enterprise is veiling a malaise of significant theological problems. While "our spiritual forebears may perhaps be pardoned for not having been aware of the fact that they were facing a crisis ... present generations, however, can hardly be excused for *their* lack of awareness."[7] As surely as the world, the church also stands at the end of a millennium and an era. What can this mean for the promulgation of the gospel and the Kingdom of God?

Globalization has blurred national, racial, ethnic, and religious boundaries, though it has certainly not erased nationalism and prejudice. The remotest natural disaster is a world event on the evening news, and the world's millions watch international sports events live. What effect has this had on the church and what does it mean? In simplest terms, "The foreign field is no longer the exotic, faraway place. It is the familiar electronic image which enters in homes almost every night."[8] The whole world lives next door and everybody is my neighbor. This removes the motivation for "conquering unknown territory, or pioneering on distant frontiers,"[9] and it raises questions about the church's view of mission, missions, and the Messiah. Globalization has had the effect of "blowing the roof off the house," so to speak, and revealing the need for the church to reconsider the whole mission enterprise from its very foundation (1 Cor 3:11).[10]

---

[7] Bosch, *Transforming Mission,* p. 7.

[8] McKaughan, *Evangelical Missions Quarterly* (July 1993): 251.

[9] Wilbert R. Shenk, ed., *Mission Focus: Current Issues* (Scottdale, PA: Herald Press, 1980), p. 42.

[10] Is there any "other name" (Acts 4:12) or any other way (1 Tim 2:5)? Pluralism has helped prompt a proliferation of literature on the question of whether salvation is available *only* through Christ. This is a critical issue but beyond my purposes. Significant works, however, include the following: William V. Crockett and James G. Sigountos, eds., *Through No Fault of Their Own?* (Grand Rapids: Baker Book House, 1991); Martyn Eden and David F. Wells, eds., *The*

As the theological issues are faced and clarified, a new era for the church appears to be opening up. As Glasser states, "Evangelicals show every evidence of growing in numbers and maturity as we approach A.D. 2000. But their response to the challenges of the days ahead means that tomorrow's missionary obedience will hardly resemble what we see around us today."[11]

The battle begins when we realize that our very vocabulary has come to betray us. Until recently, "mission" vocabulary (e.g. mission, missions, mission field, mission station, missionary) was directly associated with the church. The usage followed the Roman Catholic missionary efforts of the sixteenth century and derived from the Latin, *missio dei*, meaning God's mission. In this sense the church's going into the world with the gospel was identified with God sending His Son. However, early on, "mission" also came to be associated with the language of international diplomacy. Then a major change in its usage came about when, with World War II, "mission" or "missions" became heavily military oriented: the word "mission" identified the single or all-encompassing purpose of an operation, and "the mission"

Gospel in the Modern World (Downers Grove, IL: InterVarsity Press, 1991); Paul F. Knitter, *No Other Name? A Critical Survey of Christian Attitudes Toward the World Religions* (Maryknoll, NY: Orbis Books, 1985); John F. MacArthur Jr., *The Gospel According to Jesus* (Grand Rapids: Zondervan Publishing House, 1988); Stephen Neill, *Christian Faith & Other Faiths* (Downers Grove, IL: InterVarsity Press, 1984); Harold A. Netland, *Dissonant Voices: Religious Pluralism and the Question of Truth* (Grand Rapids: William B. Eerdmans Publishing Co., 1991); Lesslie Newbigin, *The Gospel in a Pluralist Society* (Grand Rapids: William B. Eerdmans Publishing Co., 1989); Clark Pinnock, *A Wideness in God's Mercy* (Grand Rapids: Zondervan Publishing House, 1992); William C. Placher, *Unapologetic Theology: A Christian Voice in a Pluralistic Conversation* (Louisville, KY: Westminster/John Knox Press, 1989); John Sanders, *No Other Name: An Investigation into the Destiny of the Unevangelized* (Grand Rapids: William B. Eerdmans Publishing Co., 1992).

[11]Arthur F. Glasser, "Mission in the 1990's: Two Views," *International Bulletin of Missionary Research* 13 (January 1989): 7.

was carried out by various "missions." More recently this vocabulary has been pressed into use by corporations as they have considered it important to develop "mission statements," and many Christian organizations have followed suit. With this shift in usage and change of nuance, it would seem appropriate to conclude that if the church is to continue using "mission" vocabulary, "mission" must mean something different and much more than it has.

The implication of this, of course, is that mission should be spelled with a capital "M" and be identified with *all* the church is supposed to be and do—her *raison d'être* or reason for existence. This move, however, is being vigorously opposed. It is suggested that "when mission becomes everything the church does or is supposed to do in the world, missiology loses its focus and becomes whatever reflects the mood of the hour."[12] Certainly the present situation gives little indication of any particular focus. What was historically *missio dei* became "missions"; then missions became "foreign" and "home" missions. Now *everything* has become missions: Christian service camps, Bible colleges, nursing homes, and rescue missions. Even the preacher's travel allowance and Vacation Bible School expenses have been included in the missions budget, because they are considered to be a part of the church's evangelistic outreach. Virtually *everything* the church is about has *de facto* already been made a part of "missions." In the relatively short time of this evolution of vocabulary, missions as it was first known has witnessed an unhappy loss of support.

---

[12]Hesselgrave, *Today's Choices*, p. 136. These comments are a follow-up on John R. W. Stott's position found in *Christian Mission in the Modern World*, p. 30. Dr. Hesselgrave used the Trinity Evangelical Divinity School Trinity World Forum (Spring 1990) to severely critique Stott's position. A year later Stott's gracious response was made as an open letter and Dr. Hesselgrave has a surrejoinder.

Clarifying Mission—Missions—Evangelism

In the controversy over what constitutes mission or missions, two most significant issues must be faced. First, "mission" has been virtually, if not completely, equated with "evangelism." However, such an inclination to see mission only in terms of evangelism is a limited view of mission. The question is: is this biblically acceptable? When any one of several equally essential emphases is either prioritized or neglected, difficulties will arise and intensify. As a result, the present controversy over the nature of missions is symptomatic, and it has virtually created what is now called "missiology," a theological effort to discern from the biblical text a more adequate understanding of what mission or missions really should encompass.

Secondly, from a totally different impetus we have also been driven to a theological rethinking of mission or missions. This is highlighted by the EFMA's change of name from the Evangelical Foreign Missions Association to the Evangelical Fellowship of Mission Agencies.[13] It has become necessary to adjust to the changing face of the missionary force and to what actually constitutes a mission field. Presently, more than two-thirds of evangelical Christians are from *the rest* of the world[14] and "today the church is found, at least in some small measure, in most of the major cultures."[15] This is called by some the "third wave."[16] There is a "rapid rise of the Church and missionary activity in the Two-Thirds

---

[13]"Noteworthy," *International Bulletin of Missionary Research* 15 (July 1991): 117.

[14]Larry D. Pate, "The Dramatic Growth of Two-Thirds World Missions," in *Internationalising Missionary Training*, ed. William David Taylor (Grand Rapids: Baker Book House, 1991), p. 28.

[15]Ebenezer Sunder Raj, "Missionary Training—The Indian Context," in *Internationalising Missionary Training*, p. 66.

[16]See Douglas J. Elwood, "Riding the Third Wave," *International Bulletin of Missionary Research* 16 (January 1992): 22.

World"[17] and soon "the majority of Protestant missionaries will be from the non-Western world."[18]

What were once the mission *fields* of the world have become the new force in the missions *movement*. This accords with Kenneth Scott Latourette's thesis that "new missionary communities would emerge, which would surface in unexpected places and among unexpected people."[19] From Mexico City in 1963, W. A. Visser 't Hooft spoke of how the world could no longer be divided into "missionizing" and "missionary territories,"[20] and now the initiative in missions is being passed from the hands of the West to the "missionized," not because the West failed, but because it has been successful. While this is reason in itself to rejoice, success has blurred the concept of what a mission field is and in some cases even made the mission language pejorative.

When we think of evangelism or world evangelism in terms of mission or missions, we are presented with a significant irony. North America has been sending missionaries to Europe for some time, and now missionaries are coming to the U.S. from Asia, and their numbers will increase. Lesslie Newbigin, a kind of present-day Roland Allen, exposes a disturbing truth in responding to the question, "Can the West be converted?"[21] Newbigin says:

> What we have [in the West] is ... a pagan society whose public life is ruled by beliefs which are false. And because it is not a pre-Christian paganism, but a paganism born out of the rejection of Christianity, it is far tougher and more resistant to the gospel than

---

[17]Pate, "The Dramatic Growth," p. 39.

[18]Ibid., p. 35.

[19]See Tracey K. Jones, Jr., "History's Lessons for Tomorrow's Mission," *International Bulletin of Missionary Research* 10 (April 1986): 51.

[20]See Bosch, *Transforming Mission,* p. 493.

[21]Newbigin, "Can the West be Converted?" *International Bulletin of Missionary Research* 11 (January 1987): 2.

the pre-Christian paganisms with which foreign missionaries have been in contact during the past 200 years. Here, without possibility of question, is the most challenging missionary frontier of our time.[22]

The West itself has become a post-Christian wilderness of neopaganism: first Europe, now North America! Euromerica! A mission field?

Henrik Kraemer said over thirty years ago, "We stand at the definite end of a specific period or era of mission, and the clearer we see this and accept this with all our heart, the better."[23] Can we acknowledge that, like the Sunday school, missions as traditionally conceived is but a parachurch method of fulfilling God's will? Unfortunately, "world evangelism" has been veiled within the vocabulary of "missions," and we think little about evangelizing others unless it concerns those who are distant from us. The vocabulary, however, no longer seems to be appropriate, since those to whom we used to send missionaries are our neighbors, and it may take more time to drive to the airport than to fly to a foreign country. The mission field that once was far away now surrounds us!

A Dynamic View of Missions is Needed

Acknowledging the limited nature of our traditional view of "missions" will prove beneficial if it results in a biblical search for a more dynamic missiology. A dynamic understanding of mission is needed that can serve the church in the present and with which she can grow, as she fulfills her evangelistic ministry in the world. The age has come again to leap forward in all creativeness and work toward an understanding of the mission of the church (at least insofar as present insight will allow) that is grounded in a sound biblical theology.

---

[22]Newbigin, "Can the West be Converted?" p. 6.
[23]See Bosch, *Transforming Mission*, p. 7.

Dr. Hesselgrave reminds us, "The challenge to missions ... is to keep abreast of a changing world while still embracing the eternal written and living word."[24] The "changing world" challenges the church's traditions and theologies about evangelizing the world. Viewing evangelism or world evangelism in terms of mission or missions has limited our understanding of what the church's mission truly is.

Compounding matters is the fact that the global village has been virtually created by the scientific and technological advancements of the West. Few understand the background and effect of our present materialistic-atheistic age—how science, philosophy, and the church have respectively contributed to its making, and how their combination has sapped the church's life and her potency in witness. As great minds from the seventeenth century to the present have tried to integrate our new knowledge from the sciences with the Christian faith, inadequate theology and wrong premises in and about science have resulted in distortions that have led down a terrible road away from God and to an unGodly separation between the sacred and the secular— between faith (revelation) and reason.

Not fathoming the results at the time, what was seen in part as bringing in a kind of Kingdom on earth was instead raising up of a modern "golden calf" in our midst. Humanity turned from worshipping the Creator to idolizing the creation again: self, science, and technology. However, this modern Tower of Babel came to ruins beneath the mushroom cloud over Hiroshima, leaving humanity in worse condition than before: the idolatry of science and technology was toppled; Japan was left without her gods; and the West was left without God.

Concurrent with this development of modern man was the modern missions movement with missionaries

---

[24]Hesselgrave, *Today's Choices for Tomorrow's Mission*, p. 86.

going to the far corners of the earth. However, it is generally conceded that these same selfless, sacrificing servants of God, while propagating the gospel, became (unwittingly or not) the "civilizing" agents of global "heathenism," making straight the way for the rationalism, materialism, hedonism, and the atheism of the West. This helped produce a new global secular paganism in what might be called the "new" West.[25] Over time the church lost her way, internalizing the faith in a kind of self-defense mechanism against the evolving anti-Christian forces ravaging about, and she has now existed for some time in an unholy, antiworldly, and anti-intellectual stance. Consequently, the church has propagated a *limited* salvation of an *otherworldly* nature that has undermined the significance, relevance, and credibility of the biblical message of salvation for daily life, for believers as well as unbelievers.

Nevertheless, we would do well not to condemn this missionary consequence categorically. Eugene Nida has well said,

> The world has not been won to Christ, but the lives of millions of people have been enriched and transformed through the extraordinary dedication of the selfless thousands of missionaries, beginning with the apostles themselves. Never has the world been so blessed by so few.[26]

Missionaries have not failed; they have "made it possible for us to talk today of the world church."[27]

---

[25]See H. Dan Beeby, "A White Man's Burden, 1994," *International Bulletin of Missionary Research* 18 (January 1994): 7.

[26]Eugene A. Nida, "My Pilgrimage in Mission," *International Bulletin of Missionary Research* 12 (April 1988): 65.

[27]Lesslie Newbigin, "The Enduring Validity of Cross-Cultural Mission," *International Bulletin of Missionary Research* 12 (April 1988): 50.

On the other hand, the worldwide church that has accompanied globalization has been infected by all of the West's diseases. David Stowe writes,

> Virtually everyone in the world is affected by two realities. One is the powerful attraction of the styles of life and thought exhibited in the highly 'modernized' Western nations. The other is the tenacity and staying power of traditional culture.... I believe that the perspectives and the mentality of a worldwide modernizing and Westernizing culture will dominate the mission context as we move toward the third Christian millennium.[28]

Titus Loong, writing on training missionaries in Asia, says, "English and Western ways usually predominate in missionary gatherings."[29] In light of these notions, as the non-Western world (which is two-thirds of it) assumes a more and more important role, how will evangelism, world evangelism, and the Kingdom of God fare?

Things will go well only to the extent that the "new" West successfully avoids the enculturation and marginalization of the church that has occurred in the West. Never has the warning cliché, "what you win them with, you win them to," been any more significant. The church that has won its way around the world has done it with a *limited* view of mission and a *limited* view of salvation. As we come to the third millennium and to a pivotal point for the church, a dynamic new missiology is needed to advance the Kingdom of God.

---

[28]David M. Stowe, "Modernization and Resistance: Theological Implications for Mission," *International Bulletin of Missionary Research* 12 (October 1988): 146-147.

[29]Titus Loong, "Training Missionaries in Asia: The Asian Cross-Cultural Training Institute," in *Internationalising Missionary Training*, p. 44.

A Dynamic Missiology: A Biblical Perspective

The singular missiological purpose of Messiah Jesus, if discoverable in the scriptures, must unquestionably be the mission rationale for the church (John 20:21). When properly understood, it will surely provide the *dynamic missiology* needed for the people of God. In a sense, the biblical revelation is closed and absolute, but it is also dynamic. As we interact with it, we make new discoveries, we deepen our understanding, and we extend the applications of its truth. It is especially crucial, therefore, that we look to the Word in this present day for a holistic gospel.

The Western encapsulation of the gospel has weakened its force by separating evangelism from ethics and by removing the gospel from ecological considerations. A biblical critique of this shortsightedness can only heighten the appreciation of what "Almighty" means and reveal the great need in the church to see mission from the perspective of the "whole counsel of God." Such a view is essential for a valid and effective ministry of evangelism and world evangelism as well as for fulfilling other equally important priorities or responsibilities.

Mark records that "Jesus went into Galilee, proclaiming the good news of God. 'The time has come,' he said. 'The kingdom of God is near. Repent and believe the good news!'" (Mark 1:14-15 NIV). Jesus' hearers could scarcely believe their ears. John salutes Him, exclaiming, "Look the Lamb of God, who takes away the sin of the world." In response to Jesus, the people were amazed and said, "What is this? A new teaching—and with authority!" (Mark 1:27 NIV). What drew the crowds? What drew their acclamation? The gospel! What was the gospel? In Jesus' words, "The Kingdom of God has come."

In the Kingdom parables, Jesus expresses that the Kingdom of God has entered history in our time and space—in the world we know and experience. This is a promise kept by the Creator of the universe. God created man with the high purpose of being with him forever in a meaningful existence (Gen 1-2), but men and women chose to live after their own will and way, as if they knew better than the Creator (Gen 3). The consequence was death. Into God's cosmos or orderliness came chaos; into that which was good, very good, came disorder. But before casting man from the garden, God promised that He would yet make a way for man to fulfill his created purpose (Gen 3:15). In Jesus, the promise is kept (Matt 1:20-23). This is the gospel.

From Genesis 1:26 to Revelation 11:15, God has revealed that his will for man is that he participate in His plan for the creation and the ages (Heb 1-2). The gospel is this: that which was lost in the first Adam is recovered in the second (Rom 5), so far as the curse is found. Proclaiming the gospel—evangelism and world evangelism—is showing men and women how they can be a part of God's purpose again and be sons and daughters of the Creator.

When one turns to the book of Acts, the message remains the same. Luke records that Jesus continued to speak to them about the "things concerning the Kingdom of God" (1:8). When the gospel went to Samaria, "the good news [was] about the Kingdom of God" (8:12); and when the gospel went to the "uttermost parts," it was the message of the "Kingdom of God" (14:22). When Paul spoke to the dispersion, it was about the Kingdom of God (19:8). Luke and Paul particularly emphasized the message in recording Paul's farewell address to the elders of Ephesus. He preached to them the "gospel" (20:24), the "Kingdom" (20:25), "the whole will of God" (20:27). To the end, Paul tried to persuade his countrymen "about the Kingdom of God" (28:23); and when they could not be persuaded, he "preached the Kingdom of God" to the Gentiles (28:31).

The Kingdom of God is a word about God's presence in the here and now as well as later. It is about how the purpose of God is fulfilled in His people now and in the ultimate totality of God's reign later. Jesus says that it is by the light or "lamp" of this word (Mark 4:21-22) we understand the meaning of life, history, and the future. The Kingdom of God is the hermeneutic for interpreting or understanding everything around us.

Helmut Thielicke lectured to tens of thousands during World War II (with thousands of hand copies going to the war fronts). He said, "What we were doing there was teaching theology in the face of death ... the only thing that was of any help at all was the gospel itself." He said:

> I wanted to help them see their life and the course of history from the standpoint of Christ. I wanted to show them that faith not only has something to do with our state after death or with our inner religious life, but that it also opens our eyes to a wholly new way of looking at life here and now. That when we meet Christ we see nature (the creation), history, our fellow men, our community life, the problem of law and justice, war, and even our death with new eyes.[30]

So Thielicke lectured on the only thing that mattered—the Kingdom of God.

An adequate missiology entails the *totality* of God's missiological purpose. When it does, it will bring reconciliation to every area of alienation: the spiritual (God), the personal (self), the social (others), and the material (the rest of creation). A missiology grounded in the Kingdom of God, present and yet to be, will be dynamic, restoring power to proclamation and the repossession of His whole creation, especially humanity. Such a dynamic missiology will have far more than an evangelism and world evangelism emphasis; it will serve

---

[30]Helmut Thielicke, *Man in God's World*, translated and edited by John W. Doberstein (New York: Harper & Row, 1963), p. 10.

the *whole* purpose of God. It will bring the Kingdom of God into encounter with the stronghold of Satan (Luke 4:16-19; 2 Cor 10:13-15). It will be the church's ordering impetus!

This accords with the holistic biblical worldview grounded in Genesis 1-3. Especially in Ephesians but also in Colossians, we learn that the *high calling* on humanity is to be with God forever, in this life as He indwells us, and in life as it shall be as we dwell with Him (Eph 1:3-23). Paul's theology is thoroughly cosmic, and his word about the Kingdom in Romans is a word about the whole creation (Rom 8:22). Paul's word about the whole creation is placed in the context of evangelizing the world (Rom 1:5,8; 16:26). The vastness of humanity's dwelling place is, for the most part, only knowable to the twentieth-century mind through modern technology. When considering all that creation entails, it taxes our mind to think that God did all of this for us.

From a biblical perspective, we do not see the creation awaiting its destruction as if under condemnation. Rather, it anticipates deliverance and restoration with humanity, the zenith of God's creation (Heb 2:5-8) at our Lord's return, or on the eighth day of creation (Rom 8:18-25). What modern Western Christianity has failed to recognize is that humanity is an integral part of creation and shares solidarity with it. The universe is not merely a stage for redemption, it is valued by God for itself and is also being redeemed. Our bonds of imprisonment, then, are not the creation but the sin and shame of our disobedience and the consequent inability to exist in the immediate presence of the Creator and carry out His purpose.

The Church and Her Holistic Mission

T. S. Eliot said, "A wrong attitude toward nature implies a wrong attitude toward God, and the consequence is an inevitable doom."[31] The mission of God's people in the world and particularly to the world's peoples is jeopardized by the church's limited understanding of her reason for existing. Never in world history have so many claimed to be Christian; yet never has the church been so without influence. The church is like an ancient mariner on becalmed seas! Everything appears to be in order, but her witness to the world, whether in the West or the "new" West, is unconvincing. The twentieth-century church lies dead in the waters of a post-Christian world. Why? Because the church is hampered by science, technology, and an inadequate theology about God's relationship to the creation. The advancement of our scientific knowledge and the resulting technological capacity necessitate a reevaluation of our traditions and theological notions.

It is apparent from an examination of modern missions that the church suffers from a long-standing shortsighted view of her *mission*. Correcting her understanding of mission requires correcting her *limited view of salvation*. This will restore vitality, meaning, and motivation to the church—a church which will have a dynamic evangelism and world evangelism program.

G. Campbell Morgan so long ago in *The Mission Manifesto* expressed in his message, "The Evangel to Creation," that biblical salvation in its fullest implication means that God in Christ through man was bringing restoration and newness to the whole creation (Rom 8:22). Thus God's intention for humanity from his created beginning (Gen 1:26) ever remains the rationale for our very existence. This possibility through Christ *is* the gospel and it explains *why* there is a Great Commission.

---

[31]T. S. Eliot, quoted in Dorothy L. Sayers, "Creed or Chaos," in *The Necessity of Systematic Theology*, ed. John Jefferson Davis (Grand Rapids: Baker, 1978), p. 43.

The Great Commission is grounded in God's intention for the creation, establishing both a present and eternal purpose for humankind. Therefore, the salvation goal of saving *individuals* while remaining oblivious to the groaning of creation is entirely out of harmony with the full implication of the Great Commission.

The basic affirmation of humankind's identity—his being created in the image of God toward the responsible stewardship of all creation—is affirmed in the reconciling work of Jesus Christ (John 1; 1 Cor 8:6; Eph 1:10; Col 1:16-17; Heb 1; 2 Cor 5:17-21). In affirming His authority, Jesus categorically showed power over the demonic, nature, disease, physical life, and sin. Christ is the second Adam, restoring humanity to His true and original intentions. He makes possible the attainment of our vocation; he "rehumanizes" us. The creation of God and our evangelistic responsibilities thus cannot be separated. God's mission in Jesus Christ is the restoration of harmony between the Creator and creation, between God and humanity, and between man and creation, of which he is an inseparable part.

The church has jeopardized her mission by minimizing the meaning of the gospel. The "Christian" outlook has been appallingly narrow and, with disastrous effect, has failed to see the implications of the resurrection of Jesus Christ for the whole creation. In the resurrection, Christ overcame all the destructive forces operating in creation—the forces that have blighted and spoiled humanity and marred the whole creation. The risen Lord is Himself Master—the "first fruits" (1 Cor 15:20)—above all destructive forces, and those who come into union with Him receive His strength to gain victories over these forces themselves. He is the Renewer and Restorer of all that human life entails. "'Thou hast put all things in subjection under his feet.' For in subjecting all things to him, He left nothing that is not subject to him. But now we do not yet see all things subjected to him" (Heb 2:8 NASB). The "good news" is neither understood nor can it be preached with power until we come to realize that the gospel, for our Lord, was for the whole creation and not humanity only. The final victory awaits the consummation of the age, but His redeeming and regenerating work is the goal of our service. The full redemption of reality will come, and that anticipation challenges us to meaningful commitment to God's mission today.

Unless the church reorders its evangelism and world evangelism efforts under the whole biblical mission of mankind in a *dynamic missiology*, "How shall they hear?" (cf. Rom 10:14). People cannot hear when what they are told is not relevant to the world they know. Either we show in our presentation of the Gospel how all of humanity and our scientific age fit into the plan of God, or the image of God will remain unattractive and undesirable because such a God will be perceived as not big enough. Reality will no longer allow the church to live in a "spiritual" vacuum. The church must face up to the world dominated by the scientific enterprise. As Dorothy Sayers has said:

> These sciences have done an enormous amount to expose the *nature* and *mechanism* of man's inner dislocation and ought to be powerful weapons in the hand of the church. It is a thousand pities that the church should ever have allowed these weapons to be turned against her.[32]

If the church will yet take into account the scientific enterprise and face up to an evaluation and reformulation of her theological notions, then God's people will again be the blessing presence of God in the world by which the peoples may come to know and acknowledge Him as Lord. Life is a pulpit; worship is a life style. Science, education, psychology, anthropology, economics,

---

[32]Sayers, "Creed or Chaos," p. 43.

politics, art, industry, farming—every part of reality is a fit place from which to worship and preach. Being the church means occupying the world. We can be thankful that the church has begun to stand, not only for evangelism and world evangelism (individual salvation) but also for social action (servanthood). However, a further holistic reformulation of our theology must include the stewardship of *creation*!

Conclusion

Emptiness, emptiness, all is emptiness (Eccl 1:2). Without the ordering sound of the gospel's high calling and a dynamic missiology worked out under the all-encompassing purpose of God, all will be emptiness. Without a dynamic missiology, the splendid motivation of Isaiah (Isa 6:8) will not be there, and the excuses for the church's not sending or not going will have the same hollow sound as Cain's retort, "Am I my brother's keeper?" Evangelism and world evangelism are a *sine qua non* for the church, *but* under the auspices of our Creator who endowed science, reason, creativity, and language to be His *servants* to *all* and to be used in *stewardship* to Him for the *whole creation*. As G. Campbell Morgan concluded:

> If the first note of the *Missionary Manifesto* be the proclamation of the *Lordship of Christ*, the second note is the proclamation of the risen Lord as the *Renewer of the whole creation*; and the only way in which that proclamation can be made is by passing into the kosmos [*sic*] in order to communicate to it through sacrificial service the forces of our own Christ-renewed life.[33]

If this sounds grandiose, take note of J. R. R. Tolkien's *The Hobbit*. One autumn evening the wizard,

---

[33]Morgan, "The Evangel to Creation," p. 81.

Gandolf, pays a visit to Bilbo the Hobbit. Bilbo was doing his memoirs—recording all those misadventures and adventures of a time past—and they talked of their times together, and of course Bilbo asked how things were in the lands of the Mountain. Bilbo couldn't believe his ears:

> "Then the prophecies of the old sons have turned out to be true, after a fashion!" said Bilbo.
> "Of course!" said Gandolf. "And why should not they prove true? Surely you don't disbelieve the prophecies because you had a hand in bringing them about yourself? You don't really suppose, do you, that all your adventures and escapes were managed by mere luck, just for your sole benefit? You are a very fine person, Mr. Baggins, and I am very fond of you; but you are only quite a little fellow in a wide world after all!"
> "Thank goodness!" said Bilbo laughing, and handed him the tobacco-jar.[34]

Only those who know the Creator, what He has done in Christ, and that in Christ they are a part of God's cosmic purpose—only those can laugh and enjoy life irrespective of circumstance. "For anyone who enters God's rest also rests from his own work, just as God did from his" (Heb 4:10-11). Let us therefore be diligent to enter the labor that is rest. The world is waiting, waiting, yet waiting (cf. Isa 51:4-5).

---

[34]J. R. R. Tolkien, *The Hobbit*, rev. ed. (New York: Ballantine Books, 1966), pp. 286-87.

RECOMMENDED BIBLIOGRAPHY[35]

Bosch, David J. *Transforming Mission: Paradigm Shifts in Theology of Mission.* American Society of Missiology Series, No. 16. Maryknoll, New York: Orbis Books, 1991.

Bosch is historiographical, beginning with a statement about today's crisis in mission, then tracing the paradigmatic shifts in mission from the New Testament to the present, followed by an extensive analysis of what to expect and hope for. Selective readings can be of great benefit. [Advanced]

Carson, D. A. and John D. Woodbridge, eds. *God in Culture: Essays in honor of Carl F. H. Henry.* Grand Rapids: William B. Eerdmans Publishing Co., 1993.

An important work which presents the significance of the Christian faith in various cultural arenas. [Intermediate]

Hesselgrave, David J. and Edward Rommen. *Contextualization: Meanings, Methods, and Models.* Foreword by George W. Peters. Grand Rapids: Baker Book House, 1989.

Hesselgrave is the dean of evangelical missiology and he has written on contextualizing over the years. The book presents an analytical survey, critique, and proposals. [Intermediate]

_____. *Today's Choices For Tomorrow's Mission: An Evangelical Perspective On Trends and Issues In Missions.* Grand Rapids: Zondervan Publishing House, 1988.

Hesselgrave has surveyed the trends and issues in missions and reports and analyzes what he considers to be the ten most prominent concerns. The volume is profuse with data and provides an important evangelical viewpoint. Though the format is simple and the writing well done, the material is not easy reading. [Intermediate]

---

[35]Three books would provide the concerned person with a good balanced view of what is happening in missiology today: Bosch's *Transforming Mission*; Hesselgrave's *Today's Choices For Tomorrow's Mission*; and Shenk's *The Transfiguration of Mission.*

Larkin, William J., Jr. *Culture and Biblical Hermeneutics: Interpreting and Applying the Authoritative Word in a Relativistic Age.* Grand Rapids: Baker Book House, 1988. Vital to the contextualization issue is hermeneutics. Larkin's evangelical work addresses the issues in relation to today's pluralism. [Advanced]

Newbigin, Lesslie. *Foolishness to the Greeks: The Gospel and Western Culture.* Grand Rapids: William B. Eerdmans Publishing Co., 1986. Newbigin is a modern day Roland Allen and is "must" reading. Though the work is not necessarily original nor scholarly, he incisively critiques the West, recognizing it as the church's major "mission field." [Beginning]

Senior, Donald and Carroll Stuhlmueller. *The Biblical Foundations for Mission.* Maryknoll, NY: Orbis Books, 1991. An extensive and comprehensive work on the mission of God's people based upon the Old and New Testaments. [Advanced]

Shenk, Wilbert R., ed. *Exploring Church Growth.* Grand Rapids: William B. Eerdmans Publishing Co., 1983. Disregard the publication date of this book. It is a "must." It is a compilation of essays which explores missiological issues and critiques "church growth" principles. Though uneven in quality, certain chapters are classic. In relation to the accompanying essay, Rooy's "Theology of Humankind" is especially helpful. [Intermediate]

_____. *The Transfiguration of Mission: Biblical, Theological, & Historical Foundations.* Scottdale, PA: Herald Press, 1993. In the Mennonite tradition, Shenk is a premier missiologist. Bosch is in his debt and the only reason for the difference in their titles is that Bosch went to press first. The holistic view of mission is apparent throughout these essays. [Intermediate]

Taylor, William David. *Internationalizing Missionary Training: A Global Perspective.* Grand Rapids: Baker Book House, 1991. This is possibly the best place to get a grasp of what is happening missiologically in the two-thirds world. Comprehensive, analytical, and innovative. [Intermediate]

Tippet, Alan. *Introduction to Missiology.* Foreword by Charles and Marguerite Kraft. Pasadena, CA: William Carey Library, 1987. An important older book. This is a textbook on missiology not to be overlooked in seeking a balanced awareness of missiological issues. [Intermediate]

Chapter 8:

Worldview Studies and the Bride of Christ
by
Dr. Walter Puckett

Walter Puckett is the preaching minister for the First Christian Church in Crown Point, Indiana. By his own confession, up to the age of 34, he had "rejected most pastors, because it was evident that they were out of touch with the real world." For the first time, at the age of 34, he entered college (Lincoln Christian College) and was significantly influenced by James D. Strauss.

Today, Dr. Puckett holds a B.A. from Lincoln Christian College, M.A. degrees from Lincoln Christian Seminary and Indiana State University, and a D.Min. from Trinity Evangelical Divinity School. His M.A. theses dealt respectively with "Elton Trueblood" and "Alexander Campbell and the Millennium."

His doctoral project, entitled "World Views and their Relevance to Christian Life and Witness: Lessons to Help Lay People," became the basis for a book, *Bringing the Church Off The Slippery Slope*, which was published in 1993 by Brentwood Christian Press. Published articles by Dr. Puckett have appeared in the *Christian Standard* and the *Restoration Herald*.

In addition to several preaching ministries in Illinois and Indiana, Dr. Puckett served for six years as the Campus Pastor for Indiana State University and the Rose-Hulman Institute of Technology at Terre Haute, Indiana.

[Note: We regret that during the final stages of publishing this book, Dr. Puckett lost his battle with cancer. His emphasis on developing a "world-view" has now changed to the blessedness of possessing a "heaven-view." We trust that his ministry to the Bride of Christ will continue through his contribution here.]

WORLDVIEW STUDIES AND
THE BRIDE OF CHRIST

A Tribute

I will always be indebted to Dr. James D. Strauss for bringing new life to me. He challenged me to be a student for life. My pilgrimage with Dr. Strauss commenced in the parking lot of Lincoln Christian College and Seminary on a Sunday evening in 1967. I had entered Lincoln Christian College as a thirty-four year old freshman with a marvelous wife and three wonderful children. But I was still struggling with the state of the church and the real significance of the pastoral ministry after graduating from Lincoln Christian College. Dr. Strauss challenged me to enter seminary, and he not only became a key mentor, but a brother who has journeyed with me ever since. This relationship has had a deep effect on me and my entire family.

Dr. Strauss captured me with one of his chosen texts: "We demolish arguments and every pretension that sets itself up against the knowledge of God, and we take captive every thought to make it obedient to Christ" (2 Cor 10:5 NIV). He opened to me a new world of thinking by helping me understand the need of worldview studies in the context of the Lordship of Jesus Christ and the authority of God's Word. As our culture continues in its decadent convulsions, worldview studies make the Lordship of Christ and the authority of God's Word more vital. One might even say that church leaders and congregations who do not think "worldviewishly" are not totally representing Christ and His Word.

"Buried alive" in an "avalanche of change" is an explosive truth throughout Tom Sine's *Wild Hope*.[1] It is a useful description of the anti-Christian culture war being waged in this nation. The anti-Christian forces in this culture war seem bent on destroying the spiritual, intellectual, and moral stability in the United States. This war demands that the church take with all seriousness the chosen text of Dr. Strauss (2 Cor 10:5) in equipping the bride of Christ to become a confessional, socially penetrating church in our toxic, pluralistic society.[2] Through worldview studies, the Church can be equipped as "resident aliens"[3] to bring Christian belief back into a post-modern and post-Christian world. This must happen if the church is to reclaim the higher ground in the intellectual debate casting truth against relativism, multiculturalism, pragmatism, deconstructionism, pluralism, and political correctness.

In many respects, the Church has failed in this debate. Relativism and other "isms" have created an almost totally secularistic and pagan society, because most conservative Christians develop a faith that is privately engaging but socially irrelevant. All one has to do to see this in part of the Stone-Campbell heritage is to look at the sermons and workshops of the 1993 North American Christian Convention. It was, in one respect, an opportunity missed. The theme of the convention was significant: "A Focused Church in a Fragmented World." Christ was preached as the answer, but not one workshop or sermon dealt with the questions

---

[1]Tom Sine, *Wild Hope* (Dallas: Word, 1991).

[2]Later in this essay, I will emphasize the nature and obligations of a "confessional" church. Essentially, a confessional church is one which is answerable to Christ alone, confessing Him in word and in an unconcealed lifestyle. The term "confessional" does not imply any particular allegiance to a denomination, creed, or doctrinal confession.

[3]See Stanley Hauerwas and William H. Willimon, *Resident Aliens: Life in the Christian Colony* (Nashville, Abingdon Press, 1990).

of how our nation has become so fragmented and pagan. The old myth is still alive: if enough people will become Christian, then society and the world will automatically be changed. Not true. God's Word must be preached, but the fragmentation of God's world must also be understood. The Church must be equipped to penetrate society via the transformed lives of disciples. Easy? Not at all. Imperative? Absolutely!

This approach helps answer Tertullian's famous question—one that has been asked again and again in the history of the Church, and it must be asked again now: "What does Athens have to do with Jerusalem?" By "Athens" he meant the intellectual culture, the life of the mind, the study of philosophy, literature, and history. By "Jerusalem" he meant Christianity, redemption through the blood of Jesus, faith, hope, and charity. Tertullian was responding to the erosion of the radical nature of the gospel which had been adapted to Greek thought forms. Rhetorically, the question is asking, if you are a new creature in Christ, why do you need *intellectual* culture? Let the pagan wisdom alone.

But if Jerusalem refuses to have anything to do with Athens, and if Jerusalem in general fails to display the incarnational significance of God's revelation in Christ and isolates herself from the world of the marketplace and intellectual thought with some safe eschatology, then the Church is irresponsible and ignores the dominion and witness mandates of Christ to take Him into the world.[4] Today, Athens has the upper hand. Jerusalem (the Church) limps along in a defeated manner. Intolerant secularism declares for the moment, "Let Christians have their own little compounds. We have the world!" And strangely enough, Christians who want nothing to do with Athens agree by default with

---

[4]See John F. Cosby, "Education and the Mind Redeemed," *First Things* 18 (1991): 23-28.

devotees of secularism: Athens has nothing to do with Jerusalem.

Our modern culture alienated from God is a "cut-flower civilization"[5] without an authentic working faith. Christianity is present in name but not in effective power. This situation demands that the Church raise up "history makers" who will offer society an alternative worldview that consistently and coherently gives individuals and society purpose, direction, and hope in the midst of a plurality of worldviews.

Jeremiah provides a paradigm for "history makers" consisting of five qualities crucial to worldview thinking: (1) Having a profound sense of anguish, pathos, and incongruity that touches one personally, knowing that worldviews cause the anguish in society. (2) Exuding confidence in the moral coherence of the world still held together by God, even though it does not always look like it.   (3) Asserting the raw sovereignty of God in the historical process.   (4) Possessing the capacity for social analysis and criticism as a result of worldview studies.   (5) Expressing the bold conviction that the Christian worldview is the only authentic hope for providing answers to humanity's persistent questions.[6]

The Church must be equipped for these times by understanding the crises a civilization experiences when it is without Christianity as a working faith.   Such an understanding will result from worldview studies, and it will follow the paradigm of Jeremiah by developing a confessional and effective Church in our post-Christian pluralistic society.

---

[5]D. Elton Trueblood, *The Predicament of Modern Man* (New York: Harper & Row, 1944), p. 59.

[6]See Walter Brueggeman, *Hope Within History* (Atlanta: John Knox Press, 1987), pp. 49-71.

An Imperative Call:
Worldview Awareness and Understanding

If Christians as "resident aliens" are to be powerfully confessional and penetrating in our pluralistic society in the sunset of this century and the dawn of the twenty-first century, worldview studies in Bible Colleges, Seminaries, Christian Liberal Arts Colleges, and local congregations are imperative. These studies must have a priority second only to the Word of God itself. To ignore these studies in the context of learning God's Word is morally, spiritually, and intellectually irresponsible. Worldview studies are about the complex strands of ideas that have consequences and that shape our culture. A worldview is the philosophy one accepts to deal with life. A succinct definition of worldview is: "A set of presuppositions or assumptions which we hold consciously or subconsciously about the basic make-up of our world."[7] Every person has a worldview or an eclectic worldview that dramatically affects and effects his or her everyday decisions in life and culture. These "assumptions" are what people believe to be the final truths upon which life is based and lived out. A worldview is like a stability structure, a person's attempt to make sense out of the world of ideas and experiences. A valid worldview enables one to integrate all the parts of life into a meaningful, consistent, and coherent whole. A worldview is Charles Kraft's "central control box,"[8] and whatever worldview dominates a society and affects all its cultural dimensions is its "central control box."

Until recent decades the Christian worldview was the dominant influential worldview in America. No longer is that even close to being true. In spite of the

---

[7]James Sire, *The Universe Next Door*, 2nd ed. (Downers Grove: InterVarsity Press, 1988), p. 17.

[8]Charles H. Kraft, *Christianity In Culture* (Maryknoll: Orbis Books, 1981), p. 53.

megachurch, the super-church syndrome, and church growth mania, the power of Christian influence is waning. Why? Have we lost the focus of the Gospel—God's reconciling power, which is unique to Christianity—and substituted church growth techniques? It appears that we have learned to reproduce the church as an organization, but without its transforming message. The megachurch movement seems to have three major emphases: management, therapy, and communication. At the same time, marketing (which involves product, price, place, and promotion) is the watchword. "Church" appears to be performing a service business much more than offering a systematic exposition of the Word of God. All of this produces a cafeteria spirituality where the customer is king, and where a pastor's accountability may not be based on doctrinal faithfulness but on the number of bodies and received currency. Member recruitment has replaced biblical conversion, and the myths that prop up the spate of "growthism" are crumbling and begging for something deeper—such as the transforming grace of God. Church growth strategies "waltz all around" our intense biblical and social problems which only Christ can remedy, but they "never get to the heart of the issue, content instead to appeal to the consumerism of today's religious shoppers."[9]

In worldview studies two dimensions to Christian witnessing in a confessional stance are required. First, the Christian doing the witnessing must know what he or she believes and why; and secondly, the Christian doing the witnessing must know what the person being witnessed to believes and why. Otherwise, there is very little communication that can lead to conversion. This

---

[9]George R. Hunsberger, "The Changing Face of Ministry: Christian Leadership for the Twenty-first Century," *Reformed Review* 44 (Spring 1991): 225.

worldview awareness is imperative if the confessional Church is to be adequately equipped to penetrate society. Biblical sanctions for worldview studies are prominent. In 1 Chronicles 12:23-38, David, the anointed king, looked for men raised up by God who had commitment, courage, and competence. Specifically, the men of Issachar "understood the times and knew what Israel should do" (v. 32 NIV). In Matthew 16:1-3 Jesus upbraided the religious leaders for their knowing about the weather but for not knowing how to "interpret the signs of the times" (v. 3 NIV). Luke 19:44 suggests the need for worldview understanding when it records Jesus' prophecy of destruction on Jerusalem because it "did not recognize the time of God's coming to you" (NIV). And Peter exhorts every Christian to "always be prepared to give an answer to everyone who asks you to give the reason for the hope that you have" (1 Pet 3:15 NIV). To do this, Christians need to know God's Word and God's world. Both call for exegesis. Worldview studies and apologetics cannot be separated. Neither, unfortunately, receives much attention in local congregations.

The classic text supporting the importance of worldview studies is Acts 17:22-34. Many church growth specialists are incorrect when they see Paul's effort as a failure here. In all reality he was a smashing success because of what he reveals. He knew the worldviews of his audience, challenging every assumption of the Stoic and Epicurean philosophers with the preaching about "an unknown God" who could transform their lives and answer their questions. Paul's audience included naturalists, evolutionists, universalists, and pantheists. Paul's sermon is a classic example of confronting the world with a transformed mind. As Dr. Strauss has often said, "Paul never gave up thinking and just went to preaching as many have today."[10]

---

[10]Whether these biblical sanctions will move congregational leaders to become worldview thinkers remains to be seen. Dr. Robert

My conviction is that the Christian worldview, among the plurality of worldviews, is the only one able to integrate consistently and coherently all the parts of life and of society into a whole (Col 1:17). A worldview that excludes God and His revelation will prompt one to make dramatically different decisions spiritually and morally from one that is biblically grounded. Worldview studies to equip the bride of Christ are imperative! This is a battle to the finish!

Christian education must rise above the present psyche of the novel writings of Peretti. Although they are marketed with adulation, John Seel believes that "these books are no better than pulp fiction. Yet he [Peretti] is compared shamelessly to such great Christian writers as ... C. S. Lewis" and others. The books are "repetitive—'puffed wheat' literature with small grains of content."[11]

An Imperative Cultural Awareness: A Civilization Diseased and Dis-eased By Modernity

Our culture is undergoing the most fundamental change since its inception in 1776. Just as rains and floods battered the midwest along the Mississippi River during the summer of 1993, so a philosophical storm birthed from a titanic change in worldview is shaking our society to its very core. Today, we are seeing not only what is termed the post-Christian and post-modern culture, we are also seeing and living within a

---

Lowery of Lincoln Christian Seminary has said, "The world has not seen the Christian worldview demonstrated, because the Christian worldview is rejected more by the church than the world." Indeed, the demands of living out a Christian worldview are great. As Lowery states, "The most difficult place to live out the Christian worldview is within the church." Yet meeting the demands is precisely what is required of Christian disciples.

[11]John Seel, *The Evangelical Forfeit* (Grand Rapids: Baker Books, 1993), pp. 43-44.

widespread and growing radical assault on the Judaeo-Christian values which helped form this nation. The Church has allowed these alien worldviews and culture wars to dislocate it from the center of society off onto a slippery slope away from society's center. Therefore, our task of "bringing the Church off the slippery slope"[12] requires not only worldview studies, but also an awareness of the state of our "cut-flower civilization" which is ravished by the power of modernity without the transforming faith of the Church.

Significant minds and sobering voices like Russell Kirk are suggesting that the stability of our civilization is in jeopardy. Positive-mind-benders will not listen to such prophets. But for Christians to ignore such prophets is to be irresponsible. Consider our cities and recognize the lack of moral imagination and right reason required to keep some sense of a tolerable community. Our cities illustrate our age of bewildering thinking and character. How far might we be from the end of an era—a culture that may be on the verge of being dumped into the dustbin of history? Does the Church have anything to say to that?

Is this too gloomy for "cheap grace" Christians who have invested in a pragmatic approach to church growth at the price of true Truth? A pop psyche religion that is a mere private matter and that bows to the consumer generation of gushing baby boomers and busters is not Christianity. It is a religious muddle wherein the central values are personal choice, tolerance of different lifestyles, mixing religion and psychology, and doing whatever works for them. This is nothing but a transformed narcissism that may lead to the question: "What is so special about Christianity?" The crisis, simply put, is that the social function the churches once

---

[12]See Walter Puckett, *Bringing The Church Off The Slippery Slope* (Columbus: Brentwood Christian Press, 1993).

fulfilled in American life is gone. As Kennon Callahan has put it, "The day of the churched culture is over."[13]

My British friend, the late Malcom Muggeridge, offers much to consider in the final paragraph of his essay, "The Great Liberal Death Wish."[14] In these shadow years of the twentieth century, it deserves a wider audience.

> As the astronauts soar into the vast eternities of space, on earth the garbage piles higher; as the groves of academe extend their domain, their alumni's arms reach lower; as the phallic cult spreads, so does impotence. In great wealth, great poverty; in health, sickness; in numbers, deception. Gorging, left hungry; sedated, left restless; telling all, hiding all; in flesh united, forever separate. So we press on through the valley of abundance that leads to the wasteland of satiety, passing through the gardens of fantasy; seeking happiness ever more ardently, and finding despair ever more surely.[15]

Likewise, writers such as Stanley Hauerwas and Alasdair MacIntyre concur with Muggeridge's verdict on society, emphasizing that the remnant must first come together in little communities of character "while society slides toward its ruin."[16] This is not a pretty conclusion,

---

[13]Kennon Callahan, *Effective Church Leadership* (San Francisco: Harper and Row, 1990), p. 13.

[14]Through my association with Elton Trueblood, I have had the privilege of talking at length with Muggeridge on several occasions and of sharing a meal with him at his home south of London. Based on his writings and his concerns for the church and today's culture as expressed to me, he was a true prophet in our day.

[15]Cited in Russell Kirk, "Civilization Without Religion," *Touchstone* 6 (Winter 1993): 5-6.

[16]See Kirk, "Civilization Without Religion," p. 6. Note Stanley Hauerwas's and Willimon's *Resident Aliens*; Stanley Hauerwas, *After Christendom?* (Nashville: Abington Press, 1991; and Alasdair MacIntyre, *After Virtue: A Study of Moral Theory*, 2nd ed. (Notre Dame: University of Notre Dame Press, 1984).

but we best not write it off. Before the world can be
effectively confronted with the gospel, the church must
exhibit communities of character which are different
from, though not isolated from, the world. The need for
the bride of Christ, an authentic bride of Christ, is a
desperate need!

Part of the problem is that most faith today really
does not impact the world around us. We are a society
in peril, in an advanced state of decadence, needing the
glory of Christ coming through the Church, because
fundamentally what ails modern civilization is the decay
of the authentic, life-transforming religious faith of
biblical Christianity. A Christianity controlled by
"seekers" and a Christ who is "user-friendly" will never
save society. T. S. Elliot said, "Redeem the time; redeem
the dream." In the words of Russell Kirk,

> If a culture is to survive and flourish, it must not be
> severed from the religious vision out of which it arose.
> The high necessity of reflective men and women, then,
> is to labor for the restoration of religious teachings as
> a credible body of doctrine.... It remains possible,
> given right reason and moral indignation, to confront
> boldly the age's disorders. The restoration of true
> learning, humane and scientific; the reform of many
> public policies; the renewal of our awareness of a
> transcendent order, and of the presence of an Other;
> the brightening corners where we find ourselves—such
> approaches are open to those among the rising
> generation who look for a purpose in life. It is just
> conceivable that we may be given a Sign before the
> end of the twentieth century; yet Sign or no Sign,
> Remnant must strive against the follies of the time.[17]

In all of this confusion and fragmentation, the
Trojan horse of modernity must be challenged by the
confessional church. Modernity is a key cause for the

---

[17]Kirk, "Civilization Without Religion," p. 9.

crises both in America and the American church. Modernity has contributed to the loss of authority and to the shallowness of the American church as manifested in the contemporary church growth movement. The statistics of the Church are high; the influence very low and waning.

"Modernity" (derived from the Latin word *modernus* meaning "just now" or "of today") involves not just a particular intellectual "paradigm" stemming from the Enlightenment. *Modernity is an unprecedented psychological and spiritual rupture of a people from its cultural and spiritual roots.* The result is faith's loss of authority in society. Furthermore, as John Seel observes, long before modernity changes the doctrinal content of belief,

> it alters one's assumptions about how life is to be organized day to day. Before theology is diluted, every other aspect of social life is transformed. The new is celebrated while the traditional is ridiculed. Big is presumed to be better. Meeting felt needs takes precedence over meeting real needs. Maximizing efficiency and control overtakes the slower, and more human, patterns of social organization. Images replace a respect for reading and the importance of words.... And so modernity has become the greatest challenge facing the church and discipleship since the gnosticism of the second century.[18]

Os Guinness provides a most useful analysis of the spiritual challenges which modernity poses.[19]

(1) "Modernity is the central fact of human life today." It is global and the most powerful culture in history. It is "the great alternative to the kingdom of

---

[18]Seel, *The Evangelical Forfeit*, p. 110.

[19]See Os Guinness, *Dining With The Devil* (Grand Rapids: Baker Book House, 1993), pp. 17-20.

God." Its threat is as severe as Egypt, Assyria, and Babylon in the exile of Israel.

(2) "Modernity is double-edged for human beings." It represents "the greatest human advances in history" as to benefits, power, convenience, etc., but also presents "the greatest assaults on humanness in history" such as the crises of identity and of the family.

(3) "Modernity is double-edged for followers of Christ." That is, it represents "the greatest single opportunity" equivalent to Roman roads and printing presses. It is also "the greatest single challenge the church has faced" since the apostles confronted persecution and gnosticism together.

(4) "Modernity is foundational for the character and identity of both Americans and American evangelicals." Both camps have "prospered at the growing edge of modernity,... but those most blessed by modernity are most blind to it, and those first hit by modernity are often the worst hurt by modernity."

(5) "Modernity's central challenge to America is focused in America's crisis of cultural authority. Modernity creates problems deeper than drugs, crime," etc. It creates the crisis of "cultural authority" wherein America's beliefs, ideals, and traditions are losing or have lost their compelling power in society. "What people believe no longer makes much difference to how they behave." This must be reversed or America is undone as culture unravels.

(6) "Modernity's central challenge to evangelicals is focused in the crisis of the authority of faith." This undermines the churches' capacity to demonstrate with integrity an effective faith that can provide an answer to America's crises. The churches' captivity to modernity is the prime reason faith's influence wanes more and more while culture's influence continues to keep the church dis-eased on the slippery slope of a pagan society.

(7) "Modernity is a monumental paradox to the everyday practice of faith." This is very important:

"Modernity simultaneously makes evangelism easier—more people at more times in their lives are more open to the gospel—yet makes discipleship harder, because practicing the Lordship of Christ runs counter to the fragmentation and specialization of modern life."

(8) "Modernity pressures the church toward polarized responses." Historically, liberals have generally surrendered to modernity without much effort and conservatives have tended to defy it without understanding it. This has been reversed. Progressive conservatives—megachurch—now court the "affluent consumers" of the gospel like the liberals once courted the "cultured despisers" of the gospel. "The two main examples today are the megachurch leaders marrying the managerial ... and the Christian publishers romancing the therapeutic."

(9) "Modernity's challenge cannot be escaped by the common responses to which Christians typically resort." Those recognizing the deficiencies of liberal and conservative responses often go to two further deficient responses. One resort is "pre-modernism"—looking for refreshment from the Third World that has not yet had to face modernization. The other resort is "post-modernism." However, while post-modernism recognizes that "modernism as a set of ideals built on the Enlightenment has collapsed," it fails to grasp that "modernity as the fruit of capitalism and industrialized technology is stronger than ever."

(10) "Modernity represents a special challenge to the church." The three strongest national challenges to the gospel in the modern world are Japan, Europe, and the United States. Japan has never been reached or won to Christ; Europe has been reached or won to Christ twice and lost twice; and America, "though having the strongest and wealthiest churches, is now experiencing the severest crisis, so represents the clearest test case of Christian responses to modernity."

(11) "Modernity represents a special challenge to reformation." The reason for this special challenge is its dismissal of words, replacing them with images and viewing instead of reading. The words that have remained are abstract to people. But "post-modernism further devalues words by using them to create a pastiche of effect regardless of their original meaning (for example, the multiple cultural uses of 'born-again' in advertising or new programs)."

(12) "Modernity represents a special challenge to revival." The fact is that the Church has not experienced a major nationwide revival under modernity's conditions. Modernity, on one hand, "undercuts true dependence on God's sovereign awakening by fostering the notion that [man can] effect revival by human means." On the other hand, "modernity makes people satisfied with privatized, individualistic, and subjective experiences that are pale counterfeits of true revival."

Thus, modernity has contributed to the state of our cut-flower culture without allowing an authentic transforming religious faith. As a result, three troubling dimensions of the megachurch movement call for examination.[20] The first is "the movement's challenge to theological education," which is almost a trade-off of theology for technique. The second is that, because of the accommodation to modernity within the evangelical camp, the movement has thus become "a prime, if unwitting, agent of secularism." The third is its truncated view of discipleship that "reduces not only the purpose of discipleship to evangelism, but ... fails to teach the importance of calling in the whole life" of the person evangelized. As a result of bowing to pragmatism, it seems that theology, liturgies, and messengers of God do not matter. But folksy stories, schmaltzy music, and satellite dishes do.

---

[20]See Seel, *The Evangelical Forfeit*, pp. 89-94.

In conclusion, this must be stated about modernism. Modernism is possibly dying around us, because the principles of the Enlightenment no longer work and are being discarded. Modernism has lived on a moral and intellectual capital that it has not renewed, and its foundations are eroding. What an opportunity for the church! But what if the modern church is not stronger in influence than the megachurch movement? It will miss this great occasion to recapture every inch of culture for God.

An Urgent Agenda Required:
The Confessional Church

It is an urgent call for the church equipped by worldview studies to be confessional in order to penetrate our pluralistic society and display the glory of Christ.

Pluralism in America has created a spiritual hothouse in which many more kinds of faith and fervor have flourished. Pluralism today most likely foreshadows an even more intense pluralism tomorrow. Pluralism has been no stranger to the American experience. Pluralism and its opportunities and challenges have been at the heart of this new nation and have always been a part of our American story. But postwar years have witnessed an unprecedented expansion of pluralism in our society, graduating, according to James Edwards, "from its subservience to the goals of human rights and technological specialization to an end in itself." Pluralism is a "collage of quasi-values promoted by assertion and unchallenged by reason or faith." If relativism asserts that nothing is absolutely true, pluralism asserts that all things are equally true. But to say that all things are true is to say that nothing is true, and even reasonable efforts to critique between competing claims are labeled as "elitist, patriarchal, or oppressive."[21]

Pluralism is not relativism. It does carry a doctrine that includes a belief in relativism. But in our case, as Guinness points out, "pluralism is a condition of society in which numerous different religious, ethnic, and cultural groups live together in one nation under one government." It is a social reality rather than a philosophical conclusion. It is "the end of a process [pluralization] that is at the heart of modernity and modernization."[22] This toxic pluralism makes it easy for the dominating, mindless, and destructive power of multiculturalism as a philosophy of forced equality and political correctness to grow.

In one form or another pluralism has influenced the church throughout its history, but its force is probably stronger today. The world into which Christianity surfaced was much like our culture. By Jesus' day the classical world was fragmented, the one-time-bountiful cosmos was in crisis, and the socially deteriorating forces were strong and hostile to life. Yet, as Edwards reveals,

> It was in this disintegrating world that ... the witness of Christians made legendary headway. In a fearful and capricious world, the gospel promised universal salvation in Jesus Christ; amidst cults of secrecy, the gospel was proclaimed openly in synagogues and market places; in a world searching for individual escape, the gospel took on the form of an organized church, a witnessing and sometimes suffering community of faith; and in an age when no way or truth was deemed compelling enough to demand the whole of human life, followers of Jesus

---

[21]See James R. Edwards, "A Confessional Church in a Pluralistic World," *Touchstone* 6 (Winter 1993): 17.

[22]Os Guinness, *The American Hour* (New York: The Free Press, 1993), p. 187.

Christ bore witness to their faith by the supreme sacrifice of martyrdom.[23]

In our times, however, pluralism may actually turn out to be the last, best hope for the Christian worldview rather than its inevitable destroyer. How? Because it may help demonstrate that no other worldview brings transformation, healing, and hope to our culture. It is therefore possible, in the midst of many alternative worldviews in our pluralistic society, that Christ may be recognized as the only alternative modern man has left if he is to survive individually and socially. As Guinness claims, "Pluralism could create conditions for a rebound against pluralism itself."[24]

Therefore, since pluralism is not a new but just a larger challenge, how should it affect the church? What does it mean to live by the gospel in the context of the pluralistic and cultural assumptions adopted by society today? The answer to the challenge commences with understanding the use of "confessional" in this essay. The "confessional church" understands the statement "Jesus is Lord" to mean that He is Lord of all life, creation, and peoples. This was the truth that brought the church into existence, defined Christians, and determined the missionary nature of the historic faith. A confessional faith was to penetrate every social parameter of society through the lives of transformed believers. The gospel was given to go public. It should lay claim on those who enter the truth by faith and obligate them to bear witness to Christ by word and deed. This is why having an obedient faith in Christ as Lord is personal, but never private. The church, by nature, should be confessional and missionary in

---

[23]Edwards, "A Confessional Church in a Pluralistic World," p. 17.

[24]Guinness, *The American Hour*, p. 372.

reclaiming the lost and in penetrating public life.[25] "The purpose of the church is to be a beacon of hope in a floundering culture/society."[26]

This confessional stance will develop the kind of church that is able to respond to the increasing questions over the place for truth within evangelical theology in the context of a "mega-Christianity" mentality. Answers to such questions are needed even within our own Restoration Movement heritage. That is why books like *No Place For Truth* by David F. Wells is imperative reading for church leaders.[27] This confessional stance will prevent the gospel from being reduced to a functionalism "wherein the gospel is anesthetized and the Church becomes an institution of accommodation rather than conversion."[28]

American culture has moved away from the Judaeo-Christian worldview of theism through Enlightenment deism into relativism and a "cheerful" nihilism. In fact, many modern churches have *rejected* content for style, truth and its meaning for impressions, biblical belief for games, ethical rules for social role-playing, and the gospel for therapy. Only the confessional church in a world wallowing in pluralism can turn that tide. Christians who take the confessional stance will be able to encounter effectively those who have written off the church but who advocate a new spirituality in their quest for transcendence. The church

---

[25]This confessional nature arises from the authority of Jesus as a result of acknowledging the empowerment by God at Jesus' baptism. The Spirit of God anointed Jesus with power to carry out His mission as Suffering Servant. Jesus Himself was and is the gospel.

[26]Edwards, "A Confessional Church in a Pluralistic World," p. 19.

[27]See David Wells, *No Place for Truth: Or Whatever Happened to Evangelical Theology?* (Grand Rapids: Eerdmans, 1993). Also note Os Guinness and John Seel, ed., *No God but God* (Chicago: Moody Press, 1992) and Guinness's *Dining with the Devil*.

[28]Edwards, "A Confessional Church in a Pluralistic World," p. 19.

will be able to satisfy this quest only if it operates with more than a church growth methodology that too often bypasses making committed disciples. The confessional stance will make it possible for Christians to be suffering servants who will be equipped and able to stand firm in and for Christ's truth in the midst of a hostile and relativistic society that has marginalized God and His church in our post-modern and post-Christian culture.

A poorly equipped church which affirms in theory only that "Jesus is Lord" gives cultural pluralism permission for marginalizing God and His church. The mindset of many church people has unfortunately remained since the 1950s—a time when society was not too indifferent to, but actually supportive of, the church. The church thought it was strong, but it was not. When alien worldviews entered the fray of society and began their ravaging assault in the 1960s, the church had no idea of what was happening. This has cast the church onto society's slippery slope. Without the confessional stance, Christians will never be God's subversive agents for Christ in our seductive culture. And since real evangelism is all but gone from the life of many congregations, igniting a subversive witness may be our last and best hope of cultural penetration.

The confessional stance of combined biblical studies, theological understanding, and worldview studies is imperative if the church is to reclaim the high ground of intellectual inquiry and debate in the midst of radical pluralism. Without this, the possibility of the church saying much of significance to our kind of society is small.

Through worldview studies, confessional Christians can be prepared to respond adequately when modern mindsets are more interested in what the biblical text allows than what it says; when biblical theology relies more on the social sciences than on Christ; when attacks on the transcendence and sovereignty of God from radical feminism are strong;

when the "Holy Spirit" as a mirror of human experience is more important than Christ and Scripture; and when the renewed quest for the historical Jesus is failing to find God's Son, the once-for-all revelation of God who takes away the sins of the world.

All of this is about developing a confessional church that will come alive by Christ's authority in a pluralistic society and then venture into this society armed with worldview studies to display His glory. It is about risking faithfulness to the Lord rather than seeking acceptance by culture; making disciples who understand the content of faith instead of "disciples" who merely possess paper membership; moving into boldness rather than pandering to the manufactured felt-needs of modern narcissism; risking the naming of sin—social and personal—as a first essential step to forgiveness, transformation, and holiness; reclaiming the pastoral office from mere management and psychological technique to the preaching office of biblical exposition; becoming an advocate of life from womb to the grave rather than complying with the evils of taking life; teaching a responsible sexual ethic; calling the church from rights to responsibilities; and grounding the church's total existence in the Lordship of Christ. For integrity's sake, the only alternative is taking down His name from the church and closing the doors.[29]

Alasdair MacIntyre writes, "The barbarians are not waiting beyond the frontiers; they have been governing us for quite some time. And it is our lack of consciousness of this that constitutes part of our predicament.[30] These barbarians can only be stopped by a confessional Church. "Apart from the person of Christ the Church has no existence, apart from the message of Christ the Church has no proclamation, apart from the

---

[29]Ibid., p. 20.
[30]Cited in James Davison Hunter, *Culture Wars* (Basic Books: HarperCollins, 1991), p. 315.

call of Christ the Church has no mission. Its existence, message, and mission are His; for the Church is His body"[31] called to display His glory in a pluralistic culture and world.

An Indispensable Ingredient: God's Enabling Grace

Crucial items on the challenging agenda are that we recognize the need for God's grace and understand "the special cultural situation in which grace seeks a hearing." As Oden observes,

> When sex is reduced to orgasm, spirituality to numbers, and politics to power, grace has been squandered and neglected. We treat spiritual formation as the baseball fan treats the statistic page or a broker treats computer readouts of stock averages, or television treats sweeps week, or educators treat grade averages. Spiritual growth is reduced by some to a spreadsheet operation. Bean counters and number crunchers pretend to measure personal maturation, focusing on technique and quantification at the expense of spiritual empowerment.... Therapeutic and managerial stratagems have swamped the process of listening attentively for grace.... When the church exists to satisfy immediately felt needs, it has lost the grace that makes it whole. When the Bible is treated as a vending machine and evangelization as a marketing plan, grace is tamed and reduced to routine. When preachers look to polls more than to prophets, hoping to guess what the public next wants to hear, grace becomes cheap. In all these ways the word of grace has in our time become conventional, trivial, prosaic, uninteresting, and predictable.... In a time when user-friendly religious communities have lost their distinct identity amid a maze of relativisms, the study

---

[31]Edwards, "A Confessional Church in a Pluralistic World," p. 20.

of grace · takes on new urgency and decisive meaning.... We have tried to manufacture spiritual growth while missing the very grace that would enable it.[32]

Ideas do have consequences! The war of ideas is a real war with real casualties. If the church continues to flounder and fail on the slippery slope with business as usual, the casualties will be enormous. Unless we renew what it means to be a biblical Christian in the church, the credibility needed to speak to our culture will not be found. It is crucial that we not delay our response any longer. Tomorrow's agenda is ever more urgent *today*!

------

[32]Thomas C. Oden, *The Transforming Power of Grace* (Nashville: Abingdon Press, 1993), pp. 16-19.

RECOMMENDED BIBLIOGRAPHY

Callahan, Kennon. *Effective Church Leadership.* San Francisco: Harper and Row, 1990.
One of the best treatments of the topic that builds upon the biblical qualities of leadership.

Guinness, Os. *The American Hour.* New York: The Free Press, 1993.
A massive treatment of the present and future role of faith in America. Revival is possible, but not as revival is understood by many Christians. It is true biblical revival that Guinness demands.

_____. *Dining With the Devil.* Grand Rapids: Baker, 1993.
A true picture of the dangers in the megachurch movement. It will not be appreciated by some, but the material cannot be refuted.

Guinness, Os and John Seel, ed. *No God but God.* Chicago: Moody Press, 1992.
A piercing expose and analysis of various "idols" which are influencing conservative Christianity today. Some of the idols are: the imaginations of our hearts, political activism, an appeal to a "Christian" America, blaming and victim-playing, the religion of psychology, management and marketing techniques, and an infatuation with the latest modern ideas.

Hauerwas, Stanley and William H. Willimon, *Resident Aliens: Life in the Christian Colony.* Nashville: Abingdon Press, 1990.
A very significant contribution toward making the church a colony of "resident aliens" in a day in which the churched culture is over.

Hunter, James Davison. *Culture Wars.* Basic Books: Harper-Collins, 1991.
A disturbing but thorough work in the attempt to make sense of the battles over the family, art, education, law, and politics.

Oden, Thomas C. *The Transforming Power of Grace.* Nashville: Abingdon Press, 1993.
Perhaps the best, most recent treatment of God's grace—a dynamic which is desperately needed in this era in which biblical truth is often compromised for success.

Puckett, Walter. *Bringing The Church Off the Slippery Slope.* Columbus: Brentwood Christian Press, 1993.

An excellent tool to get Christians to enter into worldview studies. It can be utilized in Christian Education in the local church.

Seel, John. *The Evangelical Forfeit.* Grand Rapids: Baker, 1993.

Imperative reading for those concerned about church growth mania and the fact of modernity within evangelicalism and the megachurch movement.

Sire, James. *The Universe Next Door.* 2nd ed. Downers Grove: InterVarsity Press, 1988.

An excellent introduction to worldview studies which accomplishes what it would take three or four other books to do.

Trueblood, D. Elton. *The Predicament of Modern Man.* New York: Harper & Row, 1944.

A classic work that is even more relevant now than when it was first published.

Wells, David. *No Place for Truth: Or Whatever Happened to Evangelical Theology?* Grand Rapids: Eerdmans, 1993.

Required reading for every pastor, elder, and college administrator. Wells describes with crushing authority and scholarly detail how evangelicalism has moved from biblical conviction to worldly accommodation in this century.

Chapter 9:

The Unmaking of the Modern Mind: Postmodern Challenges and Witness Opportunities
by
Dr. John D. Castelein

Having served as Professor of Theology and New Testament at Lincoln Christian College (LCC) from 1977-1992, John Castelein is currently Professor of Contemporary Theology at Lincoln Christian Seminary (LCS). He was born in France, raised in Belgium, and became an American citizen in 1984.
He holds a bachelor's degree from LCC and M.A. and M.Div. degrees from LCS. He received his Ph.D. from the Divinity School of the University of Chicago. His Master's thesis was "A Biblical and Historical Evaluation of the thought of the Christian Churches and Churches of Christ on Social Ethics from 1926-1976." His doctoral dissertation was "Standing on the Promises of God: The Contribution of Fundamental Theology to Peter Berger's Quest for Non-Projected Transcendence."
Dr. Castelein has published in *The Lookout*, *The Christian Standard*, *The Standard Lesson Commentary*, *The Restoration Herald*, and the *Journal of Health and Religion*. He was a contributor to the *Quest Study Bible* (Zondervan) and wrote a chapter on "The Doctrine of the Holy Spirit" in *Essentials of the Christian Faith* (College Press).
He has served as a youth minister, preaching minister, and missionary to Belgium. He is a popular preacher and teacher, whether for scholarly conferences, preaching conventions, elders' clinics, or ladies' gatherings. He delivered a key lecture ("Mentoring in Postmodern Times") for the first annual James D. Strauss Lectureship at LCS in 1995.

THE UNMAKING OF THE MODERN MIND:
POSTMODERN CHALLENGES AND
WITNESS OPPORTUNITIES

"Man is a thinking reed" (Blaise Pascal)
"I think, therefore I am" (Rene Descartes)
"I think Thy thoughts after Thee" (Isaac Newton)
"I am thought, therefore I am" (Franz von Baader)
"He is—therefore I think" (Johann Hamann)

"Edgar Brightman said: 'I believe in God <u>because</u> I believe that history represents a steady, moral progress,' to which I replied, 'I believe in God because to me history precisely <u>does not</u> represent such a progress'" (Langdon Gilkey)

"I used to think that science would save us, and science certainly tried. But we can't stand any more tremendous explosions, either for or against democracy. Only in superstition is there hope. If you want to become a friend of civilization, then become an enemy of truth and a fanatic for harmless balderdash" (Kurt Vonnegut, Jr.)

"They that have despised the word of God, from them shall the word of man also be taken away" (Merlin in C. S. Lewis)

As we were jogging around the pond at Johnson Bible College in the spring of 1968, my friend Raymond said: "There is this guy at Lincoln you ought to meet. His name's Jim Strauss, and I think you would really enjoy him." Little did I know that I would be transferring to Lincoln in the fall of that year and having my first class with "Doc" in the spring of 1969.

The class was entitled "CD 554: The Making of the Contemporary Mind"—and what an experience it was! No other class has enlarged my horizon that much at one time. This chapter seeks to express my gratitude to my teacher and colleague by examining some recent aspects of that Contemporary Mind. Specifically, I want to focus on the concept of what is being called the "postmodern" condition.[1] I believe Christian leaders in the churches and in institutions of higher education need to understand what is meant by the "postmodern" because of the opportunities and challenges this alleged new reality presents for Christianity.[2]

Locating the Postmodern

The word "postmodern" increasingly is cropping up everywhere.[3] The theologian Carl Raschke says that this term has "burgeoned, crowded, and suffused academic conversation during the last decade like so much lush, green Carolina Kudzu."[4] And, in the nineties, this word is also widely used in American popular culture. What does it refer to?

---

[1]The adjective "postmodern" can refer both to an intellectual mindset ("postmodernism") and to the specific conditions of life (economic, social, and cultural) in a given society ("postmodernity"). See David Harvey, *The Condition of Postmodernity*, for a very useful description of postmodernity.

[2]There are, however, important thinkers who deny that the human context for living today is radically different from the "modern" condition of the Enlightenment. They prefer speaking of "reflexive modernization" or late capitalism in crisis. See, for instance, John Rawls, Jurgen Habermas, Ernest Geller, Charles Taylor, Frederic Jameson, Ulrich Beck, Scott Lash, Anthony Giddens, and David Wells.

[3]Many other "post" terms related to "postmodern" (sometimes called "PoMo") are multiplying and deserving of analysis: post-Newtonian, post-Enlightenment, post-critical, post-liberal, post-industrial, post-colonial, post-structuralist, post-capitalist, post-Freudian, post-Marxist, post-Holocaust, post-communist, post-literate, and post-Christian.

[4]In "Fire and Roses: Toward Authentic Post-Modern Religious Thinking," *Journal of the American Academy of Religion* 58 (1990): 673.

As Huston Smith, a specialist on world religions, admits: "The postmodern mind is amorphous. Doubting that a deep structure exists, it settles for the constantly-shifting configurations of the phenomenal world."[5] As a result, the "postmodern" label has been appropriated by many different and even opposing groups: neo-conservatives, radical critics, utopians, as well as cynics.[6] Obviously, then, postmodern refers to a rather broad and diffuse phenomenon. But I believe it is worth trying to understand this new concept because it represents some significant dangers as well as opportunities for Christians today.[7] It seems to me that the best way to begin to understand the postmodern is to contrast it with the "modern" which it is "post" to.[8]

---

[5]In "Postmodernism's Impact on the Study of Religion," *Journal of the American Academy of Religion* 58 (1990): 653.

[6]This is the point Hans Kung makes in *Theology for the Third Millennium: An Ecumenical View* (New York: Doubleday/Anchor Books, 1990), p. 2. David Griffin delineates four basic kinds of postmodern theology: (1) Revisionary-Constructive (process thought): David Griffin and William Beardslee; (2) Eliminative-Deconstructive (based on Derrida and Foucault): Mark C. Taylor, Carl Raschke, Jeffrey Stout, Charles Winquist; (3) Liberationist: Harvey Cox; (4) Restorationist-Conservative: John Richard Neuhaus and George Rutler. This typology is found in David Ray Griffin, *Varieties of Postmodern Theology* (Albany: State University of New York, 1989), pp. 1-7.

[7]Christian leaders not directly interested in the academic context of postmodernism will benefit much from understanding the postmodern culture's impact on the generation of Baby Busters, also referred to as Generation X or Twenty-something (those born between 1965 and 1983).

[8]I use the -*ist* or -*ism* endings to indicate when a historical and cultural condition has been made into an explicit worldview and ideology. So *modern* life ("modernity") in the United States takes place in a *secular* society ("secularity") in which *plural* worldviews and lifestyles ("plurality") are available. But very few in such a society are modern*ist*s, secular*ist*s, or plural*ist*s who hold to modern*ism*, secular*ism*, or plural*ism* as their worldview.

Thus there is a distinction to be made between those who unquestioningly accept *premodern* authorities and those who explicitly advocate *premodernist* positions. The term *antimodern* can be applied

Helmut Thielicke points out that the adjective "modern" (*modernus* in Latin) was first used in the thirteenth century to castigate the new ideas of the nominalists and to distinguish those new practices which deviated from traditional medieval ways. Later, in 1687, the famous "Quarrel of the Ancients and the Moderns" occurred over the best way of doing philosophy.[9]

It is not easy to set a date for the beginning or the end of the "Modern Mind" (hereafter referred to as the MM). Different scholars propose beginning dates associated with the Renaissance, Francis Bacon, Copernicus, Galileo, Descartes, Newton, Kant, the French Revolution, or the years 1815-30. For the closing of the MM, dates have been proposed associated with Pascal, Rousseau, Kant, Nietzsche, the rise of quantum physics, Freud, World War I, World War II, or even the "Death of God" movement in the mid-1960s.

---

to anyone who has an instinctive dislike for the modern, but I use the term *antimodernist* for those who militantly oppose modernism—often with its own tools and logic—in championing a traditional cause (like David Wells, Stanley Hauerwas, Helmut Thielicke, Jacques Ellul, C. F. H. Henry, and James D. Strauss).

Some use the term "postmodern" to refer to anyone who acknowledges the demise of the Enlightenment project and realizes that life today has different intellectual horizons (including evangelical Christians like Thomas Oden, Stanley Grenz, Roger Olson, Gene Veith, Clark Pinnock, Phil Kenneson, J. Richard Middleton, Brian J. Walsh, and Leslie Newbigin). *Postmodernism* is a contemporary intellectual movement in academic circles that follows the deconstructive hermeneutics and anti-realist philosophies associated with Jacques Derrida, Michel Foucault, and Richard Rorty (like in the theology of Mark C. Taylor). Postmoderns are distinguished from antimoderns at least in two ways: (1) they are explicitly aware that they are choosing their position from a plurality of constructed and viable worldviews, and (2) they oppose modernism not merely as an outward foe but as an internalized perspective and as part of their own spiritual pilgrimage.

[9]See Thielicke's useful survey in *The Evangelical Faith*, vol. 1: *Prolegomena: The Relation of Theology to Modern Thought Forms* (Grand Rapids: Eerdmans, 1974), pp. 30-37. The root word in *modernus* is the Latin word *modo* which refers to what is recent or "just now."

Quite often the transition from the MM to the "Postmodern Mind" (hereafter referred to as PM) is dated around 1968 when radical students in Paris rejected Marxism in politics, structuralism in hermeneutics, and the principles of the Enlightenment in general.[10] Reflecting on postmodern architecture, Charles Jencks dates the passage from the MM to the PM in architecture to 3:32 p.m. on 15 July 1972, when the prize-winning modern Pruitt-Igoe housing development in St. Louis was "dynamited as an uninhabitable environment."[11] Thomas Oden dates the beginning of the MM to 1789 (the French Revolution) and its end to 1989 (the "deconstruction" of Communism's Berlin Wall).[12]

Pinpointing the Modern epoch in time is difficult because the MM is a mindset and a paradigm that has filtered down unevenly throughout the course of history into various societies (those in Europe first), cultures (those in the West first), classes (intellectuals first), academic disciplines (science and philosophy first), and artistic schools (architecture first).[13] Therefore, rather

---

[10]Where the distinctions between "modernity" and "modernism" and between "postmodernity" and "postmodernism" do not matter, I will retain John Herman Randall's classic phrase (the "Modern Mind") as well as speak of the "Postmodern Mind."

[11]See R. Bernstein's analysis and the reference to Jencks in Harvey, *Condition*, pp. 40-41.

[12]See Oden's *Two Worlds: Notes on the Death of Modernity in America & Russia* (Downers Grove: InterVarsity Press, 1992), pp. 12, 32, 51.

[13]There are many surveys of the development of the MM. See, for instance, John Herman Randall, *The Making of the Modern Mind: A Survey of the Intellectual Background of the Present Age*; Paul Johnson, *The Birth of the Modern World Society, 1815-30*; *Intellectuals*; and *Modern Times*; Robert Whittemore, *Makers of the American Mind*; J. Bronowski and Bruce Mazlish, *The Western Intellectual Tradition*; J. Bronowski, *The Ascent of Man*; Kenneth Clark, *Civilization*; Louis Untermeyer, *Makers of the Modern World*; Richard Tarnas, *The Passion of the Western Mind*; and Lawrence Cahoone, *The Dilemma of Modernity: Philosophy, Culture, and Anti-culture.*

than to try to assign some arbitrary dates, it seems more useful to analyze some *key assumptions* of the MM, the loss of which gives birth to the postmodern condition. I would like to highlight three areas of thought and life where the PM has lost confidence in the worldview of the MM. In all three areas we are faced with two options: either to proceed into greater relativism and skepticism (as in the *ultramodernism* or *hypermodernism* of deconstructive hermeneutics—most often referred to as *postmodernism*) or to return to some kind of re-affirmation of knowable truth as grounded in God as the source of human reason and the intelligibility of nature.

Loss of the MM's Rational Foundation in Epistemology[14]

The period of the MM is supremely that of the Enlightenment, the "Age of Reason" (when human rationality promises to *enlighten* the darkness of medieval knowledge). All claims to knowledge are to be anchored in the rock bottom *foundation* of universal human rationality, for it *alone*—as demonstrated in the successes of Newtonian science—has earned the following rights: (1) to question all past authorities, (2) to affirm whatever seems reasonable to it, (3) to reject whatever

---

[Note: for considerations of space, publication information will be given only for books which are cited by page.]

For Christian surveys of the MM, see C. F. H. Henry, *Remaking the Modern Mind*; David Breese, *Seven Men who Rule the World from the Grave*; C. Gregg Singer, *From Rationalism to Irrationality*; Francis Schaeffer, *How Should We Then Live?* and *The God Who Is There*; Robert Clouse et al., *Two Kingdoms: The Church and Culture through the Ages*; Tony Campolo, *A Reasonable Faith: The Case for Christianity in a Secular World*; James Marsh, Merold Westphal, and John Caputo, *Modernity and Its Discontents*.

[14]Taken from the Greek word *episteme* (knowledge, understanding), epistemology is the philosophical study of what human knowledge is, how humans can know things and other people's minds, and how they can verify and justify their claims to knowledge.

does not make sense to it, and (4) to be the one and only valid interpretation of reality which makes all other interpretations marginal.[15]

Ancient authorities always assumed that meaning was given to the universe either by (1) God, who revealed Himself in sacred scriptures, (2) the gods of Greek and Roman mythology, or (3) a divine principle (Logos) immanent in the very nature of the universe itself (Stoicism). But for the MM, universal and autonomous human rationality—as expressed in the Western Enlightenment—is the one and only Archimedean point of all knowledge, the only originating source and dependable judge of all meaning and order in the universe.

In later PM terms, Enlightenment Reason claims to be the only valid *metanarrative* of human knowledge. This stance explains the humanism[16] and naturalism so prevalent in the MM, as well as its long history of biblical criticism.[17]

As a result, in the MM, God's transcendence became a real problem; after all—how can human reason,

---

[15]Pioneers who advanced these sweeping claims on behalf of human reason include Descartes (with his new basis for truth—*Cogito ergo sum*), Locke (who urged his readers to proportion faith according to the reasonableness of the evidence presented), Hume (who demanded a book be burned if it did not deal with numbers or experimental reasoning on facts), and Kant (who advocated *Sapere aude*: "dare to think for yourself"—that is, dare to acknowledge that what you know from your own reason, apart from all traditional authorities, is indeed valid knowledge). He also believed that religion is available only within the boundaries of Reason. Other such "free thinking" pioneers are Hobbes, Spinoza, Leibniz, and Voltaire. For a Christian critique of these thinkers, see Colin Brown, *Christianity & Western Thought*, vol. 1: *From the Ancient World to the Age of Enlightenment*.

[16]The hero of Enlightenment humanism is Protagoras who said: "Man is the measure of all things."

[17]On the history of the MM's criticism of the Bible, see Henning Reventlow, *The Authority of the Bible and the Rise of the Modern World* and Hans Frei, *The Eclipse of Biblical Narrative*.

starting from reason alone, ever know it? Therefore, the biblical God was first divorced from the sphere of human experience by the deists, abandoned by early naturalists like Laplace,[18] only to be dramatically rediscovered by romantics like Schleiermacher *within* human consciousness (Gefuhl) and history.[19]

Ironically, however, Kant, the great systematizer of the MM, can also be seen as the very one who initiated the demise of the MM, for he proposed that much of human knowledge results from the way the human mind *constructs* meaning and *projects* order into human experience. The problem is that it is quite difficult to distinguish between what the mind "discovers" and what the mind "constructs" or "projects."[20] As a result, the late-modern "hermeneuticians of suspicion"—as Paul Ricoeur calls Nietzsche, Marx, and Freud—attacked the very concept of "god" as merely an ideological or psychological projection.[21]

---

[18]As is well known, the scientist Laplace felt that his scientific theories could account for all of reality without any recourse to the postulate of a "god-of-the-gaps," and so he told the Emperor Napoleon that the explanatory hypothesis of a Creator God was no longer needed.

[19]Note how the rationalism of the MM first *disengages*, then *replaces*, and finally *uses* the Other (whether it be God, nature, or one's fellow human being) for the selfish purposes of the Self. Colin Gunton develops this critique of the MM in *The One, the Three and the Many* (Cambridge: Cambridge University Press, 1993), pp. 13-15, 28-29, 69.

[20]On the difficulties of keeping the concept of God as a symbolic construction of society from collapsing into a mere human projection (wish), see Peter Berger's *The Sacred Canopy* and *A Rumor of Angels: Modern Society and the Rediscovery of the Supernatural*. These problems in Peter Berger's religious thought have been analyzed in John D. Castelein, *Standing on the Promises of God: The Contribution of Fundamental Theology to Peter Berger's Quest for Non-Projected Transcendence* (Ph.D. diss., University of Chicago, 1988).

[21]See Paul Ricoeur, *Freud and Philosophy: An Essay on Interpretation* (New Haven: Yale University Press, 1970), p. 32. On projection theories about God in Marx, Nietzsche, and Freud, see

Therefore, the PM essentially begins with the ever stronger suspicion that the alleged victory of "enlightened" human reason over God in actuality means the loss of all real meaning.[22] Whereas the MM sets itself up as judge over all past authorities and dismisses them as being hopelessly dogmatic or "enthusiastic" about matters of truth and value, the PM has questioned the MM's own epistemological foundation in human rationality.[23]

One serious blow to the alleged autonomy of modern human reason came when Kurt Gödel, a twenty-five year old German mathematician demonstrated convincingly in 1931 that even mathematics, the supreme tool of human science, is not and never can be self-authenticating. Gödel's "incompleteness theorems" mean that *no* system of thought based on supposedly certain axioms is able to explain and/or vindicate itself as a complete, necessary, and self-sufficient system of logic and meaning.[24]

Merold Westphal, *Suspicion and Faith: The Religious Uses of Modern Atheism.*

[22]We can see this growing disenchantment with the MM in the following nineteenth century figures: Schleiermacher, Blake, Wordsworth, Kierkegaard, de Sade, Dostoevsky, Wilde, Baudelaire, Arnold, Marx, Thoreau, Whitman, and Gauguin. The full nihilistic implications were first seen by Schopenhauer and most tragically by Nietzsche. Similarly, today's deconstructionist hermeneutics opposes the MM's realist epistemology as "logocentric," "ontotheological" and too "centered." As Walker Percy says in *The Thanatos Syndrome*: "This is not the age of Enlightenment, but the age of not knowing what to do" (New York: Farrar, Strauss, & Giroux, 1987), p. 75.

[23]For specific attacks on epistemological foundations, see Stanley Hauerwas, Nancey Murphy, and Mark Nation, ed., *Theology without Foundations*; Ronald Thiemann, *Revelation and Theology: The Gospel as Narrated Promise*; Jeffrey Stout, *The Flight from Authority*; John Thiel, *Nonfoundationalism*; George Lindbeck, *The Nature of Doctrine*; and Phil Kenneson, "There's No such Thing as Objective Truth, and It's a Good Thing Too" in Timothy Phillips and Dennis Okholm, ed., *Christian Apologetics in the Postmodern World.*

[24]Gödel's theorems can only be followed by people well grounded in mathematics. He used an ingenious code by which mathematical

No wonder the PM, and especially postmodernism as its most radical ideology, seeks to debunk the debunkers, to relativize the relativizers, to critique the critics,[25] and to expose the Enlightenment's own "prejudice against prejudice"![26] That is why the PM encourages today's relativizing pluralism and decentralizing globalization. The essence of postmodernism is precisely the inability or refusal (the "incredulity") to believe in any and all "metanarratives" (thereby precluding the possibility of delegitimating any and all foundations for human knowledge).[27] As a result the PM has demythologized the Enlightenment's myth of one sole universal and scientific rationality and has replaced it with a "kaleidoscopic"

---

numbers can be referred to in a self-referential way. He concluded that no logical or mathematical system built on axioms (like that in Russell and Whitehead's *Principia Mathematica*) can ever give an ultimate account of itself.

[25]For an evangelical postmodern like Thomas Oden this means the welcome criticism of the following forms of criticism of the Bible practiced by the MM: cultural, hermeneutical, literary, form, source, audience, redaction, historical, canon, pragmatic, sociology of knowledge, logical, psychoanalytic, linguistic, feminist, aesthetic, and deconstructionist. See *After Modernity ... What?*, pp. 103-132.

[26]See, for instance, Peter Berger, *A Rumor of Angels*; Hans-Georg Gadamer, *Truth and Method*; Stanley Hauerwas, *After Christendom? How the Church is to Behave if Freedom, Justice, and a Christian Nation are Bad Ideas.*

[27]See Jean-Francois Lyotard, *The Postmodern Condition: A Report on Knowledge.*(Minneapolis: University of Minnesota Press, 1984), pp. xxiii-iv. Lyotard is concerned about the condition of knowledge in a computerized age where the old metanarratives—used previously to discern and to legitimate good uses of knowledge in society—are no longer available. Postmodernism concludes that Descartes' search for an epistemological foundation in "clear and distinct ideas" has collapsed into *dualism*, Locke's attempt to found knowledge in empirical sense data has succumbed to Hume's *skepticism*, and Kant's efforts to construct a foundation for moral knowledge has been exposed as mere *wishful projection* (by Feuerbach, Marx, Nietzsche, Freud, Dewey, and Durkheim). See William's Placher's second chapter on "Foundations" in his *Unapologetic Theology: A Christian Voice in a Pluralistic Conversation.*

chaos in the area of epistemology.[28] One characteristic, for instance, especially of the recent "postmodernist" hermeneutics associated with Jacques Derrida, Michel Foucault and Richard Rorty, is its refusal to take any deep structures seriously.[29] In this sense, postmodernism is explicitly post-structuralist:[30] it understands language signs to refer only to more signs, not to any objective reality.[31] Therefore, many of these "post-

---

[28]This striking metaphor comes from Smith, "Postmodernism's Impact," p. 660. Postmodernism treats each cultural expression of meaning as if it were a Rorsarch picture in which the readers are free to see whatever they wish.

[29]See, for instance, Michel Foucault, *Power/Knowledge: Selected Interviews and Other Writings, 1972-77* and *The Order of Things: An Archaeology of the Human Sciences*; Jacques Derrida, *Of Grammatology*; *The Margins of Philosophy*; *Positions*; *Writing and Difference*; Paul de Man, *Blindness and Sight*; and Ruf, *Religion, Ontotheology and Deconstruction.* For an examination of how Foucault and Derrida have impacted on biblical studies, see Stephen Moore, *Poststructuralism and the New Testament.*

[30]The immediate occasion of the development of the PM (especially in literature) is the rebellion against the hermeneutics of structuralism. Structuralism was developed, by Claude Levi-Strauss and A. J. Greimas primarily, out of Ferdinand de Saussure's position that language, as a social construct, finds its meaning only in the agreed upon differences between words (in his influential *Course in General Linguistics*, 1916). Structuralism seeks the meaning of texts not in their historical contexts or in the intentions of their authors, but in the universal, unconscious and hidden, deep structures of all human meanings. These embedded systems of relations between words and concepts are akin to the "linguistic universals" of Noam Chomsky, the "collective unconscious" of Carl Jung, and related elements in the thought of Jean Piaget. Structuralist hermeneutics has been carried on by Edmund Leach, Dan O. Via, Daniel Patte, Edgar Knight, and the journal *Semeia*. The postmodernist hermeneutic rejects these deep structures as just more human projections and "totalizing" impositions on the text (by "dead white European males"), and prefers as it were to surf on the surface of the text.

[31]Because of Nietzsche's philosophy which was rooted in philological genealogies, Heidegger's locating of meaning in *Dasein*, and Gadamer's locating of meaning in the ongoing human conversation, *language* is where postmodernism locates all thought

modernists" play ingenious word games with surface meanings, etymologies, puns, parodies, and confusing self-referential statements.[32]

In the face of such epistemological nihilism, Christians have a great opportunity to defend human rationality in the areas of epistemology and hermeneutics.[33]

Loss of Confidence in the Objectivity of the MM's Scientific Method

One of Dr. Strauss's most repeated themes over the years has been: "It's all about science." This insight

---

and being. Therefore, to explain how deconstructionists view the nature of truth in texts, the neopragmatist philosopher Richard Rorty refers to the ancient cosmology that holds that the world rests upon the back of an elephant. It is said that one proponent defending this ancient cosmology eventually said in exasperation: "And it's elephants all the way down." So also, says Rorty, does the deconstructionist believe that all texts refer only to more words—*all the way down* (and not to some objective independent reality). See his *Consequences of Pragmatism: Essays 1972-1980* (Minneapolis: University of Minnesota Press, 1982), p. xxxv.

[32]In a very real sense, the deconstructive postmodern*ists* are more "ultra" than "post"-modernists, for they merely deepen the late modern despair of meaning and value rather than seek to overcome it. For analysis, see Nathan Scott's helpful description, "The House of Intellect in an Age of Carnival: Some Hermeneutical Reflections," in *Whirlwind in Culture*, ed. Donald Musser and Joseph Price (Bloomington, IN: Meyer-Stone Books, 1988), pp. 39-54. See also John Dominic Crossan's concept of "ludic allegory," in *Cliffs of Fall* (New York: Seabury, 1980), p. 97. Carl Raschke, in "Fire and Roses," suggests that postmodernism is what happens when Aristotle's manuscript on laughter (from Umberto Eco's postmodernist novel *The Name of the Rose*) is actually disseminated in the academic world. A striking example of this carnivalesque philosophy at play in theology is Mark C. Taylor's *Erring: A Postmodern A/theology.*

[33]See, for instance, the critiques of deconstructionism by Grant Osborne, *The Hermeneutical Spiral* and by Anthony Thiselton, *New Horizons in Hermeneutics.* Dr. Strauss has always cautioned about the dangers of a too radical *contextualization* of the truth and would urge us to explore the ways in which truths are always *context-bound* but not necessarily *context-determined.*

holds true especially for the transition from the MM paradigm to the PM paradigm. Historically it has been in the arena of science that worldviews have battled it out to determine which was fittest to survive.[34]

Newtonian science replaced the ancient Aristotelian-Ptolemaic view of the world as a purposeful organism with the MM's central vision of the world as a mechanistic machine.[35] The classical physics of the Newtonian worldview continues to be used, for all practical purposes, in the everyday world of the MM. In this paradigm, reality is made up of empirically available material bodies which: (1) consist of mass and can have motion (velocity), both of which can be precisely measured, (2) are normally at rest unless direct force is applied to overcome their inertia, and (3) are located in an "objective" manner (that is, independent of the subjective intentions of any and all observers) in a world of absolute time and absolute space (measurable by Euclidean geometry).

However, by the end of the nineteenth century, there were several phenomena that the classical physics

---

[34]The decisive battles in the MM's victory over the classical and medieval worldviews (associated with names like Plato, Aristotle, Ptolemy, Archimedes, Hippocrates, Galen, Augustine, Avicenna, Aquinas, Dante) were fought and won in the area of science by thinkers like Roger Bacon, Francis Bacon, Peter Ramus, da Vinci, Copernicus, Brahe, Kepler, Galileo, Descartes, and Newton. For a helpful survey, see Randall, *The Making of the Modern Mind*, pp. 203-81. Good surveys and histories of science for the non-scientist are Lloyd Motz and Jefferson Hane Weaver, *The Story of Physics*; Ian Barbour, *Issues in Science and Religion*; Herbert Butterfield, *The Origins of Modern Science, 1300-1800*; R. Hooykaas, *Religion and the Rise of Modern Science*; E. A. Burtt, *The Metaphysical Foundations of Modern Science*; Stanley Jaki, *The Road of Science and the Ways to God*; Stephen Mason, *A History of the Sciences*; A. d'Abro, *The Evolution of Scientific Thought: From Newton to Einstein*.

[35]See this contrast discussed in Stanley Jaki, *The Relevance of Physics* (Chicago: The University of Chicago Press, 1966), pp. 3-94.

of the MM could not account for.[36] This all came to a head on October 19, 1900 when Max Planck felt the evidence forced him to introduce a radically new radiation formula based on the "quantum of action" concept. It said energy is released in discrete and discontinuous units ("quanta") not in the kind of smooth and continuous process envisioned in Newtonian physics. Thus quantum physics was born and with it the PM.[37]

In the world of Einstein, Planck, Bohr, Heisenberg, Schrodinger, Dirac, Feynman, and Hawking, the scientific understanding of the universe and of the heart of matter has changed drastically from the reasonable and common sense view of the MM. While Einstein in his theories of Special Relativity (1905) and General Relativity (1916) did leave the speed of light as a constant amidst all frames of reference, he did in fact relativize all other "objective" measurements (of mass, velocity, length, and time). These measurements hold true only within the particular frame of reference of the observer.[38] Furthermore, he gave a radically different

---

[36]There were forces at work in kinetics (as seen in the study of gasses), thermodynamics (heat), electricity, and magnetism which did not seem to operate in exact agreement with Newtonian laws. Some such abnormalities were: (1) "action at a distance" appeared to be occurring—a notion which Newton abhorred; (2) the results of "black box" experiments of radiation emissions defied classical explanations; and (3) Thomas Young's experiments (1803) seem to have confirmed that light consisted of waves, but Michelson and Morley's experiments with the interferometer (beginning in 1887) were not able to discover the "aether" in which light waves were alleged to wave.

[37]A very useful chart contrasting the views of the world as held by Aristotle, Newton, and Einstein can be found in Gustave Weigel and Arthur Madden, *Knowledge: Its Values and Limits* (Englewood Cliffs: Prentice-Hall, 1961), pp. 72-75.

[38]A moment's reflection can show how the reality we experience at any time is bound to our particular frame of reference at that time. Since light does not propagate instantaneously, it takes light a certain time (186,272 miles per second) to get from one place to another. As a result, the star Arcturus may no longer exist, even though we still see it, for its light takes thirty-eight years to get here.

John D. Castelein

understanding of gravity than that proposed in Newtonian physics.[39]

As a result, for the PM, reality—at its very core— has become unpicturable, non-commonsensical, and no longer objectively "there," (i.e., no longer independent of the intentions of the human subject investigating it).[40] Furthermore, the PM no longer considers science to be an "objective" enterprise in which knowledge is advanced

---

[39]Ironically, Einstein, the father of relativity, opposed the radical relativism of what has apparently become the majority position in quantum physics. This position is associated with Niels Bohr and the "Copenhagen Interpretation" of Heisenberg's Uncertainty Principle. Einstein refused to believe that randomness was the ultimate foundation of reality. He believed that while God is subtle, God is not malicious, and, therefore, God does not play dice with the universe. Others who, like Einstein, have also blamed our uncertainty in quantum physics on the limitations of our human knowledge or the crudeness of our measurements are Stanley Jaki, *God and the Cosmologists*; Mortimer Adler, *Truth in Religion: The Plurality of Religions and the Unity of Truth*; and David Bohm, *Wholeness and the Implicate Order*.

[40]Werner Heisenberg's Uncertainty or Indeterminacy Principle holds that science can choose to measure either an electron's location or its velocity/mass, but not both at the same time. On the subatomic level our most careful attempts to see what is objectively there invariably interfere with what we want to observe, thus making our findings uncertain.

Niels Bohr's Principle of Complementarity, therefore, suggests that reality in essence has opposing aspects and that it is our choice of which experiment we want to use which determines which "reality" we experience (for instance, whether light is a wave or a particle). As a result Hugh Everett, for one, has theorized that each aspect of reality represents a distinctly different version of the universe: we inhabit only one of a multiplicity of universes existing side by side.

Erwin Schrodinger therefore proposed that the Copenhagen Interpretation would entail that on the subatomic level radically opposite versions of reality exist simultaneously (for instance, that a cat in a closed box is either dead or alive independent of our observation). This means the cat is in the condition of being *both* really dead and really alive *until* our act of observation makes one version the actual case ("collapses the probability"). As Niels Bohr has observed: "Anyone who is not shocked by quantum theory has not understood it."

---

by patient accumulation of empirically verified facts in accordance with strictly rational theories.[41]

The PM shares Wordsworth's horror of the Enlightenment's approach to life: the MM "murders to dissect." As one of the founders of the MM advocated: the proper way to know is (1) to abstract, (2) to dissect, (3) to reconstruct, and (4) to control (in Descartes' *Discourse on Method*). Therefore, the PM seeks a new scientific methodology that, in its treatment of evidence and in its view of the human mind, is integrative and holistic rather than fragmentary and reductionistic.[42]

Like phenomenology, postmodern epistemologies seek to get "back to the things themselves" (Husserl). They desire to expand all human avenues of perception and knowledge. This shift can be seen, for instance, in the influential philosopher Wittgenstein who later in his life advocated that we approach reality not through logic or science alone, but through various "language games," each realm of discourse appropriate to its own realm of human experience.[43]

---

[41]The growing loss of confidence in the pure objectivity and rationality of the scientific method can be traced in Thomas Kuhn, *The Structure of Scientific Revolutions*; Michael Polanyi, *Personal Knowledge*; Stephen Toulmin, *Human Understanding: The Collective Use and Evolution of Concepts*; Ian Barbour, *Issues in Science and Religion*; and Paul Feyerabend, *Against Method: Outline of an Anarchistic Theory of Knowledge* as well as his *Farewell to Reason*.

[42]See Stanley Grenz's helpful presentation of how the PM (starting from Nietzsche, Dilthey, and Heidegger) has sought to overcome the static Cartesian dualism of the MM with a dynamic understanding of the Self as embedded in history in his *Primer on Postmodernism* (Grand Rapids: Eerdmans, 1996), pp. 88-108.

[43]Concerning his enigmatic slogan, "Whereof one cannot speak, thereof one must be silent," Wittgenstein pointed out in a letter to Bertrand Russell that certain dimensions of human experience can only be *shown* (as in poetry) but not fully expressed in propositional form. This, however, does not make these dimensions of life any less real or less important. For a brief discussion see John Dominic Crossan, *The Dark Interval: Towards a Theology of Story* (Allen, TX: Argus Communications, 1975), pp. 20-24.

Terry Eagleton has well summarized the PM's rejection of science and philosophy as unifying enterprises:

> Post-modernism signals the death of such "metanarratives" whose secretly terroristic function is to ground and legitimate the illusion of a "universal" human history. We are now in the process of awakening from the nightmare of modernity, with its manipulative reason and fetish of the totality, into the laid-back pluralism of the post-modern, that heterogeneous range of life-styles and language games which has renounced the nostalgic urge to totalise and legitimate itself.... Science and philosophy must jettison their grandiose metaphysical claims and view themselves more modestly as just another set of narratives.[44]

As a result, in the PM, the "doors of perception" (Aldous Huxley's powerful phrase) are opened once again to many premodern interests and beliefs. While some PM thinkers have followed Alfred North Whitehead in his complicated "process" philosophy of quantum physics, others are using this new freedom afforded by the PM to create hybrid philosophies of Western science and Eastern pantheism.[45] As a widespread PM phenomenon, the New Age movement encompasses many revived ancient beliefs and practices: animistic spiritism, divination and mantics ("channeling"), drugs and magic ("alchemy"), astrology, occult, shamanism, gnosticism, obsession with angels, and yoga exercises. In short, the PM is open to anything and everything that promises to

---

[44]Terry Eagleton as quoted in Grenz, *Primer on Postmodernism*, p. 48.

[45]Some of the more prominent proponents of such non-Western belief systems are George Bateson, *Mind and Nature: A Necessary Unity*; Richard Pirzig, *Zen and the Art of Motorcycle Maintenance*; Fritjof Capra, *The Tao of Physics*; Gary Zukav, *The Dancing Wu Li Masters*; and Lewis Thomas, *The Lives of a Cell*.

expand our consciousness beyond the narrow confines of science as practiced by the MM. This explains the enormous interest today in the abnormal, paranormal, psychic, life after death, and UFO phenomena which is exhibited in movies, TV shows, talk shows, and the tabloids. The proper Christian apologetic response is to reaffirm the reality of the supernatural over against the naturalism that has been so dominant in the MM.[46]

Loss of the MM's Liberal and Optimistic Belief in Moral Perfectibility and Progress

A third area of crisis for the MM is the collapse of the moral universe in the West. Once Christianity provided the "sacred canopy" (Peter Berger's felicitous phrase) which sheltered all the beliefs, practices, institutions, and social roles of the Western world from chaos and meaninglessness. But along with the collapse of its foundation (i.e., autonomous reason) and its method (i.e., objective science), the Western mind also lost its canopy of meaning and value (i.e., the moral universe of Christianity).

As a result, the PM is a "mind at the end of its tether."[47] Or, as Robert Pippin observes, "Modernity promised us a culture of unintimidated, curious, rational, self-reliant individuals, and it produced ... a herd society,

---

[46]Worth examining in this area is the work done seeking to restore the plausibility of the miraculous by Norman Geisler, *Miracles and the Modern Mind*; Colin Brown, *Miracles and the Critical Mind*; Charles Kraft, *Christianity with Power*; and Jack Deere, *Surprised by the Power of the Holy Spirit*.

[47]Schlossberg in *Idols for Destruction* traces the devolution of the optimism of the MM in some of H. G. Wells's book titles: *Outline of History* (1920), *The Shape of Things to Come* (1933), and *The Mind at the End of its Tether* (1945).

John D. Castelein

a race of anxious, timid, conformist 'sheep,' and a culture of utter banality."[48]

After Hume, no serious thinker in the West could ignore what was happening to the basic values of Western civilization now that autonomous human reason was in charge. The concepts of God, self, substance, causality, immortality, duty, and community were starting to become meaningless. Hume's criticisms awakened Kant from his naive and dogmatic, rational slumbers. It was Kant's life's work to provide a viable (if not fully knowable) basis upon which to found the ethical life of practical reason. Others continued to agonize over the loss of traditional values and sought to provide new and "positive" (i.e. scientific) bases for meaningful individual and communal living: Max Weber, August Comte (positivism), Emile Durkheim (how to overcome the *anomie* of the MM), and Friedrich Nietzsche (how the "Super-human" can overcome the death of God).

But by the beginning of the twentieth century the opinion begins to prevail that these thinkers have not been able to preserve the rational foundations of Western morality.[49] The horrendous usage of the best of modern technologies (mustard gas) in Flanders' fields in World War I puts the lie to liberalism's claims of inevitable progress and human perfectibility.

---

[48]This is quoted in Gunton, *The One, The Three, and the Many*, p. 13.

[49]Besides Nietzsche, another influential voice concerned with the demise of the MM is Oswald Spengler in *The Decline of the West*. See also Miguel de Unamuno, *The Tragic Sense of Life* and T. S. Eliot's "The Waste Land" (1922), "The Hollow Men," "Ash Wednesday" (1930), and "Choruses from 'The Rock,'" in *Collected Poems 1909-1962*. When asked why he continued to study precisely those aspects of the Enlightenment tradition that were collapsing all around him, Max Weber, one of the founders of sociology, gave the chilling reply: "I want to see how much I can stand" (in Reinhard Bendix, *Max Weber: An Intellectual Portrait* [Berkeley: University of California Press, 1977], p. 9).

This is a devastating charge against the MM, for it had assumed all along that human nature and society were endlessly perfectible through the interaction of natural human evolution and the rational application of scientific technology. Since Auschwitz, Hiroshima, My Lai, Watergate, and Chernobyl, however, all of Western optimism about human progress has been tempered by a sobering realization that better technology stands in the service of the ruthless human "will to power" (Nietzsche) rather than an evolving higher morality.[50]

Nihilism, therefore, is the nemesis of the PM. The term is derived from *nihilum*, the Latin word for "nothing." This worldview accepts as indisputable fact that human existence can claim no absolute value or ultimate meaning in the universe.[51] It is the omnipresent mood of late modernism and the yawning abyss below the tightropes of all modern and postmodern philosophies.[52]

---

[50]More and more the MM is being assessed as having been in service of raw "totalizing" human power and desire, not pure human intellect. See, for instance, much of the "archaeological" work of Foucault; Paul Johnson's *Intellectuals*; and Michael Jones's *Degenerate Moderns: Modernity as Rationalized Sexual Misbehavior*.

[51]For a fuller understanding of the worldview of nihilism, the following books are recommended: James Sire, *The Universe Next Door*, chapter 5; Johan Goudsblom, *Nihilism and Culture*; Donald Crosby, *The Specter of the Absurd: Sources & Criticisms of Modern Nihilism*; Helmut Thielicke, *Nihilism: Its Origin and Nature—with a Christian Answer*.

[52]The coming of philosophical and ethical nihilism can be traced in the following authors: Ivan Turgenev, *Fathers and Sons* (1862); Fyodor Dostoyevsky, *The Brothers Karamazov* (1880); Franz Kafka, *The Metamorphosis* (1935); Albert Camus, *The Myth of Sisyphus* (1942); J. D. Salinger, *The Catcher in the Rye* (1945); Albert Camus, *The Plague* (1948) and *The Rebel* (1951); Luigi Pirandello, *Naked Masks* (1952); Samuel Beckett, *Waiting for Godot* (1954); Joseph Heller, *Catch-22* (1955); Archibald MacLeisch, *JB* (1956); Elie Wiesel, *Night* (1958); Martin Esslin, *The Theatre of the Absurd* (1961); Ken Kesey, *One Flew over the Cuckoo's Nest* (1962); most of Kurt Vonnegut, especially *Cat's Cradle* (1963), *Wampeters, Foma & Granfalloons* (1965), and *Slaughter-House Five* (1969); Richard

Thomas Oden analyzes four specific key motifs of modernity that have reached a crisis point in our world today: (1) autonomous individualism, with its clamor for sovereign individual rights, is destroying any sense of community; (2) narcissistic hedonism is rushing young people at ever younger ages into the instant gratification of sex, violence, and drugs; (3) the relentless naturalistic reductionism of all transcendent values to physical goods; and (4) the absolute moral relativism of all moral absolutes.[53]

The PM is confronted with a generation of people who live in a "naked public square" emptied of all the social institutions and structures that once embodied society's meanings and values.[54] Since so many people

---

Hooker, *Mash* (1968); Jerzy Kosinski, *Being There* (1970); Sylvia Plath, *The Bell Jar* (1971); John Irving, *The World According to Garp* (1976); Paddy Chayefsky, *Altered States* (1978); and the science fiction of Douglas Adams.

Philosophers who have wrestled explicitly with nihilism include Schopenhauer, Nietzsche, Bertrand Russell, Albert Camus, and Jean-Paul Sartre.

[53]In *Two Worlds*, pp. 33-36. William Bennett, former education secretary and director of drug control policy under presidents Reagan and Bush, gives dramatic illustration and confirmation of Oden's charges in *The Index of Leading Cultural Indicators*. Here in clear and graphic charts the evidence for the erosion of moral values in American society is irrefutable. The following statistics are way up in the last 20-30 years: crimes, prison sentences, juvenile crime arrests, children relying on AFDC, child poverty, infant mortality, teen pregnancy, abortions, births to unwed mothers, child abuse, teen suicide, divorce, single parent families, high school drop out rates, and daily TV watching.

[54]The phrase comes from Richard Neuhaus, *The Naked Public Square: Religion and Democracy in America*. Modernization has often weakened or removed entirely those intermediate social structures and cultural institutions that traditionally surround the individual's life with immediate meaning and security: the neighborhood, the family, the church, and volunteer associations. As a result, many people living in modern communities today have no immediate context and real support to give meaning to their existence. For analysis, see Peter Berger and Richard John Neuhaus, *To Empower People: The Role of Mediating Structures in Public Policy.*

are now exposed to life with this kind of a "homeless mind" (Peter Berger),[55] it is no wonder so many people live on the street or surrender to the ruthless order found in brainwashing cults and barbarian gangs.

A Closing Word on Opportunities for Christian Witness in the Postmodern World

We have dealt with three areas of crises for the MM which have given birth to the PM: epistemology and knowledge, science and technology, and morality. All three areas present very real dangers but also very real opportunities for Christian witness and service today.[56]

With the overthrow of Queen Reason from her Enlightenment throne, many other perspectives—once repressed, but more responsive to the full range of human experience—are presenting viable alternatives to the mechanism and reductionism of autonomous human rationality. There is a new willingness to let every community tell its own "story."[57] On the one hand, as we have seen, this can indeed lead to "New Age" revivals of ancient heresies. But on the other hand, there are

---

[55]See Peter Berger et al., *The Homeless Mind: Modernization and Consciousness.*

[56]For many Christians witnessing in the PM world, however, it is no longer possible to affirm the faith in an almost naive pre-modern way. They are consistently aware that they are *choosing* to believe their faith in response to what Peter Berger calls "the heretical imperative": in a postmodern society few people can take their belief system for granted (as the only possible one) any longer. See Peter Berger, *The Heretical Imperative: Contemporary Possibilities of Religious Affirmation.*

[57]There is growing appreciation for the Christian story especially in the context of the upsurge of "narrative theology." See John Dominic Crossan's *The Cross that Spoke: The Origins of the Passion Narrative* and *The Dark Interval*; Michael Goldberg, *Theology and Narrative*; Stanley Hauerwas, *A Community of Character: Toward a Constructive Christian Ethic* and *Character and Christian Life*; Stanley Hauerwas and Gregory Jones, ed. *Why Narrative? Readings in Narrative Theology*; Ronald Thiemann, *Revelation and Theology: The Gospel as Narrated Promise*; and Terrence Tilley, *Story Theology.*

new opportunities for Christians to present the Christian story, including its transcendent truths and supernatural miracles.[58] In the area of science, quantum physics has reintroduced openness, wonder, and mystery into the universe. The Newtonian world machine has been exploded by newly discovered realities that defy common sense and mechanical explanations. One scientist has observed: "The universe begins to look more like a great thought than like a great machine. Mind no longer appears as an accidental intruder in the realm of matter."[59]

Of special interest to the Christian are the possibilities for effective apologetics and witness offered by the "anthropic principle" emerging in science today. This theory takes notice of how many variables—close to forty according to Hugh Ross—in the make-up of our universe are extremely fine-tuned and would make human life impossible if they were altered even in the slightest degree. Even to a non-believer the odds are incredible that such a universe as ours supporting

---

[58]In the "charismatic" version of postmodern Christianity, the hidden, secular, naturalistic, and comfortable deistic presuppositions of North American Christianity are exposed, and a correction is attempted, by an emphasis on the "signs and wonders" and other supernatural aspects of the ongoing nature and work of Spirit in the Church today. See Ken Blue, *Authority to Heal*; Jack Deere, *Surprised by the Power of the Holy Spirit*; Charles Kraft, *Christianity with Power*; John White, *When the Spirit Comes with Power*; John Wimber and Kevin Springer, *Power Evangelism* and *Power Healing*.

Significant Christian critiques of, and calls for discernment in, this revival of the miraculous can be found in Bruce Barron, *The Health and Wealth Gospel*; Arthur Johnson, *Faith Misguided: Exposing the Dangers of Mysticism*; Edward Gross, *Miracles, Demons, and Spiritual Warfare*; D. R. McConnell, *A Different Gospel*; Michael Horton, ed., *Power Religion;* Hank Hanegraaff, *Christianity in Crisis*; Michael Moriarty, *The New Charismatics*; Norman Geisler, *Signs and Wonders*; and John MacArthur, *Charismatic Chaos*.

[59]James Jeans, as quoted in Ian Barbour, *Religion in an Age of Science* (New York: Harper & Row, 1990), p. 114.

human life could have happened by mere chance without some rational design.[60]

Finally, in the area of ethics and morality, there has never been a greater need and opportunity for Christians to defend Christian values and expose the failure of worldly beliefs and practices. The moral discourse of the PM is in total disarray and the resulting loss of individual self-esteem and commitment to communal living is evident nightly on the evening news. Thomas Oden sums it up as follows:

> The dissolution of the family, the loss of covenant sexuality, the breakdown of traditional values, the irretrievable loss of neighborhoods, the tyrannical imposition of new rules, the regulatory intrusion of government upon every aspect of private life, the loss of plausibility of religion, the loss of safe streets, the sense of homelessness in the world—modernity exacts unconscionable costs.[61]

---

[60]See John Barrow and Frank Tipler, *The Anthropic Cosmological Principle*; Paul Davies, *The Accidental Universe*; *God and the New Physics*; and *The Mind of God*; Freeman Dyson, *Infinite in All Directions*; John Leslie, "Anthropic Principle, World Ensemble, Design," *American Philosophical Quarterly* 19 (1982): 141-51; Hugh Ross, *The Creator and the Cosmos* and *The Fingerprint of God*; John Polkinghorne, *One World: The Interaction of Science and Theology*; and Stanley Jaki, *The Purpose of it All*.

[61]This quotation appears in *After Modernity ... What?*, p. 75. See also: Jeffrey Stout, *Ethics after Babel*; *The Flight from Authority*; Thomas Molnar, *The Pagan Temptation*; Alasdair MacIntyre, *After Virtue*; *Whose Justice? Which Rationality?*; and Stanley Hauerwas, *After Christendom? How the Church is to Behave if Freedom, Justice, and a Christian Nation are Bad Ideas*.

John D. Castelein

RECOMMENDED BIBLIOGRAPHY

Brown, Colin. *Philosophy and the Christian Faith.* Downers Grove: InterVarsity Press, 1975.
> No other single volume introduces the major thinkers of the modern world from the Christian standpoint as clearly and helpfully for the lay Christian. A moderate level of difficulty.

Carson, D. A. *The Gagging of God: Christianity Confronts Pluralism.* Grand Rapids: Zondervan, 1996.
> A high level, well-researched, and vigorous defense of the truth of the Christian faith against different forms of pluralism.

Castelein, John. "Ministering to Modern and Postmodern Minds." Lincoln, IL: Lincoln Christian College and Seminary, 1995. Videocassette series.
> This series of sixteen videocassettes is available through Lincoln Christian College and Seminary's Video Correspondence Department. The course can be audited or taken for seminary credit.

Dockery, David, ed. *The Challenge of Postmodernism: An Evangelical Engagement.* Wheaton: Victor/BridgePoint Book, 1995.
> A high-level survey of many crucial aspects of the postmodern condition for the church today. It contains Grenz's famous comparison between the modern "Star Trek" and the postmodern "Star Trek: The Next Generation."

Grenz, Stanley. *A Primer on Postmodernism.* Grand Rapids: Eerdmans, 1996.
> Parallels Veith's book in this bibliography but with a more demanding exposition of postmodernist philosophy and hermeneutics. I recommend this for advanced college and seminary students.

Lundin, Roger. *The Culture of Interpretation: Christian Faith and the Postmodern World.* Grand Rapids: Eerdmans, 1993.
> A demanding but very rewarding introduction to, and critique of, postmodernism especially in its relationship to literature.

McCallum, Dennis, ed. *The Death of Truth: What's Wrong with Multiculturalism, the Rejection of Reason, and the New Postmodern Diversity.* Minneapolis: Bethany House, 1996.

Spells out how postmodernity impacts on health care, literature, education, history, psychology, law, science, and religion.

Middleton, J. Richard and Brian Walsh, ed. *Truth is Stranger than It used to Be: Biblical Faith in a Postmodern Age.* Downers Grove: InterVarsity Press, 1995.

Two Christian authors try to read the Bible from a new perspective that seeks to be both evangelical and postmodern. Their pioneering attempt is bold, creative, and sure to raise some theological concerns.

Oden, Thomas. *After Modernity ... What? Agenda for Theology.* Grand Rapids: Zondervan, 1990.

One of the better evangelical expositions of why the modern mind has failed and what opportunities postmodernism affords for renewed Christian witness.

Phillips, Timothy and Dennis Okholm, ed. *Christian Apologetics in the Postmodern World.* Downers Grove: InterVarsity Press, 1995.

A collection of useful, challenging, and controversial presentations given at the Wheaton Theology Conference in 1994. Reflects different apologetic strategies evangelical Christians are using in facing postmodernity.

Randall, John Herman. *The Making of the Modern Mind: A Survey of the Intellectual Background of the Present Age.* New York: Columbia University Press, 1926, 1976.

The classic survey, still unsurpassed for clarity and comprehensibility. However, it does not take a Christian position.

Sire, James. *The Universe Next Door.* 2nd ed. Downers Grove: InterVarsity, Press, 1988.

Excellent introductory level presentation and analysis of the Christian theistic worldview and its major rivals in the modern world. Helpful introductions to nihilism and New Age worldviews.

Veith, Gene. Jr. *Postmodern Times: A Christian Guide to Contemporary Thought and Culture.* Wheaton: Crossway Books, 1994.

Another medium level introduction to the postmodern world that is very readable and quite clear. I recommend this for church leaders and beginning college students.

Chapter 10:

On the Value of the
Philosophy of Science for
Christian Faith and Ministry
by
Dr. Richard A. Knopp

Richard Knopp is professor of philosophy and inter-disciplinary studies at Lincoln Christian College and adjunct professor of Christian apologetics at Lincoln Christian Seminary. He has taught at Lincoln since 1983.

Dr. Knopp received a B.A. degree in Christian ministries from St. Louis Christian College, an M.Div. in theology and philosophy from Lincoln Christian Seminary, an M.A. in philosophy from Southern Illinois University in Carbondale, and his Ph.D. in philosophy from the University of Illinois at Urbana-Champaign. His work in philosophy has especially concentrated on two key philosophers of science, Karl Popper and Thomas Kuhn, and the significance of their thought regarding religious truth-claims and the rationality of religious commitment.

Professor Knopp was a recent $10,000 award-winner in a John M. Templeton Foundation program to develop and teach a course dealing with the relationship between science and religion. Lectures from this course, entitled "Science and Theology: Problems, Perspectives, and Possibilities," are available on video through the Lincoln Christian College media center.

Prior to teaching at Lincoln, Dr. Knopp was a youth minister in Wood River, Illinois and Florissant, Missouri; a preaching minister in McLean, Illinois; and a deacon in Champaign, Illinois. Currently, he is actively engaged in interim preaching ministries. He and his wife, Paula, have frequently served the church in various areas of music. They have two daughters and one son.

ON THE VALUE OF THE PHILOSOPHY OF SCIENCE FOR CHRISTIAN FAITH AND MINISTRY

𝕴𝖙 started at an undergraduate chapel service at Lincoln Christian College in 1974. As a new seminary student, I was perplexed when a faculty member announced that students would inevitably be hearing about the "corn-popper" debate on campus. I expected to wrestle with some difficult theological, philosophical, and cultural issues, but I was dumbfounded over how a "debate" over popcorn could prove relevant or useful. The faculty member was really referring to a major emphasis by Professor James Strauss that had permeated the · campus—the "Kuhn-Popper" debate occurring within the philosophy of science.[1] Little did I realize that the issues raised in that debate would soon capture my imagination and

---

[1]The key players in this "debate" were Thomas Kuhn, who had been professor of science history at Princeton, and Karl Popper, noted philosophy of science professor at the London School of Economics. The debate developed because of the "revolutionary" ideas about science presented by Thomas Kuhn in *The Structure of Scientific Revolutions*, 2nd ed. (Chicago: University of Chicago Press, 1962; 1970). Although there were precursors to Kuhn, Kuhn's ideas soon engendered extensive discussions among all major academic disciplines. Note Gary Gutting's vast bibliography exposing Kuhn's earlier influence in philosophy of science, the history of science, sociology of science, sociology, political science, economics, psychology, history, theology and philosophy of religion, art and literature, and education (in *Paradigms and Revolutions: Appraisals and Applications of Thomas Kuhn's Philosophy of Science* [Notre Dame: University of Notre Dame Press, 1980]).

Popper's key works at the time included the *Logik der Forschuung* (1934) which was translated as *The Logic of Scientific Discovery*, 2nd ed. (New York: Harper and Row, 1959); *Conjectures and Refutations*, 2nd ed. (New York: Basic Books, 1965); and *Objective Knowledge* (Oxford: The Clarendon Press, 1972).

guide the rest of my academic career.[2] More than twenty years later, I am even more convinced of the importance of knowing about the philosophy of science for the Christian faith and ministry. I believe that it can offer immeasurable insights to a Christian leader in his or her understanding of theology, philosophy, hermeneutics, apologetics, psychology, communication, culture, social dynamics, education, etc.

Professor Strauss was a pioneer in recognizing the relevance of post-Kuhnian philosophy of science for Christian concerns, advocating it years before the connection became prominent in print.[3] He understood that the issues have critical implications not only for the rationality of science but for the rationality of religious belief. I am convinced that, of the wide-ranging insights one might reap from the mind of Jim Strauss, as many were germinated in the field of the philosophy of science as anywhere else (except the Bible). In what follows, I want to survey this field, cultivate its significance, and harvest some applications for Christian leaders who face the tasks of understanding the world and influencing it for the cause of Christ in their preaching and teaching.

---

[2]My master's thesis dealt with "Karl Popper's Concept of Rationality in Science" (Southern Illinois University at Carbondale, 1983), and my Ph.D. dissertation applied the ideas of Thomas Kuhn and Karl Popper to the nature of religious belief, specifically as they affect the truth-claims of religion and the rationality of religious commitment (University of Illinois, 1991).

[3]Some of the earliest (and still valuable) material is Basil Mitchell's *The Justification of Religious Belief* (New York: The Seabury Press, 1973); Ian Barbour's *Myths, Models, and Paradigms A Comprehensive Study in Science and Religion* (New York: Harper & Row, 1974); and Nicholas Wolterstorff's *Religion Within the Bounds of Religion* (Grand Rapids: Eerdmans, 1976). (Also note the sources included in footnote 23 below.)

THE KUHN-POPPER DEBATE AND
CONTEMPORARY PHILOSOPHY OF SCIENCE

The Demise of Neo-Positivism

Prior to the revolution in the philosophy of science which was fostered largely by Thomas Kuhn in the 1960s, the predominant picture of science was a "foundationalist" one with a "neo-positivist" emphasis.[4] This picture presented the following general beliefs: (1) Scientific theories are empirically grounded in a foundation of empirical certainty and are empirically

---

[4]"Foundationalism" as used here refers to the basic idea that all rational beliefs must be ultimately based in an epistemic (knowledge) foundation of certitude. "Neo-positivism" suggests that the ultimate foundation for rational (and even meaningful) beliefs must be *empirical* in nature. Historically, neo-positivism is grounded in the Logical Positivist view, as expressed by A. J. Ayer, that "a statement is held to be literally meaningful if and only if it is either analytic or empirically verifiable" and "if [one's statement] is so interpreted that no possible experience could go to verify it, it does not have any factual meaning at all" (*Language, Truth, and Logic,* 2nd ed. [New York: Macmillan & Co., 1946], pp. 9,15). Ayer and others intended that this criterion be used, not just to render *false* any kind of metaphysical or religious assertion which would refer to non-empirical entities like God, but to render them *meaningless.*

The original project of the Logical Positivists to use the empirical criterion as a *general* criterion for *meaning* has now essentially disintegrated. Its thesis could not be coherently held in any strong form. One obvious problem was that the very *statement* of the thesis could not satisfy its own requirement of being either analytic (i.e., true by definition) or empirical! Hence, by its own stipulation, it lacked meaning.

However, the continued influence of this perspective, especially as it pertains to religion, is still seen in such neo-positivist writers as Kai Nielsen, J. L. Mackie, and Antony Flew. See Mackie's *The Miracle of Theism* (Oxford: Clarendon Press, 1982), esp. pp. 2-4. Also note the debates in Terry L. Miethe and Antony Flew, *Does God Exist? A Believer and an Atheist Debate* (San Francisco: Harper-SanFrancisco, 1991) and J. P. Moreland and Kai Nielsen, *Does God Exist: The Debate between Theists and Atheists* (Buffalo, NY: Prometheus Books, 1993).

verifiable or falsifiable. (2) Science is an "objective" enterprise which is not entangled in personal, social, or metaphysical presuppositions, values, or commitments. (3) Science is a "rational" program with universally accepted methods and established criteria for rationally choosing among competing theories. (4) Science progresses cumulatively "closer and closer to the truth" because a scientific theory is only replaced by a better and "truer" theory on specifiable rational grounds.

This neo-positivist (and foundationalist) picture of science created a real problem for biblical Christianity partly because it was generally espoused by those who stressed the radical *difference* between science and religion on each of the above points. (1') Religious beliefs lack the necessary empirical ("factual") basis and merely concern themselves with *values*. As such, they are not empirically verifiable or falsifiable. (2') Religious beliefs are *subjective* in nature and embroiled in all kinds of personal, social, and metaphysical presuppositions and commitments. Commitment to religious beliefs must be *absolute* in nature and differs, therefore, from the *tentative* approach by scientists to their hypotheses and theories. (3') Religion has no universally accepted methods or established criteria for rationally choosing among competing religious perspectives. (4') Any change in religious perspective (or toward a religious perspective) must be made by a "leap of faith" since no rational grounds exist for getting closer to *religious* "truth."

In sum, according to this perspective, religious "truth"-claims are entirely different from scientific truth-claims, and they are irrationally believed, having no basis other than that of an *absolute* and uncriticizable faith-commitment.[5] But as Dr. Strauss might say, "Even

_____

[5]My doctoral dissertation offers an extensive response to these two basic claims. See my "Religious Belief and the Problems of Cognitivity and Commitment: A Reappraisal Based on Contemporary

a truck driver on Route 10 would understand the devastating implications of this for the Christian faith and apologetics."

Fortunately, the advocates of the neo-positivist approach to science were not only mistaken in their views of *religion*—at least *biblical* religion—they were shown, by Kuhn and others, to be incorrect in their understanding of *science*. (Other than that—a Straussian sarcasm here—their views were perfectly acceptable!)[6] Kuhn led the charge in challenging the basic tenets of this neo-positivist (and widely held) view of science. As a notable historian and philosopher of science, Kuhn attempted to *describe* actual scientific practice, past and present. He did not merely make a radical proposal for the way he thinks science *should* be done. One of the reasons for Kuhn's significance, therefore, is his conclusion that the *history* of science does not support the neo-positivist *picture* of science.[7]

Kuhn argued that most of scientific practice— what he calls "normal science"—is guided by strong *commitments* to a particular interpretive model or "paradigm." A paradigm (which consists of methodological, psychological, and even metaphysical assumptions) often determines what the paradigm practitioner regards as relevant, true, and acceptable. Kuhn further contended that the shift from one paradigm to another is *not the rational affair* it is generally pictured as being; the shift is better characterized as a "revolution" (hence the title

---

Philosophy of Science" (Ph.D. diss., University of Illinois, 1991).

[6]I can imagine professor Strauss saying something like, "The main weakness is it isn't true" or "The French word for that is 'le bunk'" or "Like cheap clothes, it was bound to come apart."

[7]Murphy, *Theology in an Age of Scientific Reasoning*, p. 56. In addition to the resources mentioned in footnote 3 above, other helpful presentations of this turn in the philosophy of science can be found in Harold I. Brown, *Perception, Theory and Commitment* (Chicago: University of Chicago Press, 1977) and Frederick Suppe, ed., *The Structure of Scientific Theories*, 2nd ed. (Urbana, IL: University of Illinois Press, 1977).

of his book, *The Structure of Scientific Revolutions*). The move from one paradigm to another is described by Kuhn as a "gestalt switch" and a "conversion experience"; a decision that can often "only be made on faith"; and one which "cannot be justified by proof."[8] In addition, Kuhn stressed the "incommensurability" of paradigms—the notion that competing paradigms are often not subject to some straightforward comparison, because the meanings of key terms are sometimes radically different,[9] and because methodological and metaphysical assumptions greatly affect what one even considers as a relevant "fact." It is as though scientists working within the context of a paradigm are wearing a particular type of colored glasses which influences both their interpretive conclusions as well as what they consider as "facts." Scientists in different paradigms are set at "cross-purposes" and they tend to "talk through one another."[10] *"Bare facts"* do not exist *independently* of the way they are perceived; the *"facts" themselves are, in a sense, "theory-laden."* If this is true, then no "fact" is a *bare* fact.

Therefore, a scientific theory can only be evaluated in light of the entire "nest of commitments"[11]—the paradigm—within which it is a part. So when an empirical theory is falsified, one may not know for sure whether what is falsified is the empirical theory *itself* or some other (perhaps metaphysical) aspect(s) of the associated paradigm. Therefore, the demarcation between the *"empirical"* and the *"metaphysical"* is thus not at all clearly drawn.

In my opinion, Kuhn's views have often been greatly exaggerated and misinterpreted. The "strong"

---

[8]See Kuhn, *The Structure of Scientific Revolutions*, pp. 150-152, 158; cf. p. 148.
[9]Consider, for example, the term "mass" in the Newtonian and Einsteinian view.
[10]Ibid., p. 148; cf. p. 109.
[11]Ibid., p. 41.

interpretation of Kuhn—which I reject—portrays him as espousing an *irrational* and relativistic philosophy of science that advocates a kind of "mob-psychology."[12] His idea of the "incommensurability" of paradigms is frequently taken to mean that competing scientific theories cannot be rationally compared and selected. According to this interpretation, the "Kuhn-Popper" debate pitted the *irrational* and *non-progressive* notion of science (by Kuhn) against Popper's view that science is *rational* in its development and leads closer to *objective truth*. After all, the English titles of two important works by Popper were *The Logic of Scientific Discovery* and *Objective Knowledge* (emphasis added).

As I recall, Dr. Strauss favored this characterization of the debate and clearly sided with Popper on these points. However, he also communicated—as paradoxical as it appears—that many of Kuhn's ideas were valuable in establishing a *biblical* approach to science and to knowledge in general. For a time, I must admit, I could not really understand how my beloved teacher was able to fuse Kuhn and Popper together in any coherent way. Exactly what *did* he like and what did he *not* like in these thinkers? That question was not so easy to answer. In a way, the situation was typical of many exchanges that I and other students had with Dr. Strauss: we would often come away from class or a conversation feeling immensely inspired and overwhelmed with insight, but we would somehow end up asking ourselves, "Now what did he say?" (I suspect that this reflects his genius or the actual complexity of the real world more than it denotes any indecisiveness or simple eclecticism on his part.)

---

[12]See Imre Lakatos's "Falsification and the Methodology of Scientific Research Programmes," in *Criticism and the Growth of Knowledge*, ed. Imre Lakatos and Alan Musgrave (New York: Cambridge University Press, 1970), p. 178; and J. P. Moreland, "Kuhn's Epistemology: A Paradigm Afloat," *Bulletin of the Evangelical Philosophical Society* 4 (1981): 33-60.

I was able to reconcile this paradox by concluding that Kuhn can, and should, be given a "softer" reading, even though he does make some strong statements against the notion of "truth" as something which is "out there" that scientists should be working "toward."[13] Yet in spite of some of Kuhn's own statements and numerous misinterpretations of his actual views, Kuhn continues to have a lasting influence on how science is perceived. As Del Ratzsch characterizes it:

> The general philosophy of science community, after a brief, albeit rocky honeymoon with Kuhn, pulled back a bit from several of Kuhn's positions.... By the late 1960s and early 1970s, philosophy of science was clearly steering away from any sort of straight [I would say "strong"] Kuhnianism.
> But ... his influence and legacy are still substantial.... [W]hat Kuhn did was to advance the idea that the involvement of things [like "broad metaphysical and value convictions"] beyond merely the empirical is both inevitable and legitimate in science.[14]

J. P. Moreland's summary also analyzes the lasting impact of Kuhn:

> Kuhn has taught us how difficult it is to get at the facts and how central the role of theory is in such an endeavor; how important social perspective and pressure have been in the history of science; and how much of the history of science can be interpreted as a sequence of theory replacements, not refinements.[15]

---

[13]See *The Structure of Scientific Revolutions*, pp. 170-171; Kuhn's "Postscript—1969," printed in the 2nd edition of *The Structure of Scientific Revolutions*, p. 206; and Kuhn's "Reflections on My Critics," in *Criticism and the Growth of Knowledge*, ed. Imre Lakatos and Alan Musgrave (London: Cambridge University Press, 1970), pp. 264-266.

[14]Ratzsche, *The Battle of Beginnings*, pp. 118-119.

[15]Moreland, *Christianity and the Nature of Science*, p. 202.

When Kuhn is viewed in this "softer" light, the atmosphere of the "Kuhn-Popper" *debate* is altered considerably, especially when one considers that Popper eventually made some significant concessions that led him much closer to Kuhn's views.[16] I have argued elsewhere that Kuhn and Popper can be seen as offering complementary contributions to the "new" philosophy of science which have effectively impugned the neo-positivist concept of science.[17]

This "new" philosophy of science contrasts with the foundationalist picture of science at every point.

---

[16]For example, Popper originally proposed that "falsifiability" should be the decisive criterion for demarcating genuine scientific statements from metaphysical ones: "falsifiability" is used "solely as a criterion for the empirical character of a system of statements" (*The Logic of Scientific Discovery*, p. 86). But his emphasis on falsifiability was supplanted by the more general notion of "criticizability." He says, "I no longer think, as I once did, that there is a difference between science and metaphysics regarding this most important point [i.e., regarding claims to truth]. I look upon a metaphysical theory as similar to a scientific one .... *[A]s long as a metaphysical theory can be rationally criticized*, I should be inclined to take seriously its implicit claim to be considered, tentatively, as true" (*Quantum Theory and the Schism in Physics* [Totowa, NJ: Rowman and Littlefield, 1982], p. 199). He has also stated, "I do not think it possible to eliminate *all* 'metaphysical elements' from science: they are too closely interwoven with the rest" (*Realism and the Aim of Science* [Totowa, NJ: Rowman and Littlefield, 1983], p. 179).

[17]In Chapter Two of my dissertation I interpret Kuhn and Popper in a dialectical fashion and produce an approach to science very similar to that of Imre Lakatos (note Lakatos's "Falsification and the Methodology of Scientific Research Programmes," in *Criticism and the Growth of Knowledge*, ed. Imre Lakatos and Alan Musgrave [New York: Cambridge University Press, 1970], pp. 91-196). Some recent works dealing with science and religion use Lakatos more as a beginning point for their comparative analyses. See Nancey Murphy, *Theology in the Age of Scientific Reasoning* and Philip Hefner, *The Human Factor: Evolution, Culture, and Religion* (Minneapolis: Fortress Press, 1993).

Neo-Positivist Science	Post-Kuhnian Science
1. Scientific theories are empirically grounded in a foundation of empirical certainty and, unlike metaphysical (and religious) beliefs, are empirically verifiable or falsifiable.	1. Empirical "facts" are not just "given"; they are perceived through an interpretive scheme and are thus "value-laden." No "rock solid" empirical foundation exists. "Empirical" and "metaphysical" assertions can no longer be sharply distinguished on the basis of their empirical verifiability or falsifiability.
2. Science is an "objective" enterprise which is not entangled in personal, social, or metaphysical presuppositions, values, or commitments.	2. Scientific theories and practice include many methodological, sociological, and metaphysical presuppositions and commitments. Science is not purely "objective."
3. Science is a "rational" program with universally accepted methods and established criteria for rationally choosing among competing theories.	3. Science is not the monolithic, rational enterprise it is often thought to be. Fundamental disagreements arise over methods and basic assumptions. Choosing a scientific theory is not simply a matter of applying some preestablished set of criteria and following logical rules.
4. Science progresses cumulatively "closer and closer to the truth" because a scientific theory is only replaced by a better and "truer" theory on specifiable rational grounds.	4. Switching from one scientific paradigm to another requires a fundamental shift in perspective that is often not demanded by empirical evidence. "Anomalies" might prompt one to consider a different paradigm, but the shift entails a "faith-commitment"—one that may possess rational considerations but not one decisively determined by them.

In light of the fact that religious beliefs have often been accused of having no epistemologically certain foundation and of being empirically unfalsifiable, irrational, and subjective, it is now quite ironic that science must defend itself against the same charges.[18] As a result of the "new" philosophy of science, it appears that scientific statements look more and more like those of religion. And when the historical and empirical emphasis of Christianity (as opposed to other religions) is properly acknowledged, many of its assertions look more and more like scientific ones. The "new" philosophy of science has indeed opened up promising possibilities for a more positive relationship between science and religion, particularly the Christian faith. This is so, because of the demise of neo-positivism.

The Rise of Contextualism

Before evangelicals join in a chorus of "Ding Dong the Witch is Dead," they should be aware that the "stronger" reading of Kuhn has fanned the flames of another perspective which, I believe, is equally lethal to biblical Christianity. I will refer to it as "contextualism." Although they are, in some senses, at opposite ends of a spectrum, the neo-positivism and contextualism share a common platform regarding science and religion: they both view science and religion as occupying totally separate domains. But whereas neo-positivists stress the *rationality* of science and the *irrationality* of religion, contextualists maintain that science and religion can

---

[18]See Henry B. Veatch, "A Neglected Avenue in Contemporary Religious Apologetics," *Religious Studies* 13 (1977): 29-48. John Miller suggests that this is what constitutes, in part, the "logical similarity" between science and religion: "Exactly the criticism directed toward religion could be directed toward science .... Their first-order principles are hardly more open to falsification by "contrary instances" than are those general religious propositions which take the brunt of criticism .... If one admits the legitimacy of Flew's falsification argument against religion, one would find it exceptionally difficult to defend *scientific discourse* against the same charge." See Miller's "Science and Religion: Their Logical Similarity," *Religious Studies* 5 (1969): 68. Paul Feyerabend (e.g. *Against Method*) is particularly known for his attacks against the unique rationality and superiority claims of western science.

both be rational, but that their respective criteria for truth and rationality are entirely different. Context-ualists emphasize that the criteria for truth and rationality are determined by, and applicable only *within*, each respective context. Accordingly, no single standard for truth and no extra-contextual criteria for rationality exist. Instead, we must speak of multiple *rationalities*. Each context has its own "truths" and its own "rationality."[19] Contextualists readily acknowledge the demise of the foundationalism which has grounded the neo-positivist view. No context—including the scientific one—has any ultimate foundations; all contexts are truly "groundless."[20]

One consequence of the contextualist account is that any "conversion" from one context to another will require a commitment *prior to* the appeal to evidence or argument. Since the criteria for evidence and rationality are *internal* to a paradigm, one cannot use evidence or argument rationally to persuade anyone *outside* a given context. When this perspective is assessed, it should be

---

[19]Although I have used the terms "neo-positivism" and "context-ualism," I want to suggest a respective correlation between these terms and the perspectives of "modernism" and "postmodernism." Modernism is built upon the ideals of the Enlightenment which stressed having certain foundations for knowledge and powerful, universally-possessed capacities of human reason. Postmodernists contend that the Enlightenment ideal is implausible. They seek to construct (through "deconstruction"!) an approach to the world which denies universally acceptable (or available) foundations or rational criteria. In a sense, therefore, any consistent postmodernist "approach" to the world must entail the view that it can, at best, only be *one* approach among many.

Most analyses of postmodernism at least mention Thomas Kuhn as being connected with it. In a recent treatment of postmodernism, Stanley Grenz highlights the postmodernist role that Kuhn holds. See Grenz's *A Primer on Postmodernism* (Grand Rapids: Eerdmans, 1996), pp. 54-56. (For a more complete treatment of postmodernism, see John Castelein's chapter earlier in this volume.)

[20]See Norman Malcolm, "The Groundlessness of Belief," in *Reason and Religion*, ed. Stuart Brown (Ithica, NY: Cornell University Press, 1977), pp. 143-157.

clear that Christian apologetics, in the "positive" sense of offering arguments and evidences, would be annihilated.[21]

The violence of Kuhn's storm has passed, but it has left a landscape that will never be the same. One of the crucial challenges now is how one can avoid the contextualist's relativism without the foothold of foundationalism.[22] Presently, many philosophers of science

---

[21]"Negative" apologetics refers to those attempts to respond to and refute arguments against faith. "Positive" apologetics attempts to persuade an unbeliever why he or she *should* believe. See Ronald Nash, *Faith and Reason: Searching for a Rational Faith* (Grand Rapids: Academie Books, 1988), pp. 14-18.

Increasingly (and unfortunately in my view) some evangelicals are attempting a type of "apologetic" which rejects the notion of "objective truth" altogether. They emphasize, instead, the need and value of having lives of integrity and Christ-like love in the church to authorize its witness. Note the various approaches to apologetics in Timothy Phillips and Dennis Okholm, ed. *Christian Apologetics in the Postmodern World* (Downers Grove: InterVarsity, 1995) and especially the chapter by Philip D. Kenneson, "There's No Such Thing as Objective Truth, and It's a Good Thing Too," pp. 155-170. Cf. Stanley Hauerwas et al., ed. *Theology Without Foundation: Religious Practice and the Future of Theological Truth* (Nashville: Abingdon Press, 1994).

[22]Alvin Plantinga, one of the most influential living Christian philosophers, has provided an interesting attempt at rejecting foundationalism while avoiding relativism. Especially note the following works by Plantinga: "Is Belief in God Rational?" in *Rationality and Religious Belief*, ed. C. F. Delaney (Notre Dame: University of Notre Dame Press, 1979), pp. 7-27; and "Reason and Belief in God," in *Faith and Rationality*, ed. Alvin Plantinga and Nicholas Wolterstorff (Notre Dame: University of Notre Dame Press, 1983), pp. 16-93.

Plantinga has argued that one does *not need* to have arguments or evidence in order for one's religious beliefs to be "rational," because belief in God is a "basic belief" that does not require such. Thus, the unbeliever cannot legitimately charge the believer with irrationality simply because she fails to satisfy the foundationalist's demands for argument and evidence.

But if all Plantinga shows is that belief in God *can* be properly basic for the *believer*, he has not at all shown that it is, or should be, an acceptable basic belief for *everyone*, or that a nonbeliever is somehow "mistaken" in excluding it. At best, it seems that the

---

(and many within other disciplines) are seeking to find a moderate climate between the implausible certitudes of foundationalism and the undesirable vicissitudes of relativism. It is within this intellectual atmosphere that Christian leaders live. Challenges as well as vast opportunities are in the forecast.

Implications for Theology, the Christian Faith, and Ministry

Increasingly, authors (many of which are evangelicals) are recognizing the impact of Kuhn and contemporary philosophy of science in areas critical to the Christian faith. Applications have been made, for example, to the nature of religious language and the rationality of religious commitment (Trigg; Knopp); the nature of theology in relation to science (Austin, Knopp, Murphy, Moreland, Van Huyssteen); creation and evolution (Ratzsche); and to the areas of social science (Gaede), psychology (Van Leeuwen), and hermeneutics (Poythress).[23]

---

believer can only say, "It is rational *for me*." But this implies that there are multiple (and even conflicting) legitimate rationalities. Therefore, Plantinga's view may be quite helpful as a "negative" apologetic, but as it stands, it does not provide a sufficient basis for a "positive" apologetic.

Of course, one should not condemn a position for failing to do what it never intended. This point is exposed by Ronald Nash when he says, "How does Plantinga's position *on this point* [i.e., giving the believer a right to profess belief in God as properly basic] convince an agnostic or atheist that he should take belief in God as properly basic? How does Plantinga's view *on this matter* show the non-Christian that his basic beliefs are incorrect? The answer is simple: Plantinga's views *on this subject* were never intended to do *that!*" (Nash, *Faith and Reason*, p. 90). (A forthcoming book on Plantinga's thought will be published by Eerdmans and edited by James Sennett, one of the contributors to this volume.)

[23]See Roger Trigg, *Reason and Commitment* (Cambridge: Cambridge University Press, 1973); Knopp, "Religious Belief and the Problems of Cognitivity and Commitment: A Reappraisal Based on Contemporary Philosophy of Science" (Ph.D. diss., University of Illinois, 1991); William H. Austin, *The Relevance of Natural Science*

But all this may still strike some as being "too intellectual to be of any real value for me or my church." Even the erudite Jim Strauss would have asked his students, "What good is it if you can't preach it?" Perhaps one way to help show the relevance of the philosophy of science is to list some significant questions to which this material can bring useful insight.

1. Is the Christian faith "rational" and, more generally, what does it mean to accept a system of belief "rationally"?
2. Is every Christian belief equally important?
3. Why do people disagree so much over biblical interpretation?
4. Why is there such disagreement over interpreting "evidence" for God and the Christian faith? Why don't evolutionists reach the same conclusions as creationists?
5. How can I best defend the Christian faith? What is the best approach to apologetics?
6. What is involved in the process of "conversion? How might I understand the dynamics involved between the believer and the unbeliever?
7. How should I understand and present the relationship between science and the Christian faith?
8. How can churches and church leaders allow themselves to be so closed to new ideas?

to *Theology* (NY: Harper & Row, 1976); Murphy, *Theology in an Age of Scientific Reasoning*; J. P. Moreland, *Christianity and the Nature of Science* (Grand Rapids: Baker Book House, 1989), pp. 195-202; Wentzel Van Huyssteen, *Theology and the Justification of Faith* (Grand Rapids: Eerdmans, 1985), pp. 3-15, 57-75; Ratzsch, *The Battle of Beginnings: Why Neither Side is Winning the Creation-Evolution Debate*, pp. 103-135; S. D. Gaede, *Where Gods May Dwell: On Understanding the Human Condition* (Grand Rapids: Academie Books, 1985); Mary Stewart Van Leeuwen, *The Person in Psychology: A Contemporary Christian Appraisal* (Grand Rapids: Eerdmans, 1985); and Vern Poythress, *Science and Hermeneutics* (Grand Rapids: Academie Books, 1988), pp. 39-72.

These questions are (or at least should be) critically important for the concerned Christian in the modern world. In the remaining part of this chapter, I want to suggest how knowing something about the philosophy of science can contribute to our answers, not just to "intellectual" and esoteric issues, but to significant "practical" questions like these. I will pursue this by identifying some key "values" that philosophy of science can bring to the areas of theology, the Christian faith, and leadership ministry. One desired by-product is to demonstrate that the typical sharp dichotomy between the *theoretical* and the *practical* is improper—to show that theoretical pursuits need to have practical objectives, and that practical solutions need sufficient theoretical underpinning.

(1) *One of the values of knowing about philosophy of science is that it can help us comprehend key issues and representative positions among competing theological perspectives and alternative apologetic methodologies.* One of the reasons why philosophy of science needs to be understood is because theologians— from liberal to conservative—have been consciously or unconsciously influenced *by* it or they exemplify positions *within* it. For example, some prominent representatives of both "neo-positivism" (or "foundationalism") as well as "contextualism" have lodged within the house of Christian faith.

Theology has its own types of *neo-positivists* and *foundationalists.* Some neo-positivist theologies *accept* the rational standards and truths established by science and concede that religious belief is "irrational" and "uncriticizable." Kierkegaard, for instance, says that "there is only one proof—that of faith," and that "reasons and proofs ... must be done away with."[24] Barth and

---

[24]Soren Kierkegaard, *Concluding Unscientific Postscript,* trans. David Swenson and Walter Lowrie (Princeton: Princeton University Press, 1941), pp. 500, 496.

Richard A. Knopp

Tillich also portray religious belief, if evaluated by the criteria established by modern science, in a very similar fashion to Kierkegaard.

Another neo-positivist approach to theology adopts a foundation of "biblical authoritarianism" and *dismisses* science—at least at those points where it conflicts with religion—as misguided and mistaken. Certainly those who argue for an earth no more than about 10,000 years old fit into this category.

A third type of theological neo-positivist or foundationalist can also be identified. This group would include those who might be classed as "naive evidentialists" in the area of apologetics—those who say or imply that defending the Christian faith requires little more than pointing to the "facts" of history (e.g. miracles, prophecy).

One underlying problem with all three of these approaches is that they are based upon a foundationalist epistemology and a neo-positivist understanding of science whose plausibility is greatly in question. (1) Kierkegaard and others relegate religion to irrationality on the basis of a naive (and misdirected) acceptance of the rational normativeness of science. (2) The foundationalism of the biblical authoritarians is problematic, in part, because it ignores or undervalues the inescapable role of presuppositions in biblical interpretation. (3) And evidentialist apologists fail to recognize the critical importance of interpretive paradigms in their appeal to the "facts" of history.

But theology not only includes neo-positivists and foundationalists, it harbors an array of *contextualists*—those who consider the criteria for rationality and truth as *internal* to each theological paradigm. In a sense, theologians like Barth and Tillich reside in this camp. Tillich says, for instance, "There is no criterion by which faith can be judged from outside the correlation of faith."[25] And Barth asserts that

> there is no sense in which we have to answer for the Bible really being God's Word. Any wish to answer for it would here be a denial of what we wished to answer for. We can say no more than this, that in this matter the Bible can answer for itself.[26]

In addition to theologians like Barth and Tillich, the contextualist camp also holds some conservative thinkers, particularly in the Reformed (Calvinistic) tradition. One influential spokesman for this view was Cornelius Van Til.[27] After stating that God is the most basic and final reference point in human interpretation, Van Til asserts:

> This is the question as to what are one's ultimate presuppositions. When a man becomes a sinner he made of himself instead of God the ultimate or final reference point.... The sinner has cemented colored glasses on his eyes which he cannot remove. And all is yellow to the jaundiced eye. There can be no intelligible reasoning unless those who reason

---

[25]Paul Tillich, *The Dynamics of Faith* (New York: Harper & Brothers, 1957), p. 59.

[26]Karl Barth, *Church Dogmatics*, vol. 1, pt. 1, *The Doctrine of the Word of God* (Edinburgh: T & T Clark, 1936), pp. 302-303. Barth asserts that historians, educationists, and philosophers who use any criteria for judgment other than the single criterion of the Word of God improperly "judge the Church's language about God on principles foreign to it, instead of on its own principles" (Ibid., p. 5).

[27]Cornelius Van Til (1895-1987) left his teaching post at Princeton Theological Seminary to become long-time professor of apologetics at the more conservative Westminster Theological Seminary in Philadelphia where his influence was felt by many notable evangelical scholars, including Gary North, Rousas Rushdoony, Vern Poythress, and Francis Schaeffer.

together understand what they mean by their words.[28]

The similarities between Van Til's *theological* statement and the characterization of *science* by Thomas Kuhn are astonishing. Recall that Kuhn talks of the switch from one paradigm to another as a "conversion experience," one that can "only be made on faith," and one that "cannot be justified by proof." Further, Kuhn holds that those in different paradigms are set at "cross-purposes" and they tend to "talk through one another."

Van Til's own theological emphasis is that if one does not *start* with belief in God, he or she cannot engage in intelligible reasoning with those who have this belief, and he maintains that the colored glasses (of unbelief) cannot be removed by man. He claims that there is no epistemological *common ground* between the believer and the unbeliever upon which legitimate persuasive arguments can be exchanged, so no argument or evidence is *possible*, much less necessary or even appropriate, to lead one to believe in God.[29] As a consequence, *God* is the only one capable of removing the colored glasses.

By way of summary, we have two families, neo-positivists and contextualists, with considerably diver-

---

[28]Cornelius Van Til, *The Defense of the Faith*, 3rd ed. (Phillipsburg, NJ: Presbyterian and Reformed Publishing Co., 1955; 1980), p. 77.

[29]Summarizing the Reformed position, Plantinga says, "Like Calvin, Kuyper, and Bavinck, Barth holds that belief in God is *properly basic*—that is, such that it is rational to accept it without accepting it on the basis of any other propositions or beliefs at all. In fact, they think the Christian ought not to accept belief in God on the basis of argument;... What the Reformers held was that a believer is entirely rational, entirely within his epistemic rights, in *starting with* belief in God, in accepting it as basic, and in taking it as a premise for argument to other conclusions" (Alvin Plantinga, "Reason and Belief in God," in *Faith and Rationality*, ed. Alvin Plantinga and Nicholas Wolterstorff [Notre Dame: University of Notre Dame, 1983], p. 72).

gent perspectives. Each family has its sons and cousins, and even some unexpected bedfellows. Using this interpretive structure, a useful comparative analysis of a variety of theological and apologetic positions becomes possible.

Neo-Positivist Foundationalism	Contextualism
Science offers the "foundation" for what is known; religion is irrational. [modernism]	Neither science nor religion has any ultimate "foundation"; each has its own criteria for truth and rationality. [postmodernism]
Religion offers the "foundation" for what is true; science, when in conflict, is mistaken. [fundamentalism]	In a sense, both religion and science lay their own ground-rules and both can be "true" in their respective senses. [neo-orthodoxy; existential theology]
Persuasion is done by an appeal to "facts" or evidence. [evidentialism]	No appeal to argument or evidence is necessary, appropriate, or even possible. [neo-orthodoxy; existential theology; "radical" presuppositionalism]

The problem, stated in ironic metaphorical terms, is that both of these families have been sired by what turns out to be a father who was impotent! Both have relied on an unjustified perception of science in developing their approach to the relationship between science and religion. To change metaphors—both family trees continue to display some beautiful foliage on their branches, even though the nourishment to their roots is depleted or at least severely polluted. Yet both families have a sustained lineage which is very much alive, even if not well. And knowing about the philosophy of science can aid the Christian in knowing better how to understand and respond to those who must face an impending "family crisis."

(2) *The philosophy of science can enhance our understanding of the nature of revelation, of conversion, and of the relationship between the believer and the unbeliever.* Christian theology is sharply divided over

Richard A. Knopp

questions pertaining to the nature of revelation and conversion. (a) Is revelation "propositional" or is it "dynamic"? *Is* the Bible the "Word of God" or does it *become* the "Word of God" when one is personally "encountered" by God?[30] (b) Regarding conversion, does genuine conversion occur when one looks objectively at the factual claims of the Bible, intellectually assents to these claims, and volitionally commits *oneself* to them, or does the Holy Spirit effect the conversion of the unbeliever?

Extending the earlier claim of Alexander Campbell,[31] the tradition of the Stone-Campbell movement has tended to over-emphasize the propositional side to revelation and down-play, if not practically ignore, the divine initiative in conversion. After all, it has been a top priority to repudiate the existentialists and the neo-orthodox (who stress non-propositional revelation) and

---

[30]"Propositional" revelation stresses the idea that God communicates informational truth-claims about Himself, humanity, and the world; and God does this through the medium of human language. More properly viewed, as Ronald Nash points out, this notion does not mean that *everything* truly "revealed" by God is propositional; it only means that *some* information about God, humanity, and the world has been revealed in human language. It opposes the position that God does *not* reveal *any* specific information or commands through human language. In their own ways, many influential theologians (e.g. Brunner, Bultmann, Tillich, Richard Niebuhr) take the non-propositional line, as expressed by Bultmann, that "God's revelation ... is no longer a communication of teachings, nor of ethical or historical and philosophical truths, but God speaking directly to me ..." (Bultmann, *Myth and Christianity*, trans. Norbert Gutermann (New York: Noonday, 1958], p. 69). For a good overview on this issue, see Ronald Nash, *The Word of God and the Mind of Man* (Grand Rapids: Zondervan, 1982), pp. 35-54.

[31]Alexander Campbell (*Millennial Harbinger*, 1846) said that "the fact that God has clothed his communications in human language, and that he has spoken by men, to men, in their own language, is decisive evidence that he is to be understood as one man conversing with another" (Royal Humbert, ed., *A Compend of Alexander Campbell's Theology* [St. Louis: Bethany Press, 1961], p. 51).

---

sharply distinguish ourselves from the Calvinists (who laud the point that it is *God* who elects and regenerates).

But one benefit of my interaction with the philosophy of science is that I have been aroused to ask whether my restricted diet has led me to a condition of "theological anemia." I have been prompted to ask whether I have been open to the *entirety* of the biblical record or more concerned with sustaining a commitment to *my* particular theological paradigm. The point that Kuhn and others make about the scientific "establishment" (i.e., those who accept and staunchly defend the existing paradigm within "normal science") forces me to wonder whether I am really open to looking at data in *new* ways. More generally, it helps me comprehend how some church leaders are so easily subject to the same kind of "paradigm posture." They continue to "*see* it and *do* the same way," and they are critical of anything or anyone who challenges the paradigm that *they* authoritatively certify. Of course, this application of Thomas Kuhn only reinforces something Jesus said centuries earlier: "New wine must be put into fresh wineskins" (Luke 5:38).

With respect to the issues concerning conversion and revelation, perhaps the options are not so mutually exclusive. Does an *exclusive* acceptance of the first option in each case (i.e., "*all* revelation is propositional"; "the Bible *is* the Word of God"; "conversion is simply *my* response to historical facts and the identity of Christ") do adequate justice to the entirety of the biblical data?

My response to this question is "no." As a *completed* written document, the Bible *is* the Word of God; *yet*, as Hebrews 3:7-8 asserts, "Just as the Holy Spirit *says*, '*Today* if you hear His voice, do not harden your hearts ...'" (emphasis added). On the one hand, to come to God in conversion, one "must believe that He is" (Heb 11:6), and one must confess that Jesus Christ who has come in the flesh is from God (1 John 4:2). But on the other hand, no one can come to Jesus, Jesus says, "unless the Father who sent [Him] draws him" (John 5:44). And Paul relates that the "natural man" who has the "wisdom" of this world and who rejects the wisdom of God as "foolishness" does "not accept the things of the Spirit of God ... and he cannot understand them, because they are spiritually appraised" (1 Cor 2:14). Calvinists, most assuredly, have a special affinity for these passages (and others like them).[32] These verses seem to bolster the view that *God* alone decides who will become a believer.

One prominent view is to think that the tensions evident here are unique to *theology*. But I believe that the context of current philosophy of science is significant, in part, because it reveals that the difficulties of communication and rational persuasion between adherents of conflicting paradigms are not a uniquely *theological* problem; other critical factors are involved in "not seeing" a different perspective, beyond attributing the incapacity to God's refusal to grant "illumination." It also suggests that if communication and rational persuasion within post-Kuhnian science are still possible (even if very difficult), then the same possibility exists for conflicting theological and philosophical perspectives. The fact is that "successful" communication *does* occur between competing scientific paradigms, and rational choices for different scientific paradigms *are* made. In the same way, even though the religious believer and

---

[32]Other particularly relevant passages include Matthew 11:27 ("... no one knows the Son, except the Father; nor does anyone know the Father, except the Son, and anyone to whom the Son wills to reveal Him"); Matthew 13:10-11 ("And the disciples came and said to Him, 'Why do You speak to them in parables?' And He answered and said to them, 'To you it has been granted to know the mysteries of the kingdom of heaven, but to them it has not been granted"); Romans 11:8 [citing Isaiah 29:10] ("God gave them a spirit of stupor, eyes to see not and ears to hear not ..."); and John 12:37-40 ("But though He had performed many signs before them, they were not believing in Him;... For this cause they could not believe, for Isaiah said again, 'He has blinded their eyes, and He hardened their heart ...'").

the unbeliever hold incompatible (and perhaps even incommensurable) paradigms, yet common ground does exist for rational argumentation to be a part of the persuasive process.

On the other hand, the conversion to another paradigm involves *more than* mere rational analysis. It includes more than a presentation of "data" from which one "robotically" makes logical inferences and subsequent commitments. In other words, the conversion from one paradigm to another, while not "mystical," is also not *exhaustively* explained in purely rational categories.

What this means, in sum, is that revelation and the process of conversion can possess an importantly *rational* (and propositional) component; yet we do not need to feel overly constrained to delimit the range or the method of God's revelatory and converting Word. In more common parlance, it can be expressed this way: "Something's probably wrong if you find yourself telling God what He can and cannot do. You might try sending Him UPS, but He's very difficult to put in a box."

(3) *The philosophy of science can guide us toward a more effective apologetic methodology.* Traditionally, two contrasting apologetic approaches predominate: evidentialism and presuppositionalism. These approaches (as discussed earlier) have sided with neo-positivism and contextualism respectively and are subject to numerous criticisms as a result. The evidentialist perspective has been advocated and popularized by Josh McDowell and John Montgomery. The presuppositionalist stance in its extreme form has been propagated by Cornelius Van Til.[33] (Van Til

---

[33]See John McDowell's *Evidence that Demands a Verdict: Historical Evidences for the Christian Faith* (San Bernardino, CA: Campus Crusade, 1972. A good collection of McDowell's writings can be found in *The Best of Josh McDowell*, compiled by Bill Wilson (San Bernardino, CA: Here's Life Publishers, 1990). More recent work from Montgomery's perspective is in his edited work, *Evidence for Faith:*

believed, in fact, that he was one of the few "consistent" presuppositionalists.) A more popular, but "modified," presuppositionalist was Francis Schaeffer. Schaeffer claimed that "presuppositional apologetics would have stopped the decay" that led to modern secular thought, and he claimed that "now for us, more than ever before, a presuppositional apologetic is imperative."[34]

I also believe that a presuppositional apologetic is imperative. However, the particular form of this apologetic must be such as to give an appropriate place to the use of *intercontextual* argument and evidence. As many philosophers of science are now trying to develop a perspective that accounts for values and presuppositions as well as empirical evidences, so must Christian apologists do much the same thing. The real challenge is articulating a coherent apologetic that does justice both to the role of presuppositions, while maintaining the significance of evidences for Christian belief. Some attempts have commendably been made toward this objective.[35] Applying principles from the philosophy of science can be extremely productive toward this goal.[36]

One practical upshot of all this is that it should have a dramatic effect on a college (or seminary) curriculum, on the way specific classes dealing with

---

Deciding the God Question (Dallas: Probe Books, 1991). Van Til's approach is presented in his *The Defense of the Faith*.

[34]Francis Schaeffer, *The God Who Is There* (Downers Grove: InterVarsity, 1968), p. 15.

[35]Note Ronald Mayers, *Both/And: A Balanced Apologetic* (Chicago: Moody Press, 1984) and Ronald Nash, *Faith and Reason*. Nash refers to his own approach as a kind of "inductive presuppositionalism" (p. 61).

[36]The avid evidentialist, John Montgomery, argued in a conference paper at the 1995 Evangelical Theological Society that no logical "half-way house" exists between evidentialism and presuppositionalism. However, after he heard a paper by Kenneth Harper on applying principles from the philosophy of science to the "Evidential-Presuppositional Impasse," he acknowledged in private conversation that such insights can be "very fruitful" and are "gaining great force" in the area of jurisprudence.

apologetic issues are developed, and on the way we personally defend our faith to an unbeliever. Serious consideration should be granted to requiring (or at least offering) courses in *philosophy of* science and to approaching apologetics as more than just naively marshaling "evidences" for one's faith.

(4) *Understanding the philosophy of science can facilitate a more rational attitude toward our own faith and can contribute toward a more effective defense of the rationality of that faith in contrast to competing worldviews and religions.* The philosophy of science convincingly demonstrates that what is crucial for rationality is not whether a particular theory is empirically verifiable or falsifiable, but whether it and the rest of its associated belief system are *intersubjectively criticizable.*[37]

Some years ago, the philosopher of science, W. W. Bartley, raised serious and legitimate questions about the rationality of much of modern theology, especially the approaches of Barth and Tillich. His notable 1962 book entitled *The Retreat to Commitment* was extensively revised and enlarged in a second edition published in 1984. Bartley's basic thesis did not change: it was that religious believers hold *irrational* beliefs because they have "retreated" to a domain of *uncriticizable commitment.*

I would suggest that Bartley is right—at least he is right about many types of religious belief and religious believers, within Christianity as well as outside it. Ironically, a Christian may experience deep frustration when unbelievers refuse to analyze critically *their* belief system, but the same Christian may never consider the appropriateness (and necessity) of being genuinely open to criticizing his or her *own* beliefs.

---

[37]Philip Clayton rightly puts strong emphasis on this criterion of rationality. See his *Explanation from Physics to Theology* (New Haven, CT: Yale University Press, 1989).

In spite of Bartley's own conclusion that religious commitment *per se* is irrational, he has highlighted a criterion of rationality that is particularly useful for the Christian who believes that God has revealed substantive information about Himself, about humanity, and the world. Bartley's rationality criterion of "criticizability" can be effectively utilized by the Christian to defend the rational superiority of *biblical* theism.[38] In contrast to neo-orthodox and existential theologies and the major alternative world religions—all of which profess that the uncriticizability of religion is a *virtue*, and all of which possess negligible empirical content—*biblical* theists can welcome rational criticism and respond enthusiastically to those who rightly demand sufficient evidence to accompany one's life commitment.

(5) *The philosophy of science can aid us in understanding the nature of a "belief-system": it consists of a more or less coherent web of numerous beliefs, some of which constitute the indispensable "core" of the paradigm and some of which lie on the periphery.* Even if one (rightly) rejects the relativism associated with the strong interpretation of Kuhn, the philosophy of science still correctly underscores the idea that individual beliefs (or even "facts") cannot be taken in isolation from the rest of the system; their warrant is greatly dependent upon the viability of the system as a whole. This is one reason why I strongly advocate the use of "worldview" studies in Christian education and apologetics.[39] It

---

[38]In the last chapter of my doctoral thesis, I attempt to develop the basic structure for this approach.

[39]One of my "staple" classes at Lincoln Christian College (also available on video) is "An Introduction to Worldviews." Fortunately, various evangelical authors are making important contributions with this approach. See James Sire, *The Universe Next Door*, rev. ed. (Downers Grove: InterVarsity, 1988); Ronald Nash, *Faith and Reason* and *Worldview in Conflict* (Grand Rapids: Zondervan, 1992); Arthur Holmes, *Contours of a Worldview* (Grand Rapids: Eerdmans, 1983);

allows theological doctrines and specific factual and historical claims to be assessed within a larger context. This *worldview* orientation would be much more productive, for example, in the debate between creationists and evolutionists. This dispute, in its most significant dimension, is inevitably not as much a dispute over "evidence" as it is over conflicting worldviews.[40] However, evolutionists as well as creationists frequently seem to be operating with an outdated conception of science. The popular prophet of science, Carl Sagan, appears as ignorant of this as do many well-meaning but misguided members of various creationist societies.[41]

To apply this worldview emphasis to teaching and preaching, we must recognize, much more than we have, the critical necessity of communicating *perspectives* in the classroom and from the pulpit in addition to the "facts" of biblical history. The "particulars," as Francis Schaeffer would remind us, are of little value in them-

---

and Norman Geisler and William Watkins, *Worlds Apart: A Handbook on Worldviews*, 2nd ed. (Grand Rapids: Baker, 1989).

[40]This point is especially emphasized by the Berkeley law professor, Phillip Johnson, in *Darwin on Trial*, 2nd ed. (Grand Rapids: InterVarsity, 1993) and by Norman Geisler and J. Kerby Anderson in *Origin Science: A Proposal for the Creation-Evolution Controversy* (Grand Rapids: Baker, 1987). J. P. Moreland and others attempt to revitalize the plausibility of understanding creation from a scientific perspective that does not necessitate "methodological naturalism." See J. P. Moreland, ed. *The Creation Hypothesis* (Downers Grove: InterVarsity Press, 1994). The critical role of worldviews is also stressed by a recent and important evangelical response to the Jesus Seminar, which is a movement designed to propagate the view that Jesus never *said* nor *did* most of what the Gospels attribute to him. See Michael Wilkins and J. P. Moreland, ed. *Jesus Under Fire* (Grand Rapids: Zondervan, 1995).

[41]Del Ratzsche's recent book cogently presents the case that evolutionists and creationists rely heavily on "substantial assumptions and presuppositions concerning philosophy of science," and many of their arguments and assumptions "fail to withstand close scrutiny" (see *The Battle of Beginnings: Why Neither Side is Winning the Creation-Evolution Debate*, especially p. 11).

Richard A. Knopp

selves without a framework within which to integrate them into one's entire conceptual and cultural experience. Teachers and preachers must address, not just "what 'facts' does this passage convey?" but "how do they fit within the entire scope of the Christian worldview?" and "how should it uniquely affect my attitudes and actions in the modern world with its array of philosophical and religious options?" An "effective" Christian is not just committed to "facts"; he or she is committed to an entire worldview.

Furthermore, philosophers of science (particularly Imre Lakatos) underscore the idea that some beliefs are indeed "essential" to maintain the paradigm—they constitute the "core" of the system—while others, though important, are not the *sine qua non* of the paradigm's plausibility. If Christians understood this point, *it might help us advance the persistent debate over inerrancy.* The belief in inerrancy has been a divisive criterion within the Christian community. Some persons unabashedly preach it (and require it); others balk because of the semantic hurdles of the term, although they might not (publicly) assert that the Bible contains errors.

My initial response is that the emphasis of the former group is misplaced; it tends to "major in minors" by making the viability of the *core* of the Christian faith contingent upon the accuracy of the biblical record in every single *detail.* The apprehensions of the second group, I sometimes feel, border on the "cowardly." Let me hasten to say that I am not contending that the Bible contains specific "errors." But I do wonder whether it is really *necessary* for the Bible to be "true" in every detail (including history) before its *truth* can be uncompromisingly proclaimed. It is the *paradigm* of Christian theism—the paradigm which centers on Christ as the "truth," the *logos* (John 1:1,14), the integrating focus around which all thought should be affected and directed (Col 2:8; 2 Cor 10:5)—which is the indispensable message from God to the world. As science illustrates, the "truth" of a paradigm is not necessarily rendered untenable, and a commitment to it is not necessarily irrational, simply because the paradigm possesses some anomalies. Paradigms are not rejected because of anomalies; they are rationally rejected because of an accumulation of *severe* anomalies, and only then in the face of some promising better alternative paradigm.

It is my conviction that the truth and explanatory superiority of Christian theism would remain intact *even if*, for example, Paul is *correct* when he says that he and those with him on the way to Damascus had "all *fallen* to the ground" (Acts 26:14) and Luke is *mistaken* when he says that the men with Paul "*stood* speechless" (Acts 9:7). Please do not infer that I believe that these are necessarily "errors." I am suggesting, following an analogy from science, that problems in details do not demand the conclusion that the belief system itself is false or that some alternative explanation must necessarily be empirically or rationally superior.

If we judiciously implemented this principle that "core" beliefs are indeed indispensable and "peripheral" beliefs are potentially negotiable, we might discover that the world is a *big* place and that the philosophical and religious alternatives to biblical Christianity are *radically* different. We might more properly identify the real "enemies" of the cross (and recognize that they are probably not the Presbyterians and Pentecostals down the street). We might even powerfully demonstrate the relevance and genius inherent in a prominent motto of the Stone-Campbell movement: "In essentials, unity; in opinion, liberty; and in all things, love."

RECOMMENDED BIBLIOGRAPHY

Barbour, Ian. *Myths, Models, and Paradigms: A Comparative Study in Science and Religion.* New York: Harper & Row, 1974.
   An excellent comparative analysis of science and religion. Barbour's focus on models and paradigms is very helpful, although he eventually directs his support toward the "process" view of God derived from A. N. Whitehead. [Beginning]

Johnson, Phillip E. *Darwin on Trial.* 2nd ed. Downers Grove, IL: InterVarsity, 1993.
   This Berkeley law professor created much turmoil with his initial (1991) edition of this book which sharply questions the evidential support for naturalistic evolution. This slightly modified edition has a new, very interesting epilogue which recounts, and responds to, the varied reactions to the first edition from both the secular and Christian worlds. Johnson's position is expanded in his *Reason in the Balance: The Case Against Naturalism in Science, Law, and Education* (Downers Grove: InterVarsity, 1995). [Intermediate]

Knopp, Richard A. "Religious Belief and the Problems of Cognitivity and Commitment: A Reappraisal Based on Contemporary Philosophy of Science." Ph.D. diss., University of Illinois at Urbana-Champaign, 1991.
   A comprehensive attempt to justify the rationality of Christian truth-claims and commitment in the context of the predominant perspectives of neo-positivism and contextualism. The views of Kuhn and Popper are analyzed, synthesized, and applied to religious belief. The argument is made that some forms of religion (notably Christian theism) make comparable truth-claims to those of science because they are rationally and empirically testable. Hence, religious commitment can be rational rather than blind. [Advanced]

Kuhn, Thomas. *The Structure of Scientific Revolutions.* 2nd ed. Chicago: University of Chicago Press, 1970.
   The watershed work which decisively and irreversibly challenged the view that science is totally objective and rational. [Advanced]

Mitchell, Basil. *The Justification of Religious Belief.* New York: The Seabury Press, 1973.
   A very useful approach to justifying religious belief. Mitchell discusses what it means to "prove" or "disprove" God's

existence, and he utilizes the work of Thomas Kuhn to develop a cumulative case for the rationality of theism. [Beginning]

Moreland, J. P. *Christianity and the Nature of Science: A Philosophical Investigation.* Grand Rapids: Baker Book House, 1989.

A carefully presented work by a leading evangelical philosopher. It includes chapters on the definition of science, scientific methodology, the limits of science, scientific realism, alternatives to scientific realism, and the scientific status of creationism. [Advanced]

Nash, Ronald. *Faith and Reason: Searching for a Rational Faith.* Grand Rapids: Academie Books, 1988.

A useful apologetic work which discusses the rationality of religious belief, arguments for God's existence, the problem of evil, and miracles. Nash adopts a worldview approach. [Intermediate]

Ratzsch, Del. *The Battle of Beginnings: Why Neither Side is Winning the Creation-Evolution Debate.* Downers Grove: InterVarsity, 1996.

Armed with a solid awareness of philosophy of science, this Calvin College professor cogently exposes many misunderstandings and mistakes by both creationists and evolutionists. In Jim Strauss's terms, this book is "indispensable" for those interested in any portion of this discussion. (Of course, according to Strauss, nearly *every* book is "indispensable"!) [Intermediate]

_____. *Philosophy of Science: The Natural Sciences in Christian Perspective.* Contours of Christian Philosophy, ed. C. Stephen Evans. Downers Grove: InterVarsity, 1986.

A brief introduction to the post-1960 developments within philosophy of science and their relevance for Christianity. [Beginning]

Wolterstorff, Nicholas. *Reason Within the Bounds of Religion.* Grand Rapids: Eerdmans, 1976.

This 115 page book is referred to by Wolterstorff as a "tract for Christians." Formerly professor at Calvin College, this current Yale professor invites Christians to integrate their scholarship with their faith. He argues for the legitimacy of Christian commitment, even though he rejects "foundationalism," whether it be a foundationalism based upon philosophical or empirical principles or a foundationalism based upon the Bible. [Beginning]

Chapter 11:

Plato's Metaphysics: His Contribution to a Philosophy of God
by
Dr. Terry Miethe

Terry Miethe holds degrees from Lincoln Christian College (A.B.), Trinity Evangelical Divinity School (M.A.), McCormick Theological Seminary (M.Div.), Saint Louis University (Ph.D in philosophy), the University of Southern California (A.M. and Ph.D. in theology and social ethics), and the University of Oxford (D.Phil. in history).

Topics for his theses and dissertations range from Friedrich Nietzsche to Alexander Campbell. His authored books include: *The New Christian's Guide to Following Jesus*, *The Christian's Guide to Faith and Reason*, *The Compact Dictionary of Doctrinal Words*, *Living Your Faith: Closing the Gap between Mind and Heart*, and *A Believer's Guide to Essential Christianity*. His co-authored books include: *Does God Exist? A Believer and Atheist Debate* (with Antony Flew), and *Why Believe? God Exists!: Rethinking the Case of God and Christianity* (with Gary Habermas).

Dr. Miethe has written chapters for *The Grace of God/The Will of Man*, *Biblical Errancy: An Analysis of its Philosophical Roots* (Zondervan), *Dictionary of Christianity in America* (InterVarsity Press) and has published articles in such journals as *The New Scholasticism*, *The Modern Schoolman*, *Augustinian Studies*, *The Presbyterian Journal*, *Faith and Reason*, *Journal of the Evangelical Theological Society*, *Cornerstone*, *The Christian Standard*, *Bulletin of the Evangelical Philosophical Society*, *The Restoration Quarterly*, and *One Body*.

PLATO'S METAPHYSICS:
HIS CONTRIBUTION TO A PHILOSOPHY
OF GOD

Introduction

Before I transferred to Lincoln Christian College from a state university in 1967 and met James D. Strauss. I did not know what the word "philosophy" meant. In my second semester at Lincoln, I took History of Philosophy under professor Strauss and my life was changed forever! In one semester I felt as if I learned more than I had in my entire life. The next semester I took Strauss's course in New Testament Theology with similar results. Thus, I figured that if I could learn so much in just one class, think what I could learn in four classes under his direction in one semester. In the spring of 1969, I enrolled in four Strauss classes. In all, undergraduate and graduate, I had the pleasure of taking twelve classes from Jim Strauss.[1]

Indeed, I learned much from Professor Strauss. He communicated the necessity of loving the Lord above all else,[2] the challenge of spiritual and academic excellence, the importance of commitment to the local church,[3] the great value of knowing philosophy (all of

---

[1]The other classes were: The Making of the Contemporary Mind; Christology; Roman Catholic Theology; Theological Themes in Contemporary Literature; Nietzsche; Biblical and Theological Ethics; Process Philosophy; Philosophical Ethics; Existentialism and Phenomenology; and Theology of Hope. I received my introduction to these subjects from Strauss.

[2]See Terry L. Miethe, *The New Christian's Guide to Following Jesus* (Minneapolis, MN: Bethany House Publishers, 1984).

[3]See Miethe, *Living Your Faith: Closing the Gap Between Mind and Heart* (Joplin, MO: College Press Publishing Company, 1993); and

philosophy, but most specifically metaphysics), the need for theology, the vital task of missions and evangelism, and the challenge of living as a Christian in today's world. Professor Strauss started me on a lifelong quest to study philosophy, theology, history, and the Bible. In a real sense, my life's commitment to learn as much as possible about Ultimate Reality and to share this in meaningful ways with as many people as possible had its beginnings in those days.

Since it was James Strauss who introduced me to philosophy and since it is often said, following Alfred North Whitehead, that the European philosophical tradition consists of a series of footnotes to Plato (and that there is no road one can travel in philosophy where one does not meet Plato coming back), it is quite appropriate for me to intertwine my "tribute" to Strauss with an analysis of the world's first great philosopher—Plato—and his contribution to metaphysics.

What is "Metaphysics" & Why is It Important to the Christian?

Metaphysics is that area of philosophy in which one studies the nature of being *qua* [as] being, or ultimate reality. It is traditionally referred to as "the science of being as such."[4] To the "uninitiated" in philosophy, metaphysics may seem the "most mysterious and foreboding of all the branches of philosophy. The name alone elicits images of abstract and difficult

Miethe, *A Christian's Guide to Faith & Reason* (Minneapolis, MN: Bethany House Publishers, 1987).

[4]"The term, 'science,' is here used in its classic sense of 'knowledge by causes,' where 'knowledge' is contrasted with 'opinion' and the term cause has the full signification of the Greek *aitia*. The 'causes' which are the objects of metaphysical cognition are said to be 'first' in the natural order (first principles), as being found in no higher or more complete generalizations available to the human intellect by means of its own natural powers." Dagobert D. Runes, *Dictionary of Philosophy*, 15th ed., rev. (New York: Philosophical Library, 1960), p. 196.

doctrines."[5] Certainly, there is a sense in which this is true. Metaphysics is concerned with discerning what can be known of reality as such; it even considers whether there *is* such a thing as "ultimate reality."[6]

The word "metaphysics" actually comes from the Greek *meta ta physika* which literally means "after the things of nature." It was the rather arbitrary title traditionally thought to have been assigned by Andronicus of Rhodes around 70 B.C. to a certain collection of Aristotle's writings (i.e., those works which came after his *Physics*).[7] Aristotle called the subject matter of these texts first philosophy, theology, or sometimes wisdom. So originally, the term had reference to those problems Aristotle treated which were neither "physical" nor, so Aristotle thought, reducible to observable physical phenomena.[8] Later, both classical

---

[5]Norman L. Geisler and Paul D. Feinberg, *Introduction to Philosophy: A Christian Perspective* (Grand Rapids, MI: Baker Book House, 1980), pp. 34-35.

[6]Some examples of traditional metaphysical questions are: What are the ultimate objective constituents of reality? Is there a God? What is being? What is the nature of space and time? Must every event have a cause? Are there such things as universals, and what are they? Is the human will free or determined?

[7]The phrase *ta meta ta physika biblia* (or "the books after the books on nature") was not used by Aristotle himself but apparently by the editors who classified and catalogued his works centuries later.

[8]The "exact" relationship of "metaphysical" or "spiritual" reality to "physical" or "sensible" reality is of course actually a very important central question of the whole philosophical discipline known as "metaphysics." It is my contention that metaphysical or spiritual reality is *not* separated by an inseparable gulf from the physical world, as in Plotinus or Kant, and that Hume was wrong in his analysis about what we can or cannot, and do or do not, experience in our world. My contention is that if Hume had been more "empirical" than he was, he would have had an altogether different view of physical reality.

See the seminal debate between Terry L. Miethe and Antony Flew, *Does God Exist? A Believer and an Atheist Debate* (San Francisco: Harper Collins, 1991); and Terry L. Miethe and Gary R. Habermas, *Why Believe? God Exists!: Rethinking the Case for God*

and medieval philosophers used the term to refer to the subjects discussed "after the things of nature" because they thought these subjects were further removed from sense perception, and as such were more difficult to understand.[9]

Metaphysics is *vital* for the Christian because it is essentially the philosophy of God. It is identical with it really. There are metaphysics which are atheistic or even agnostic which may claim to arrive at first principles which are different from God (and I believe inferior to God). But at least traditionally, Western metaphysics is the study of reality as such—of being as such. It must be consummated by some kind of theory of God.[10]

Yet, most unfortunately, even some Christians do not understand the importance of metaphysics or see the need for a philosophy of God. They *act* as if it can all be taken for granted! In recent years it has *not* been fashionable to talk as if one could "prove" the existence of God.[11] One of the arguments often given as to why one does not need to try to prove that God exists is: "The Scripture does not argue for God's existence. The Bible just assumes God's existence." I have answered this claim with three lines of argument.[12] But basically, it is simply *false*—and even if it were true it is irrelevant to our apologetic need today! Certainly the

---

and Christianity (Joplin, MO: College Press Publishing Company, 1993), especially "Part One: Evidence from Philosophy," pp. 15-104.

[9]The Greeks did not make a distinction between what we call "natural science" and "metaphysics." As recently as the period of the American Civil War, the term "natural philosophy" was still used in reference to mathematics and science, which led to the modern science of physics.

[10]See Terry L. Miethe, *The Metaphysics of Leonard James Eslick: His Philosophy of God* (Ann Arbor, MI: University Microfilms, Inc., 1976) and Miethe, *The Compact Dictionary of Doctrinal Words* (Minneapolis, MN: Bethany House Publishers, 1988), p. 137.

[11]Of course, this depends in large part on what one means by the word "prove." See Miethe, *Living Your Faith*, pp. 49-51.

[12]Miethe and Habermas, *Why Believe? God Exists!*, pp. 16-18.

Bible indicates that man has a "natural knowledge of God." It is clear in Romans 1:18-23 that men knew through nature God's attributes, power, and nature (cf. Rom 2:14-15). "It will not do to say that in such passages the author is only arguing to God's nature ... not his existence. For arguing that a god is good and powerful is arguing that there is a god who is God (i.e., omnipotent, omniscient, etc.), and so that there is a God."[13]

Every once in a while, I used to hear the comment: "That'll preach." It is much past time that we realized the "preacher" needs a great wealth of knowledge other than just that which he can actually use in his next sermon! It was Jim Strauss who helped me see that preachers would have a much sounder message and the Church would be much more "empowered" as an institution if they—the preachers and church members—could articulate and defend a viable philosophy of God. For Strauss, teaching and preaching were really inseparable from philosophy and theology. Issues that flow directly out of the subject matter, questions of philosophy, and discussions in this regard are often used as excuses by non-believers to keep them from seriously examining the scriptures or the claims of Christ. Philosophical apologetics is at the very least "pre-evangelism" and can often lead to, and be a part of, actual evangelism!

Even issues as "abstract" as Plato's contribution to a philosophy of God, in the right hands, at the right moment, can be used mightily by the Spirit to remove obstacles in the path of faith! The general orientation and background necessary for such knowledge is essential to really understand a Christian worldview and will form a much needed base to articulate this worldview to believers and non-believers alike. I have

---

[13]Richard Swinburne, *Faith and Reason* (Oxford: Clarendon Press, 1981), p. 86.

seen this time and again! Yes, philosophy and apologetics is of *vital importance* for preaching and teaching alike.[14]

God in Plato

Plato was born in 428-427 B.C. and died, according to the best information, in 348-347 B.C. The impact of Plato upon Western philosophy and theology is greater, perhaps, than any other single philosopher. It will not be until the thirteenth century that Aristotle will begin to have as formidable an influence in the West as Plato. I have personally known more than one twentieth-century philosopher who believed that Plato was the greatest philosopher who ever lived.

Plato is famous for his theory of the Forms or Ideas, and his theory of reminiscence, which is the process of learning. Plato accepted the theory of Heraclitus through Cratylus, his teacher, that the sensible world is in constant flux and that there is nothing which is "self-identical"—something which would require "being" as distinct from "becoming." But can this theory be true for reality itself? Plato thought that the physical world, being always in flux, could not be the object of scientific knowledge or rationality. Thus Plato reasoned that there has to be something besides the world of becoming which has being, a type of reality which is eternal and immutable.

Plato was trying to synthesize two radically opposed points of view in Greek thought (i.e., the Heraclitean and the Parmenidean positions). Parmenides thought that everything was One, without any change whatever and without any qualitative or

---

[14]In fact, a number of ministries today really use philosophy and apologetics as essential parts of their approach in both preaching and teaching. Examples would be Dr. D. James Kennedy of Coral Ridge Presbyterian Church and "Truths that Transform" (which airs on over 430 radio stations weekly).

quantitative differentiation. The only difference from "being" would be "non-being" which is unthinkable and cannot exist. Consequently, that which exists is Being without difference or any kind of multiplicity. It is One.[15]

But pre-Socratic Greek philosophy ended in an apparent insoluble dilemma. Either the world is total flux (Heraclitus), or the world is total unitary Being exclusive of differentiation and change (Parmenides). In neither case is rational knowledge of the world possible.[16]

The task of Plato was to reconcile the two extremes. Plato tried to show that both are correct in some sense. Reality consists of a kind of Being which is eternal and immutable and also a kind of existence which is process itself. One must have both to render the physical world of flux scientifically knowable. The physical world of flux must be interpreted in terms of Being which is eternal, self-identical, and indivisible.[17]

This gives rise to Plato's famous theory of the Forms, or the Ideas. The word *eidos* can be translated "idea," but this is a rather misleading translation. We tend to think of ideas as mental concepts—thoughts in the mind. But Plato is talking about the ultimate Forms

---

[15]Yet the very nature of a judgment of being involves both sameness and difference with respect to the subject and the predicate. This must be true if one is going to give a reason which is capable of saying something that is not a tautology. There must be something in the predicate which is not simply identical with the subject. Plato's insight on this matter is extremely important for the history of natural theology in the West: if one is to take the subject just by itself, there is nothing whatever one can say about it. See Leonard J. Eslick, "The Platonic Dialectic of Non-Being," *The New Scholasticism* 29 (January, 1955): 33-49.

[16]If everything constantly changes, it changes immediately after the moment one claims to "know" something. If everything is simply One and unchanging, it is obviously a world totally separated from our bodies and physical senses.

[17]See Leonard J. Eslick, "The Dyadic Character of Being in Plato," *The Modern Schoolman* 31 (1953-54): 11-18.

of reality, the "archetypes" of reality itself (e.g., "justice with a capital "J"). The Forms which are eternal and unchanging are the points of self-identity to which the physical world of becoming only refers. Without a reality of this kind, the world in which we live would be essentially meaningless.

In the physical world of becoming there are many things which are beautiful that share or partake of Being. All are beautiful in the finite way. There is something about them which is flawed or imperfect. This is why we can think about such things as being more or less beautiful. However, they only "participate" in true Beauty. What makes this possible is a reality—the Forms or Ideas—which is essentially beautiful; it is Beauty of its very essence—a Beauty which has no otherness (as compared to physical beauty).

The physical world is a world in process. That which becomes does not exist in itself or in its own right. Ultimately what underlies its existence becomes in Plato's *Timaeus* the "Receptacle."[18] This is the universal subject of all becoming which produces flowing images of the Forms themselves. The Forms are the real substantive entities. After Plato, the hallmarks of Being and Reality become its eternal, immobile, self-identical, and necessary nature. The physical world is a mysterious blend of Being and non-being. Existing things in the physical world *are*, and they are *not*, simultaneously. They are images of Being, just as time is the moving image of eternity. Their existence is temporal rather than eternal.

If something were essentially Being, there would be nothing to limit or make finite the being which it is. This will eventually become the traditional formula for

---

[18]Plato, *Timaeus*, 49a, in *Plato: The Collected Dialogues*, ed. by Edith Hamilton and Huntington Cairns, Bollingen Series LXXI (Princeton: Princeton University Press, 1961), p. 1176. All future references to Plato's writings, unless otherwise indicated, are taken from this edition.

Divine Being—Being who is being by its very essence (i.e., pure infinite Actuality). This Being would be necessary and uncaused. If creatures exist that are beings in a limited way (e.g. a man or a horse), such creatures, since they are not Being by their very essence, must have their being caused by another. The problem is: what can cause the participation in Being of finite beings? (The type of causality operating here for Plato is not efficient causality, but formal causality.) Finite beings must be caused to be the kind of things they are by Forms which are Being itself, Justice itself, etc.[19]

Plato's Forms are separated from the physical world because of his theory of knowledge. One of the chief reasons is the absolute distinction between the objects of *knowledge* on the one hand and *opinion* on the other. Knowledge for the ancient Greeks deals with what we would call "science" in the strictest sense. Science, for the ancient Greeks, always deals with things that cannot be other than they are. So Being is the object of knowledge, but opinion is notoriously fallible. Opinions deal with things that change, the world of becoming, which are true at one time but not true at another.[20]

This is stated in Plato in terms of the famous figure of the divided line. The first and the weakest level of cognition is equivalent to sense perception. Plato holds what we might call a "double motion" theory

---

[19]See Robert John Henle's *Saint Thomas and Platonism* (The Hague: M. Nijhoff, 1956) on the idea of formal causality in Plato. In the Christian view of God, Thomas Aquinas's for example, all of these perfections which do not involve limiting factors are synthesized into One Divine Being, God. They all become names of God. This is not a step that Plato takes.

[20]There is an essential rule in Platonism with respect to verifying or falsifying something. Verification is always from above, never from below. One does not verify the truth or falsity of an opinion by looking downward to sense perceptions. One has to look upward to the higher reality of enduring and necessary truths and Being—to the world of the Forms.

of sense perception. There is the external motion outside of us—the event which is happening at a particular time—and the eternal organic motions in terms of our sense organs. These two motions go together and produce a third motion which is the sense image itself. Thus, what we perceive through our senses exists only in relation to the individual who is perceiving it. There is not any *public* world which is disclosed by sense perception at all.

The real events or actual physical motions that are causing sense perception must be seen through the mind. This is not an act of sense perception itself, but an intellectual inference beyond sense to the supposed causes of sense images. The things that are really causing one's sense perceptions are hidden behind one's back as it were. One can reach them only through some kind of intellectual inference. This is a very important point in terms of Plato's later theory of Divinity. In terms of the famous allegory of the cave, the hidden men who are causing the actual physical motions are souls, self-moving movers.[21] Soul is not itself perceptible through the senses. But for Plato all physical motions are ultimately caused by the self-motion of Soul. This is profoundly important in terms of Plato's theory of God. When Plato comes to his formal proof of the existence of God in the tenth book of the *Laws*, this is the way he will argue.[22] He proves the existence of souls as self-moving movers, as spontaneous sources of motion. The physical motions that are produced are moved movers. Their motion is received from without. Plato believes that every kind of physical motion ultimately must have its origin in the self-motion of Soul which is in some way divine.

Reality is ordered ultimately in terms of what Plato calls the Good. All order flows from the Good.

---

[21]See Plato's *Republic*, Book 7.514, p. 747.
[22]Plato, *Laws*, p. 1440.

Plato has the Divine Mind as the paradigm of Cosmic order. (Science for Plato is thoroughly teleological.) God (i.e., Soul) causes the order of being and of physical nature by looking to the Good or to the Best. The Good is the Form of all of the Forms. The Forms themselves are images or reflections of the Good, and their ordering is a functioning of the Good. The Good is in Platonic science the first principle of reality. Does not this imply, therefore, that the Good is God, the supreme God? Most interpreters of Platonic theology would simply identify the Good with God.

But such an identification is a mistake with very significant consequences. God is always to be found for Plato in terms of Mind or Soul, ultimately as the highest of all souls, the God Plato calls the "Demiurge" in the *Timaeus*,[23] a God who is looking at the Forms and fashions the world physically after these Archetypal Models.

In Plato, one can exclude all other possible causal hypotheses only by a process of dialectical transformation of reason. This process is made possible by the supreme principle of all dialectic and of the Forms themselves. The supreme principle of all being is called the Good. The world is ordered by mind for the Best or the Good. There is a passage in the sixth book of the *Republic* in which Plato says that the Good is beyond Being, Essence, and Knowledge.[24] The achievement of real knowledge on the level of dialectic is in terms of the illumination which the soul of the philosopher ascending to the truth receives from the Good. It is only in the light of the Good that one can ascend in this way.

This gives some idea of the importance of divinity for Plato. Divinity performs the intelligent and rational ordering of nature. Without an indwelling God, there

---

[23]Plato, *Timaeus*, pp. 1162-ff.
[24]Plato, *Republic*, p. 740.

would be no such ordering. Divine Reason is ultimately the cause of all regular motions of the cosmos. The task of Divine Reason for Plato is to make a rational order out of what is primordially disordered and chaotic. Basically the creative task of divinity will be described in the *Timaeus* of Plato as reason persuading necessity in order to make chance or random motion play as small a part as possible.

The *Timaeus* is a creation myth for Plato. It does not mean anything at all like the Christian doctrine of creation *ex nihilo*.[25] The making of the cosmos is the making of an order.[26] The Platonic *Demiurge* does this by creating the soul of the world. The whole life of immortality is a life in which souls, ever moving and self-moving, participate in the eternity of the Forms. In the *Timaeus* the Demiurge is presented as if he were transcendent and metaphysically prior to his creation of the world. But this is mythical language and this is not literally the case for Plato. The Demiurge is a way of talking about the World Soul itself which had for Plato no radical origin. "God" in the highest sense for Plato is to be understood in terms of immanent reason in nature itself.

---

[25]"Creation is the Christian teaching based on Genesis 1-2 that God formed the universe and everything in it by a direct act: 'In the beginning, God created the heavens and the earth' (Gen 1:1). Many interpret this creation to be 'ex nihilo,' which means that God spoke the world into existence 'out of nothing.' The Fourth Lateran Council (1215) made the term 'ex nihilo' an official part of the teaching of the Church." Miethe, *The Compact Dictionary of Doctrinal Words*, p. 65.

[26]Lucretius, the first-century Roman poet, wrote in *De Rerum Natura* of the creation of the world: *Nil posse creari de nilo*, "nothing can be created out of nothing," which is also rendered as *ex nihilo nihil fit*, suggesting that every effect must have a cause. Lucretius agreed with the fifth-century B.C. Greek philosophers who theorized that the world could not have been made from nothing. Today the Latin phrase is applied rather broadly to suggest that a dull mind cannot be expected to produce great thoughts, anything worth doing requires hard work, you can't get blood from a stone, and so on—all of which are quite true!

For Plato, there are three main levels in which things exist. The Forms and physical world are the highest and the lowest respectively. God is not to be found in either of these levels. God is not a Form for Plato. He is not the Form of all the Forms (i.e., Goodness). The intermediate level is where we should look for Platonic divinity. God is Soul, the highest and best of all souls. (Souls are souls because they are self-movers and the origin of all physical motion for Plato.) God is in the intermediate level between physical becoming on the one hand and the eternal and immutable Forms on the other.

If one takes away the idea of real relatedness from the notion of anything whatever, there is nothing left which could possibly exist. As a result of this reasoning, Plato revised his earlier theory of Forms, according to which the Forms were thought to be simple, unrelated unities, as just themselves and nothing else whatever. But Plato shows in the first hypothesis of the *Parmenides* that if this were the case, then nothing can be said about them.[27] There could be no dialectic of knowledge about the Forms of reality themselves. In fact, they could not be real. They could not even exist. If one is going to have anything which really exists, it must involve Power—an ability to make a difference to others, and of having others make a difference to oneself.

Unfortunately, the Neo-platonic tradition eventually associated the Good or the One, simple unity, with God.[28] And some early Christian theologians under the influence of Neo-platonism not only thought of God as utterly simple, but as not really related to the world at all. This utter simplicity was regarded as part of the Divine perfection. But Christian theologians should

---

[27]Plato, *Parmenides*, p. 935.
[28]See Miethe, *The Metaphysics of Leonard James Eslick*, pp. 60-70.

have associated God with the Platonic doctrine of the Soul which has relatedness and Power.

The Meanings of Power

It has been posited that the traditional doctrine of divine omnipotence comes from Greek metaphysics. In the Greek view, which I do not accept, divine omnipotence "is thought of as the imposition of the necessity of remorseless reason, resulting in the iron determinism of essentially subordinated causal series, or of a descending syllogism."[29] This view is at the root of the problem in historical theology of reconciling the freedom of God's creatures with His omnipotence.

The metaphysical problem one faces is how to establish a viable meaning of "power" that retains God's unlimited creativity and grants true freedom for His creatures. There are at least two ways in which this is not possible if one adopts the standard doctrine of divine omnipotence. (1) True power cannot be the kind of power of the oriental despot who has the life and death of his subjects at his command. This is arbitrary "power" and is a debased and dishonorable weakness according to Plato. This is related by Plato in a classic text in the *Gorgias*:

> Imagine that I'm in the crowded marketplace with a dagger concealed under my arm and I say to you, "Polus, I have just acquired an amazing sort of tyrannic power. If I think that anyone of these men whom you see ought to die this very instant, die he shall, whomever I choose! And if I think that any of their heads should be bashed in, bashed it shall be right on the spot! or if a coat should be slit, slit it shall be! That's the sort of power I hold in this city!" Then if you didn't believe me and I showed you my dagger, you might look at it and say, "Why Socrates,

---

[29]Leonard Eslick, "Omnipotence: The Meanings of Power," *The New Scholasticism* 42 (Spring 1968): 289.

everyone can have that sort of power. In this way you might burn down any house you pleased, and even the Athenian dockyards and the man-of-war and all the ships, both public and private." But surely this is not what one means by having great power: to do anything one pleases.[30]

For Plato genuine power is seen in goodness and the knowledge of it. Power alone is *free* and it gives the gift of freedom to others. In this case God in His goodness gives His freedom and allows creatures to participate in and have creativity.[31]

(2) True power cannot be manifested in the imposition of mechanical determinism. The Greeks valued the regularity of motions too highly. Because nature was regular in its normal functioning, events were predetermined. Even Plato failed to realize that such laws

> ... far from expressing the fullness of divine power, may only be the averagings of dead and habitual repetitions in nature, so that the power of the past, imposed upon the present, evokes only conformity without novel creative response. The forms of "necessary" relatedness expressed in laws may therefore exhibit only the weakness of matter unable to create or innovate, rather than the power of creative spirit.[32]

Thus, true power, as in Plato's *Sophist*, must be *dynamis* (i.e., the power of acting and of being acted upon in relation to others). True power is the ability to make a difference to another and of that other being able to make a difference to the original thing. I do not think that this formula has ever been improved upon as

---

[30]Plato, *Gorgias*, Trans. by W. C. Helmhold (Indianapolis, IN: The Bobbs-Merrill Co., 1952), pp. 466-70.

[31]Eslick, "Omnipotence: The Meanings of Power," p. 290.

[32]Ibid., p. 291.

a metaphysical definition of power. The fact *that* we affect others is not as important as *how* we do. I believe it is the *kind* of difference made to others which is most important:

> To the extent to which the power exerted attains its effect by force imposing conformity, that effect has a diminished ontological status and value, proportioned to the inferior metaphysical level of the agent. Slavery begets slavery; freedom begets freedom. The creativity of violence and compulsion is minimal; it is weakness engendering weakness.[33]

Permit me to give two analogies from experience of the creative power of God: (1) In literary art the writer has always been thought of as creating a fictional world of his own. But there are two kinds of literary creativity: (a) the bad literary craftsman who manipulates lifeless puppets in a predetermined pattern with no room for surprise; and (b) writers like Shakespeare or Cervantes whose creatures like Falstaff or Don Quixote exhibit a mysterious life and freedom of their own. I suspect that even their creators could not always have predicted in advance what these two would do. (2) In the relationship of teacher and student, the teacher who only produces carbon copies of himself and of his opinions has the least *power* or ability of teaching. The students are not given any independent power of judgment. Teaching as indoctrination is a betrayal or failure of the true power of the art. For example, Jim Strauss taught me to think on my own, to dream, and to act on rational evidence to fulfill the dreams! As ironic as it seems, Plato was at his height in producing an Aristotle who so disagreed with this teacher.[34]

God, by unlimited authentic power, can produce independently existing creatures who share in the liberty

---

[33]Ibid.
[34]Ibid., p. 292.

of deity and can become co-creators with Him in their own measure. This is true *power*! God's divine creative power is synonymous with the divine names of Freedom and Love. God is Freedom and Love and He imparts these to His creatures because it is His very nature to do so. Existence with freedom is itself the gift of divine power. And God is "really related" to His creatures. Power in its active dimension is self-relating. God wills us and knows us from eternity as persons made in His own image.[35] We do make a difference to God. Because of God's creative power, we have an authentic share in His creativity. As Genesis records, "Then God said, Let us make man in our image, according to our likeness; ... And God created man in His own image, in the image of God He created him; male and female He created them" (Gen 1:26-27).

Plato and the Philosophy of God

There are two very valuable insights in Plato which are important here and which need to be incorporated into a philosophy of God. (1) The historic Plato revised his theory of the Forms. One cannot associate the One or the Good, of which there is no knowledge, with Platonic divinity. The importance of divinity for Plato is precisely the intelligent and rational ordering of nature. Divinity in Plato is found in the self-movement of souls.[36] (2) Plato's doctrine of *dynamis*

---

[35]See Miethe, *Living Your Faith*, pp. 49-60.

[36]The very notion of self-motion, the self-moving mover in terms of soul, means that with respect to knowledge and everything else, soul itself has an agency—self-motion. This makes it ridiculous to hold that there is nothing in the intellect that is not first in the senses (i.e., the dogma of empiricism).

I think this is precisely the point where Whitehead fails. He attempts to retain his own British empiricism. (The empiricism of Aristotle and Aquinas is much better than that of the seventeenth and eighteenth century British tradition.) Whitehead supposed that in all actual entities except God, the physical pole entirely precedes the mental pole. In order to make that stick, Whitehead has to bring

or power says that for any one thing to really exist, it must have the ability to make a difference to something else and of other things to make a difference to it. Thus, divinity for Plato must be in real relationship to the physical world. These insights are important foundations of a viable metaphysics in the twentieth century.

We see in Plato an insight that is extremely important for the history of natural theology in the West. Simple unity cannot exist. The very nature of a judgment of being involves both sameness and difference with respect to the subject and the predicate. For the world to be scientifically knowable or the object of rationality, there has to be something besides the world of becoming which has a type of reality that is eternal (i.e., Being). Thus, metaphysics has a very important task for Plato. This is the task of reconciling two extremes: either the world is total flux (in which case we can have no rational knowledge), or the world is total unitary being which excludes differentiation and change (in which case we can have no rational knowledge).

One finds rationality in the universe only in the existence of a rationally ordering *nous* or Spirit. This is finally absurd and self-contradictory to deny. Indeed, modern physical science itself could not exist without positing the uniformity of nature,[37] and the uniformity

---

God in as a kind of divine illumination. One cannot really account for knowing or being, or for the knowledge which creatures have or the being which they have, unless there is some kind of primacy in them of agency. It is a matter of degree, to be sure, but every being, whether they be God or creatures, must have some underived mentality, which is precisely what Plato was maintaining.

My main criticism of Whitehead's metaphysics (as well as that of Augustine) is that he removed any genuine independent agency from creatures in order to glorify God. This is not the proper way to glorify God. If God is a creator who is impotent to create free creatures, He is thus demeaned rather than glorified.

[37]See C. S. Lewis, *Miracles: A Preliminary Study* (New York: Macmillan, 1947), pp. 108-109 and Alfred Whitehead's even stronger statement in *Science and the Modern World* (New York: Mentor

of nature cannot be known unless there is a rational Spirit beyond nature ordering it according to reason.

This points to the second and equally important insight. This spiritual (i.e., nonphysical) entity must be really related to the physical world. Anything which really exists must involve the ability to make a difference to it (i.e., have power). If one takes away the idea of real relatedness from one's notion of anything whatever, one has nothing left which could possibly exist.

Thus this spiritual entity performs two very important functions in the world: (1) it orders the world according to reason; and (2) it is really related to the physical world as is seen by radical creativity or newness in the human mind. These have very important implications for every problem in the history of natural theology in the West. Thus, God by His very nature is both transcendent and immanent. He is eternally there and really related to the physical world. This is of extreme importance in developing a metaphysical system for the twentieth century.

Building a Philosophy of God

Building a philosophy of God is an important and complex project, a project for which many people, perhaps most, in our comfortable world are not prepared to pay the price. Yet the world needs such an effort even more than ever before. I believe that we must draw on history, philosophical reasoning, revelation, personal experience, and all possible claims to knowledge and truth.

It is clear that the nature of God as expressed in Greek philosophical thought is not sufficient. Certainly, the Christian concept of God is much richer than the

---

Books, The New American Library of World Literature, Inc., 1925), pp. 13-14. For general background, see the chapter on "The Limits of Science" (pp. 105-113) in Miethe and Habermas, *Why Believe? God Exists!*

Greek view. If one views God as utter and simple unity—that which does not admit to degrees—the problem arises as to how the many physical things can participate in that which is without parts. The identification of God with the One of Plato, as interpreted by Plotinus, gives birth to negative theology in the history of Western Christian thought.[38] The traditional theory of the nature of God has always strongly emphasized the utter simplicity and the utter transcendence of God. Thus God is indivisible and transcendent in relation to everything beneath Him. Yet it is clear that this is not the God of the Christian revelation,[39] or of Plato. We should have been emphasizing His real relatedness and immanence, not just His transcendence!

The "philosophy of God" must be the very capstone of one's metaphysics. It is also foundational in that it holds it together. I think there are at least three very important philosophical "indicators" of God (1) It is evident that the world and all that is in it cannot be independent. That which is clearly an effect cannot account for itself. Contingent existence is supported on all sides. It is ultimately absurd to hold that everything in the world is mechanical and a result of chance. There are then cosmological reasons for positing God's existence.[40] (2) The rationally inescapable must be the real.[41] The laws of logic in fact originate not just from

---

[38]See Miethe, *The Metaphysics of Leonard James Eslick*, pp. 60-70.

[39]See Miethe and Flew, *Does God Exist?*, pp. 117, 119.

[40]See Ibid., pp. 127-37, 181-86; and Miethe and Habermas, *Why Believe? God Exists!* pp. 83-93.

[41]By "rationally inescapable" is meant a non-contradictory view the only possible alternatives to which are contradictory. Of course, what is rationally inescapable is not necessarily psychologically or volitionally coercive. One may believe or affirm a position which is really logically contradictory. But one cannot avoid a rationally inescapable position *if* one wishes to be logical. See the Appendix on the "Law of Non-Contradiction" at the end of this chapter.

the nature of the mind but from an analysis of ontology—from an examination of reality itself. Thus, the very concept of an absolutely perfect being or necessary being demands that such exist. Reason itself "points" to God. (3) Radical creativity can only be a result of the immanence of the spiritual in the physical world. We do not have experience of the purely physical as such. Life itself, and certainly intelligent life, is proof positive that Materialism is untenable. Our "empirical" experience itself shows us that reality is made up of both the physical and the spiritual.

Theological reasoning for the existence of God is implicit in philosophy and extremely important. The historical evidences of the Christian faith are evidential. They do not go against reason or fact. They are as historically reliable as any claims of history. I do not, and cannot, subscribe to "religious modernism" or relativism. "Faith" is not irrational and definable only by the personal feelings of individual subjects. Faith, the Greek word *pistis*, means literally to accept or trust and act on something based on evidence.[42] Biblical faith may be *above* reason, but it cannot go *against* reason. That is, the object of our faith, God, cannot be totally comprehended by man, but that does not mean He cannot be to some extent known or that He cannot reveal himself to us! After all, the ultimate question is not whether the finite mind of man can reach God, but whether an infinite and yet immanent God can reveal Himself to us. The answer to this question must be "yes He can, and yes He has."

Thus the philosophy of God is fundamental to a metaphysical position. God must be all powerful in an absolute sense and be the prime example of perfect relationality. God must be immanent in, and really related to, the world in which we live. This is consistent with the Christian Scriptures. The Gospel of John (3:16)

---

[42]See Miethe, *Living Your Faith*, pp. 21-31.

reads: "For God so loved the world, that He gave His only begotten Son, that whoever believes in Him should not perish, but have eternal life." *To be* is to be free, and to be free is to be able to create, both for God and man.

Epilogue

Socrates has been accused of corrupting the youth of Athens and "with making new gods, and not believing in the old ones."[43]

> ... they say Socrates is some sort of criminal, and that he has a bad influence on the young.... But since they don't want to lose face, they come out with the standard accusations made against all philosophers, the stuff about "things in heaven and things under the earth," and "not recognizing the gods" and "making the weaker argument stronger."[44]

Very interesting, indeed! In the *Apology*, we have Plato's famous record of Socrates' defense before the citizens of Athens. It is a beautiful—an incredible—piece of prose! Here, in this most famous dialogue, we read one of the most famous platitudes in history. A longer quote is most appropriate:

> If on the other hand I say that really the greatest good in a man's life is this, to be each day discussing human excellence and the other subjects you hear me talking about, examining myself and other people, and that *the unexamined life isn't worth living*—if I say this, you will believe me even less."[45]

---

[43]Plato, *Euthyphro* in *Ancient Philosophy*, Philosophic Classics, Volume I by Walter Kaufmann and Forrest E. Baird (Englewood Cliffs, NJ: Prentice Hall, Inc., 1994), p. 72.

[44]Ibid., p. 89. This is from Plato's *Apology*.

[45]Ibid., p. 99 (emphasis added).

This is certainly not contradictory to what Jim Strauss taught me. Again, it was professor Strauss who constantly challenged us to attempt to live for Christ and to strive toward "spiritual and academic excellence."

In the *Apology*, Socrates relates that his mission in life is to search for wisdom. He tells us that one of his friends went to Delphi—yet today an incredibly beautiful place—and asked the oracle if anyone was wiser than Socrates. "The priestess of Apollo replied that there was no one wiser."[46]

Knowing that he had no wisdom, Socrates sets out to verify or falsify the oracle's claim! He approached three classes of people who "seemed to be wise." First, he examined a politician: "... the result of my examination ... was this, I decided that although the man seemed to many people, and above all to himself, to be wise, in reality he was not wise." Socrates goes on to say:

> In all probability neither of us knows anything worth knowing; but he *thinks* he knows when he doesn't, whereas I, given that I don't in fact know, am at least *aware* I don't know. Apparently, therefore, I am wiser than him in just this one small detail, that when I don't know something, I don't *think* I know it either.

After that he began approaching people in a systematic way. He found "those with the highest reputations seemed ... to be pretty nearly the most useless."[47]

Second, he examined writers. Plato recalls:

> Practically anyone present could have given a better account than they did of the works they had themselves written.... I realized that their achievements are not the result of wisdom, but of natural talent and inspiration, like fortune-tellers and

---

[46]Ibid., p. 87.
[47]Ibid., pp. 87-88.

clairvoyants, who also say many striking things, but have no idea at all of the meaning of what they say. Writers, I felt, were clearly in the same position. Moreover, I could see that their works encouraged them to think that they were the wisest of men in other areas where they were not wise.

Third, Socrates examined the craftsmen. "Each one, because of his skill in practicing his craft, thought himself extremely wise in other matters of importance as well; and this presumptuousness of theirs seemed to me to obscure the wisdom they did have."[48] Like Socrates, it was Jim Strauss who first made me profoundly aware that I was truly ignorant. As I have already stated, it was also Strauss who—at least initially—started me on the road to try to discover knowledge, truth, and—yes—perhaps even "wisdom." The more I have learned, the more I have to acknowledge how little I *do* know. In fact, in the last few months, and as I write this, I have been wondering if I know anything at all!

Socrates claimed that it would be "the most reprehensible folly" to think one knows what one does not know. Further, he said, "Would it not have been very illogical of me, when *god* deployed me, as I thought and believed, to live my life as a philosopher, examining myself ... then to be afraid of death—or anything else at all—and abandon my post?"[49] (cf. Psalm 23).

Ultimately, I must credit God, who used James Dean Strauss (in part) to make my way—HIS way—known to me! It has been over a quarter of a century since I met Jim Strauss who taught me, not of new gods, but of the one true God and of His son, Jesus. He

---

[48]Ibid., p. 88.
[49]Ibid., p. 93.

taught me the centrality of the Resurrection;[50] the adequacy of the Christian message; the importance of history, philosophy, and apologetics.[51] He taught me the Christian worldview. This is a debt for which I am eternally thankful! I pray I will not abandon my post!

APPENDIX ON
"THE LAW OF NON-CONTRADICTION"

In an earlier footnote, I stated that "one cannot avoid a rationally inescapable position *if* one wishes to be logical." The basis of rational inescapability is the law of non-contradiction. In order to prove that the rationally inescapable is really true, one must show that the principle of non-contradiction must apply to reality. That is, one must show that the principle of non-contradiction must be true apart from our knowledge about it. This view is called "cognitive independence." A major question, however, is how can this be shown?

To say as A. J. Ayer that "our justification for holding that this world could not conceivably disobey the laws of logic is simply that we could not say of an unlogical world how it would look" is insufficient. This is only to say that the law of non-contradiction is *linguistically* necessary but not that it is *ontologically* so. But if it is to be contended that the rationally inescapable is real, it must be shown that what is rationally inescapable is also *ontologically* necessary.

Furthermore, it will not suffice to argue that "the law of non-contradiction must apply to reality, because there is no way to deny the principle of non-contradiction without using it in the very denial." All this argument proves is that the principle is rationally undeniable or inescapable; it does not show that it is ontologically

---

[50]See Terry L. Miethe, ed., *Did Jesus Rise From the Dead: The Resurrection Debate*, with Gary Habermas and Antony Flew (San Francisco, CA: Harper & Row Publishers, 1987).

[51]See Miethe and Habermas, *Why Believe? God Exists!*

necessary. That is to say, something might possibly be unreal even though it is not possible to think of it as unreal. For example, one might agree that the ontological argument shows that it is rationally necessary to posit an Absolutely Perfect Being without agreeing that this being really exists. So then, in order to show that the rationally inescapable is real, one must prove that it is not possible that something can really *be* false even when we must inescapably *think* of it as true.

Another unhelpful approach would be to say simply that a denial of the applicability of the principle of non-contradiction is contradictory. This would amount to saying no more than "the denial of the principle is not true because it contradicts the principle." But this would be arguing in a circle: it would be *using* the law of non-contradiction *to prove* the law of non-contradiction. In other words, no *reductio ad absurdum* argument— disproof of a principle or proposition by showing that it leads to an absurdity when followed to its logical conclusion—can be used to prove the law of non-contradiction. To say that the denial of the law of non-contradiction is absurd is to say that it is contradictory, and this is *assuming* the law of non-contradiction *in order to prove* the law of non-contradiction.

Is there any way out of this impasse? Is there any way to prove that the principle of non-contradiction must apply to reality and, therefore, that the rationally inescapable must be real? That is, is there any way to prove that the rationally inescapable is real without using the law of non-contradiction in the proof? The answer seems to be that there is no *direct* way to do so. Every rational proof would have to use the law of rationality (i.e., the law of non-contradiction) in the very proof of it; otherwise the proof would not be a rational proof. What other kinds of proofs are there but rational ones?

If there are no direct proofs of the law of non-contradiction, are there any *indirect* proofs? Certainly, there are no valid indirect proofs of the law of non-contradiction of the *reductio ad absurdum* variety; for as has been shown, this is arguing in a circle.

However, all is not lost. There is yet another indirect way to substantiate the ontological validity of the law of non-contradiction. Francis Parker,[52] for example, argues that any denial of the reality of the rationally inescapable is "self-defeating." To deny its independent reality is to affirm it in the same breath in which it is denied by implying that the principle of non-contradiction is true independently of our knowledge of it. That is, in order to deny its reality, one must assume that the denial is itself true of reality. But the only way one's denial of the law of non-contradiction could be true of reality is on the condition that the law of non-contradiction cannot be denied of reality; otherwise, the very denial would make no sense.

Of course, this does not "prove" that the principle of non-contradiction is true of reality, but only that it cannot be consistently or meaningfully denied of reality. There could still be some strange sense in which the rationally inescapable might *be* unreal even though it cannot be *thought* or *asserted* to be unreal. The reason there is no way for anyone to think or say that the principle of non-contradiction does not apply to reality is that the very act of thinking or affirming implies that the principle is really true apart from our thought about it. In other words, there is no way for anyone to think or state a consistent position apart from the principle of non-contradiction. If the denial of the principle is *no position at all*, then the skeptic has, as Aristotle pointed out, reduced himself or herself to a vegetable; he or she is not really saying anything at all.

---

[52]See Francis H. Parker, "The Realistic Position in Religion," in *Religion in Philosophical and Cultural Perspective*, ed. Clayton Feaver *et al.* (Princeton, NJ: Van Nostrand Company, Inc., 1967), pp. 78-112.

In sum, the basis for believing that the law of non-contradiction does apply to reality (and therefore that the rationally inescapable is real) is that the position is literally undeniable and its opposite is unthinkable. One may affirm its validity consistently, but one cannot deny it consistently. The law of non-contradiction is not only used when one *affirms* it, it is used when one *denies* it. It is inescapable. In other words, in the very act of denying it, the principle of non-contradiction affirms itself. There is no way for one to *think* otherwise than that the principle does apply to reality. The very "question" as to whether non-contradiction applies to reality is no question; it has no meaning unless the law of non-contradiction does apply. It is impossible even to think or question the position that non-contradiction necessarily applies to reality. (I end this musing with this most appropriate saying: *semel insanivimus omnes!*)

RECOMMENDED BIBLIOGRAPHY[53]

Burtt, Edwin Arthur. *The Metaphysical Foundations of Modern Physical Science: A Historical and Critical Essay.* The International Library of Psychology, Philosophy, and Scientific Method. 2nd ed. rev. London: Routledge and Kegan Paul Limited, 1932.

A classic attempt "to plunge into the philosophy of early modern science, treating its key assumption[s] ... and following them to their classic formulation in the metaphysical paragraphs of ... Newton." Includes chapters on "Copernicus and Kepler," "Galileo," "Descartes," "Seventeenth-Century English Philosophy," "Gilbert and Boyle," "The Metaphysics of Newton," [some one hundred pages] and a conclusion. [Advanced]

*Collins, James. *God in Modern Philosophy.* Chicago, IL: Henry Regnery Company, 1959.

Called a "brilliant work of clarification and synthesis." Examines the main philosophical approaches taken toward God since the beginning of the 1600s. Includes such diverse thinkers as Cusanus, Calvin, Bruno, Montaigne and Charron, Gassendi and Huet, Mersenne, Descartes, Spinoza, Leibniz, Malebranche, Bacon, Locke, Berkeley, Hume, the Common-Sense Reaction, Bayle, Wolff, Kant, Voltaire, Rousseau, Hegel, Feuerbach, Marx, Nietzsche, Heidegger, James, Pascal, Newman, and Whitehead. [Advanced]

*Hartshorne, Charles. *Creative Synthesis and Philosophical Method.* La Salle, IL: The Open Court Publishing Co., 1970.

The foremost advocate of "process philosophy," Hartshorne here gives his classic treatment of metaphysics, the Idea of God, and creative synthesis. His most important work. [Advanced]

*Hartshorne, Charles and William L. Reese. *Philosophers Speak of God.* Chicago, IL: The University of Chicago Press, 1953.

A classic treatment of the philosophy of God in three parts: "Classical Views," six chapters; "Modern Views," four chapters; and "Skeptical or Atheistic Views, Ancient and Modern," in four chapters. Treats both Eastern and Western views, Pantheism, Emanationism, Temporalistic Theism, Religio-Pragmatic Skepti-

---

[53]An asterisk * indicates the most highly recommended sources.

cism (Buddhism), Logico-Metaphysical Skepticism, Nietzsche, Freud, and Dennes. [Advanced]

*Klubertanz. George P., S.J. *Introduction to The Philosophy of Being.* Second Edition. New York: Appleton-Century-Crofts, 1963.

Perhaps the best introduction to the philosophy of being/metaphysics ever written. Even though Klubertanz claims that "this is an introductory textbook of metaphysics, whose aim is to help a beginning student" and that it is "not a profound study directed to the scholar," it will be difficult for the beginning student to handle. [Advanced]

Klubertanz, George P. and M.R. Holloway, S.J. *Being and God: Introduction to the Philosophy of Being and to Natural Theology.* New York: Appleton-Century-Crofts, 1963.

A combination of Klubertanz' *Philosophy of Being*, minus the last four chapters (9 and 11-14) and Holloway's *Natural Theology* with seven chapters on the existence and nature of God, etc. Intended to be a textbook for a one-semester class in theoretical metaphysics and natural theology. An excellent book. [Advanced]

Miethe, Terry L. *The Compact Dictionary of Doctrinal Words*: Easy-to-Understand Definitions of Theological Words for all who Study, Teach or Preach. Minneapolis, MN: Bethany House Publishers, 1988.

Over 570 theological terms succinctly identified and briefly explained, often with helpful bibliography for further research. Has sold tens of thousands of copies and judged an excellent resource for preachers, teachers, undergraduate and graduate students. [Intermediate]

*_____. *Living Your Faith: Closing the Gap Between Mind and Heart.* Joplin, MO: College Press Publishing House, 1993.

Examines the relationship between faith and reason. Emphasizes the Christian's need to attain a balance between what the *mind* knows to be true and what the *heart* desires to express. Gives practical ministry suggestions. [Beginning]

_____. *The Metaphysics of Leonard James Eslick: His Philosophy of God.* Ann Arbor, MI: University Microfilms, Inc., 1976.

Examines God and the great metaphysical issues in the history of philosophy in an attempt to build a viable modern philosophy of God. [Advanced]

*_____ and Antony G. N. Flew. *Does God Exist? A Believer and an Atheist Debate.* San Francisco, CA: Harper Collins Publishers, 1991.

A highly acclaimed debate on the existence of God. Foreword by Hans Küng, contributions by A. J. Ayer, Richard Swinburne, and Hermann Häring. Being translated into Spanish. [Advanced]

*_____ and Gary R. Habermas. *Why Believe? God Exists! Rethinking the Case for God and Christianity.* Joplin, MO: College Press Publishing Company, 1993.

An examination of the newest evidence as to why one should believe in God and the truth of Christianity. In four parts: "Evidence from Philosophy," "Evidence from Science," "Evidence from Morality," and "Evidence from History." Being translated into Korean. [Intermediate]

*_____, Editor. Gary R. Habermas and Antony G. N. Flew. *Did Jesus Rise from the Dead: The Resurrection Debate.* San Francisco, CA: Harper & Row Publishers, 1987.

The award winning debate on the historicity of the resurrection of Jesus, with responses by Wolfhart Pannenberg, Charles Hartshorne, James I. Packer, and Terry L. Miethe. [Intermediate]

Pannenberg, Wolfhart. *Metaphysics and the Idea of God.* Grand Rapids, MI: Eerdmans, 1988.

Pannenberg is one of the dominant figures in contemporary theology and perhaps the most comprehensive theologian at work today. He arranges this book in two parts: "The Idea of God" and "Metaphysics and Theology." It is a short, succinct introduction to the "crisscrossings of theology and metaphysics over the last 2000 years." [Intermediate]

*Plato. *Plato: The Collected Dialogues.* Edited by Edith Hamilton and Huntington Cairns, Bollingen Series LXXI. Princeton, NJ: Princeton University Press, 1961.

The classic scholarly edition of the complete works of Plato including the letters "with Introduction and Prefatory Notes." A must for scholars interested in Plato's thought. [Advanced]

*Swinburne, Richard. *The Coherence of Theism.* Oxford: Clarendon Press, 1977.

Investigates what it means, and whether it is coherent, to say that there is a God. Swinburne's classic argument is that Christian theism is coherent in spite of philosophical objections. [Advanced]

*Thompson, Samuel M. *A Modern Philosophy of Religion.* Chicago, IL: Henry Regnery Company, 1955.

The finest book in the philosophy of religion and metaphysics I have found. Eight parts treat: "Religion and Philosophy," "Faith and Knowledge," "Truth," "The Nature of Man," "The Idea of God," "The Existence of God," "Our Knowledge about God," and "God and the World." Very highly recommended. [Intermediate]

Chapter 12:

Still Lost in the Moral Malaise Without Christ
by
Dr. Paul McAlister

Paul McAlister received the M.Div. degree in theology and philosophy from Lincoln Christian Seminary in 1972 and his Doctor of Ministry (D.Min.) degree from Bethel Theological Seminary in 1978. He has taught at Minnesota Bible College since 1972, teaching Theology and Ethics, and directing the mission program at the College.

Dr. McAlister also serves on several Community Corrections Committees as well as the Ethics Committee at the Federal Medical Center, U.S. Bureau of Prisons. He is an ethicist for the Institutional Review Board for the Olmsted Medical Group, and, for four years, an ethicist for the required Medical Ethics course for second year students at the Mayo Medical School.

He acknowledges his gratitude to Lincoln Christian Seminary and especially to his friend, colleague, and professor— Dr. James Strauss. According to Dr. McAlister, "Dr. Strauss's interdisciplinary insight and Christian worldview have encouraged me and helped prepare me to enter the world of dialogue and decision-making as a Christian caught by the vision of a Christ who takes all things captive!"

STILL LOST IN THE MORAL MALAISE
WITHOUT CHRIST

The Development of Ethical Theory:
An Overview

We need go no further than the newspaper, the television news, the entertainment world, the streets, or the inner recesses of our own lives to see the uneasy reality of moral stress. Almost everyone would agree with Dr. Strauss that we are "lost in a moral malaise."[1] Whether we lament the tragedy of violence, wrestle with hard choices in the fields of bio-ethics, or struggle to make decisions regarding personal relationships, the moral weakness of our world sets before us an overwhelming threat. Answers to guide us out of the malaise have not been easy to find in a society seeking answers within itself. Modern civilization has turned away from any "word from God" and has looked in vain for human words capable of providing clarity and resolution.

Where did this situation come from? What has happened throughout the history of the West which has led to the deafening of human ears to the word of God as the source of moral judgment and behavior? A helpful, and very readable, overview of the history of ethics can be discovered in the book, *Thinking about Ethics*, by Richard Purtill. He confronts us with several questions which will need to be answered in the effort to understand the variety of ethical approaches evidenced in Western civilization.

1. What question was this theory trying to answer?

---

[1]See James D. Strauss, "Lost in the Moral Malaise of Situation Ethics," in Strauss's *Newness on the Earth Through Christ* (Lincoln Christian Seminary Press, 1969).

2. What answer does this theory give to that question?

3. How is this answer related to our contemporary ethical problems and concerns?[2]

Though people from the beginning of time have, no doubt, questioned the meaning of right action, to understand the contemporary Western world we start with the Classical world. The Sophists answered the question of "how does one live the good life?" by suggesting that the "good life" was attained by being "successful." The definition of success varied with the user, and therefore the Sophists were essentially "nominalists."[3] The word "success" had no inherent meaning beyond whatever meaning one chooses. This clearly does not give objective insight into what is good.

Plato, in contrast to the Sophists, argued that there must be some effort to conform our thoughts to the unchanging, perfect world of ideals. Plato saw the practices and stereotypes of his world as universally valid, and thus believed that societal roles should reflect the ideal of virtue differently. Slaves should practice virtue as a faithful slave and so forth. Only the adult male could exercise freedom and initiative. For Plato, this ideal was to be recognized through reason.

Aristotle, unlike Plato, saw universal principles present in concrete cases, not existing in a separate ideal world. For Aristotle, the good life was to be found in doing—doing in accord with good principles. Aristotle, as other Greeks, admired moderation. The good could be

---

[2]Richard Purtill, *Thinking about Ethics* (Englewood Cliffs: Prentice-Hall, 1976). Compare his survey with Strauss's incisive comments in *Newness on the Earth*, pp. 195-201.

[3]"Nominalists" essentially deny the reality of "universals." They do not recognize the reality of abstractions, such as the idea of "goodness." The "good" would simply be what the individual, or God, wills. One does not, therefore, will something *because it is good*; rather, something would be good because one *willed* it. This leads to a word having only the meaning attributed to it by the user.

attained by striking a balance between extremes. His doctrine of the "Golden Mean" expresses this balance. But questions regarding why one should avoid either extreme, or whether one can clearly define the point of balance are never finally resolved.

The Stoics and Epicureans attempted to identify the "good life," yet they presented discordant views as to what constitutes the "good." The Epicureans held that the good life was a life of pleasure. It must be noted that this "pleasure" was more mental pleasure than wild sensuality. Nevertheless, that pleasure was still self-serving. The good life would seek pleasure and avoid pain.

The Stoics sought to find satisfaction through the avoidance of dissipating desires and wants. They rejected elaborate wants, but approved the natural wants and needs such as family and citizenship. Roman citizens were somewhat confused by the moral positions of the Epicureans and the Stoics which led many toward the Eastern "mystery" religions.

Judeo-Christian influence had a very different starting point from Greece and Rome. The Judeo-Christian position arises from a commitment to "revelation" as the primary source of moral obligation and criteria for the "good." This view holds that morality flows from meta-ethical realities. Biblical ethics assumes that the good is conformity to the will of God. Ethics, in the biblical view, is more than seeking the satisfaction of one's private "good." Indeed, the "good" is found in relationship to a personal God. (I shall return to this view in the next section of this essay in considering the elements necessary for ethical theory.)

A major concern in this essay is the development of secular ethics as evidenced in the modern world. We necessarily focus upon major people and positions to describe this development. Due to the limitations of this essay, I will merely summarize people and issues which deserve much fuller treatment. It is my hope that a summary of the crucial points will be sufficient.

In the development of the secular models of ethical theory, I begin with British Empiricism. The idea that ethical criteria arise from experience contributes a major plank in the platform of contemporary thinking. The "good" is distilled from experience. The names of Hobbes, Hume, Price, and Reid all need to be mentioned. Key developments in the contemporary world can be attributed to Bentham and Mill. Experience-based values became associated with "Utilitarianism." This view, popularly understood as "the greatest good for the greatest number," has dominated much of ethical discussion in the modern era. But defining the "good" was still an unresolved matter. Furthermore, it would take a substantial calculus to be able to measure the consequences of an action even if a definition of the good were offered. Prominent concerns include these: who should determine what "good" consequences are, and is the "good" to be calculated over the long-term or the short-term? An act may well provide a significant number of benefits to people, perhaps more benefits than some other decision; yet the total number of benefits may be lacking any sense of distributive "justice." The minority may virtually be forgotten.

"Utilitarianism" drives many contemporary decisions which may fall within the political sphere or within "medical ethics." Utilitarianism is a form of "teleological" ethics which uses the "ends" or outcomes of decisions to determine their ethical status. But such decisions are unknown and even unknowable at the time of the decision. Thus, for the criteria to determine what is "good" and what is "just," utilitarianism needs something beyond itself.

If British thought was controlled by experience, then Continental (European) theory was controlled by reason. I shall only comment here on Immanuel Kant.

Kant's "Categorical Imperative" and "Hypothetical Imperative" structure much of his ethical theory. Kant recognizes that experience is limited and therefore cannot provide a comprehensive moral theory. He seeks to find some "deontological principle"—a principle which identifies our moral duty with reference to an action itself, without reference to the goodness or badness of the *consequences* of that action. Based on this principle, Kant asserts that we ought always to treat people as "ends" and not merely "means."

While this is commendable, it is not sufficient. He suggests that whatever one chooses, one ought to be willing to have that choice universalized. The result of Kant's position is to grant ethical decisions to "autonomous" man. But Kurt Baier in *The Moral Point of View* points out that Kant's idea that people of "good will" choose noble things is a major and disputable assumption.[4] Baier argues that moral decisions reflect societal roles and privileges and that the human inclination is prompted by self-interest and not by a sense of moral duty to others. It could thus legitimately be argued that human beings cannot produce *absolute* ethical norms, and they do have within themselves the motivation to be moral. Kant leaves us with a process for making moral decisions but neither the motivation nor the criteria for knowing what we ought to do. On the one hand, Kant demonstrates that basing moral decisions upon experience fails to lead us out of the cultural relativism of our experience. On the other hand, Kant leads us to an autonomous ethics without content.

The effect of Kant is to leave ethical decision-making to the individual and, therefore, without obligation outside oneself. Ethical decisions are right on the basis of the individual's intent. If the individual is

---

[4]See Kurt Baier, *The Moral Point of View: A Rational Basis for Ethics* (Ithica, N.Y: Cornell University Press, 1958).

content with the thought that the decision be universalized, it would be right. Since Kant separated moral decisions and values from knowledge, values are based in subjective decisions. Kant's intent may be other, but the result of his view leads to the subjective notion that if people make decisions by their good will, then those decisions are moral. Here again the issue is that ethical deliberation involves the individual's intention, not some source outside of the self.

This "autonomy" is another plank in the platform of contemporary ethics. An extension of this is evidenced in this century's "existential" ethics. According to existential ethics, one brings no ethical criteria into the situation; rather one seeks only to act in a loving way within the situation. This, of course, relativizes ethical decisions. It leaves undefined what it means to do the loving thing. Love is without content. The popular work of Joseph Fletcher exemplifies the problem of "situation ethics." In a culture like ours, where ethical theory is rooted in the individual, words like love, good, right, etc., have no correspondence to anything outside of the user's intent. Therefore, such words have no meaning and generate the nightmare of a culture capable of generating contradictory behavior, with everyone able to defend their behavior as moral or right. No private ethical criteria are available and no social ethic is possible. Thus, relativism is yet another plank in contemporary ethics.

Elements Necessary for Ethical Theory

The difficulties expressed in the preceding summary of ethical theories lead inescapably to the need for certain foundational elements to be recognized. If there is the possibility of ethical guidance—for the identification of "normative" standards for what we "ought to do"—then the following elements must be present. Arthur Holmes has stated the elements well.[5] The first element pertains to "cases." The "case" refers to specific acts and seeks to determine whether such an act is justifiable. The decision is based upon "Moral Rules." These "rules" are guidelines which apply to certain areas of life (for example, to medical decisions, to relationships, and to property issues). Holmes goes on to describe "Moral Principles" which underlie the "rules." These principles are broad ethical concepts which bridge all "cases" and areas. Such "rules" as "Love" or "Justice" would be included. The fourth element for ethical theory is cited as "bases." The "rules," "principles," and concerns about specific actions are rooted in some "base." The base is philosophical or theological in nature and is the foundation of the theory. It answers the question, "Why should I seek to do the right thing?"[6] Moral issues disclose the presence of "good" and "evil," or "right" and "wrong." Ethics becomes more systematic and provides "normative" guidance.

The Christian locates the "base" in theology. The ought of moral intent is motivated by God. The content of principle and rule are structured by Scripture. Scripture also offers certain "cases" which bring guidance. It is obvious that specific acts (i.e. cases) may change throughout history. Technological development confronts society with cases not confronted before. The ethical decision for the Christian is, nevertheless, still informed by the "rules" and "principles." It is clear that all ethical theories, in order to provide a dependable

---

[5]See Arthur Holmes, *Ethics: Approaching Moral Decisions* (Downers Grove: InterVarsity Press, 1984).

[6]An example may help distinguish these elements. In the area of medical ethics, a dilemma may arise concerning whether to disclose a potential negative outcome for a medical procedure. The "case" involves whether or not to inform the patient. The "rule" may be the patient's right to "informed consent." The "principle" may be "honesty." The underlying "base" may be the value and dignity of human life.

structure for decision making, must include all the elements above.

Ethical Theory and Medical Ethics

In what follows, I will reflect upon the history of modern medical ethics as a way to illustrate the need for the fourfold approach described above. I will then reflect upon the elements entailed in biblical ethics in order to offer biblical ethics as the need of the hour to resolve conflict and provide the motivation as well as guidance for ethical decision-making.

The field of "Medical Ethics" has grown substantially over the last few decades. The rise of new technology and the tragedy of human violence, both international and national, have highlighted the crisis in medicine around decision-making. Perhaps the most famous code of medical ethics in history has been the "Hippocratic." This code reflects many of the concerns of ancient Greek philosophic schools. Many see the work as the product of the ascetic philosophy of Pythagoras. The code speaks of key precepts, such as beneficence and nonmaleficence as well as prohibitions against abortion, euthanasia, and sexual relationships with patients.

These Hippocratic precepts have informed decision-making for 2500 years. Though modified somewhat through the years to remove some of the evidence of pagan influence, the Hippocratic ethic, along with Stoic notions of duty and Christian and Jewish teachings, contributed greatly to the first American Medical Association code in 1847.[7] These precepts and the notion of gentlemanly virtue controlled medical ethics. However, major challenges have occurred in the recent decades of this century.

---

[7]For an excellent survey of the changes in medical ethics, see Edmond Pellegrino, "The Metamorphosis of Medical Ethics," *Journal of the American Medical Association* 269 (March 3, 1993): 1158-1162.

To suggest a few of the forces which precipitated the changes, I would first point to the historic contribution of Kant. As Dr. Strauss often commented: in Kant, ethics became autonomous. While this philosophical development is crucial to understand, its force was not widely manifested in our culture as long as there remained a moral consensus derived from Judeo-Christian values. Kant's influence can be seen in medical ethics as clearly stated in the following:

> In Philosophy, autonomy derives from Kant's attempt to ground ethics upon logical necessity, thereby securing for it universal, unchanging, and certain status. These goals were achieved at enormous cost, however .... The autonomy principle is, then, a way of separating ethical thinking from the empirical world and placing it in the rationalist realm of metaethics. Such a philosophic move has enormous practical consequences. In emptying ethics of content, it makes adherence to procedural matters the test of ethical validity.[8]

I shall return to the above insightful comment. First, I must note other developments in our century which have manifested Kantian influence. I will note only two factors which have influenced the struggles in medical ethics. Cut off from the base values of the Judeo-Christian tradition, and influenced more by the "will to power" of Nietzsche, the horrors of the "Holocaust" threw the world into turmoil. Values were challenged at each level of society. What was so overwhelming with regard to the Holocaust experience was that even Nazi doctors justified their involvement in the brutality with an appeal to research and the betterment of society. Therefore, it seems that an

---

[8]Colleen Clements and Roger Sider, "Medical Ethics' Assault Upon Medical Values," *Journal of the American Medical Association* 250 (Oct 21, 1983): 2011.

application of a utilitarian ethic, at least as applied to the greatest number of Germans, led to medical exploitation.[9]

Another key to understanding the rush to and confusion of medical ethics is to be found in the explosion of new technologies. We are confronted with choices unthought of only decades ago. The cases we face are complicated by the technologies at our disposal. That we can do new things technologically does not necessarily imply we ought to do them. As many seek to justify decisions by appeal to their results, we must ask the following kinds of questions: how can one know the results before an action is performed? What results are relevant? Should one consider long-term or short-term consequences?

In light of the many issues of the twentieth century and the inability of the relativism of culture in general to provide answers, medical ethics turned to a form of decision by principles. Many writers have discussed issues such as abortion, suicide, and euthanasia. Little attention was paid to larger moral bases. Now, much energy is expended on the applications of certain principles. Those principles especially include nonmaleficence, beneficence, autonomy, and justice. These seemed to provide a way to avoid the subjectivity of the past and to provide a way to analyze decisions through a medical-ethical "work-up."[10] The climate of cultural autonomy has been very influential in medical ethics. In many respects the idea of patient autonomy had become dominant.

---

[9]See Robert Jay Lifton, *The Nazi Doctors* (New York: Basic Books, 1986).

[10]A medical-ethical "work-up" normally includes a consideration of the following elements: the relevant clinical facts (including the nature of the disease and options for treatment), the ethical issues (such as who makes the decision, and upon what basis), and justifying the decision on the basis of all these factors.

The problem is that autonomy, cut off from medical norms, may often conflict with other principles, such as beneficence. When resolution is sought among these abstract principles, there needs to be an appeal to yet some other principle. Many have offered ways to prioritize these *prima facie* principles, but to this point, the limitations and lack of consensus remain.

Some ethicists have moved to a virtue-based theory. This view highlights the character of the agent. Virtue and character have traditionally been important until the turbulent period I have described. But the definitions of "virtue" and "good character" are inadequate without some substantive reference point. What the physician deems to be the "good" may not agree with the patient. Therefore, the issue of trust becomes crucial. But why should I trust someone's virtue unless I accept that person's conception of the right or good? Other ethicists move to an "ethics of care," with some of the same difficulties. Once again, how does one trust someone else's definition of caring? Yet others adopt an "ethic of casuistry." These ethicists look for cases which by extension can inform one as to the right thing to do. But as Pellegrino states, "When there is no consensus, as when the moral viewpoint of a society defines what it considers a dilemma or a paradigm case, casuistry encounters difficulties." Again, Pellegrino says:

> Clearly, the proposed alternatives to principlism can enrich any theory of medical ethics. None is independent of principles, rules, or obligations, without which they would succumb to the debilities of subjectivism and relativism. What is required is some comprehensive philosophical underpinning for medical ethics that will link the great moral traditions with principles and rules and with the new emphasis on

moral psychology. This obviously calls for more than an affable eclecticism.[11]

Moral dilemmas cannot be recognized, let alone resolved, without a comprehensive theory which entails all of the elements mentioned earlier. Our culture is without consensus, because it has no base. We have tried to survive upon a theistic (and essentially "Christian") heritage which has now been rejected in theory and practice. As a result, the pluralism and relativism in society cannot offer a base to provide the moral "ought" or the principles and rules to provide sufficient guidance to remove the ambiguities of relativism. For instance, the concern over ethical issues in the whole field of health care is growing: no "ought" can be provided for base values such as the value of human life, the purpose of life, and the nature of "good" and "right." A further problem relates to the belief in integrity and the good intentions of man. These things are assumed, but clearly without evidence. Knowing what is right and choosing to do the right should not so quickly be assumed to be natural in mankind.

The above discussion describes the great difficulties exhibited in the field of medical ethics. The point is that this field, while vital, is only one example of the larger problems in a culture without consensus. The relativism of the modern era cannot provide the comprehensive theory to resolve the moral conflicts. The theories suggest solutions but cannot provide the base or principles of substance to apply to conflict. Our culture has no clear way to prioritize the varying values, and therefore, to make or defend its ethical decisions.

Any ethical theory able to provide a comprehensive normative approach to moral issues has to account for base values and provide principles and purpose for moral behavior. Such a theory needs to

---

[11]Pellegrino, "The Metamorphosis of Medical Ethics," p. 1161.

provide understandable norms and have a sensitive awareness of moral conflicts and the difficulties involved in resolving them. Since many charge that a Christian or biblical ethic is too simplistic to provide a comprehensive framework, it is to the nature of biblical ethics that I now turn. Could a biblical ethic offer a legitimate source of hope for the moral difficulties of our day? If so, what is its nature? And is it feasible?

The Hopeful Word of Biblical Ethics for the Modern Malaise

When one begins to examine biblical teaching regarding ethics and morality, invariably one begins with the Law of the Old Testament. The beginning of biblical moral teaching is rooted in the character of God. For example, Isaiah 6:3 declares the holiness of God. And in Leviticus 11:13 the writer declares that those who belong to God are to reflect His holiness. These elements can be used to construct the base for a biblical view of morality. These elements provide a standard outside of ourselves to which God holds us responsible. The standard reflects the very character of God, and it is, therefore, no mere convention or ad hoc solution to the question of social and personal behavior.

The commandments of Exodus 20, begin with man's relationship to God, then extend to man's social relationships. Note several caricatures of the Law. Some declare that the Law was concerned only with externals. This, however, is not very convincing in light of the prohibition against "coveting." Some argue that the Law is simplistic and has no application in a world of ethical conflict. Yet for some reason, such critics ignore Exodus 21:12, where we see that the application of the prohibitions is not at all simplistic. This section clearly deals with the circumstances of an action as well as with an agent's intent! God has revealed Himself to His people out of love and expects that His people will respond out of love to His holy will.

This theme of law and love is reflected in the New Testament as well. In John's gospel we confront Jesus' identification of love and obedience. John expresses Jesus' claim that if we love Him, we will keep His commands (14:15). Jesus further states that because of our love, the world will know that we belong to Him (see John 13:35). In the entire context of John, witness is very important. In 15:27 the fact that His disciples are to bear testimony to Jesus ties together behavior and witness.

Another frequent assumption is that biblical love is somehow unrelated to ethical norms. Love has been existentialized to the extent that it provides no content for moral decision-making. But note the statement of the Apostle in Romans 13:9, where he explains that far from rejecting law, love summarizes the law. Paul's use of the phrase, "summed up in," discloses that biblical love indeed does have normative content.

It seems, therefore, that the biblical material presents a base for ethical theory in the nature of God. The Bible presents principles, such as that we should love, and it offers rules which tell us how love acts in various contexts. The final moral measure of human behavior is not derived from individuals, but from the revelation of God's character and intent.

Biblical ethics reflects the character and love of God. It is grounded in Him. Unfortunately, some declare that obedience calls for a merit system. But Paul argues consistently that the Law does not save us. In fact, the law informs us as to our need for salvation. Biblical ethics takes seriously the character of broken and weak people. We are given a standard to be followed, norms to be accepted, but we are given these in relationship to God and His redeeming purpose.

An interesting part of the New Testament teaching relates to a misunderstanding of some concerning the "Golden Rule." Jesus said that this is the "law and the Prophets." As Yoder points out in *The*

Politics of Jesus, after giving the Sermon on the Mount, Jesus did not repeat the "Rule" as the basis for all decisions. It was not a first-century form of Kant's "Categorical Imperative." The rest of the gospels is saturated with statements such as: "Do as I have done," "love as I have loved," "serve as I have served." Jesus becomes the model for ethical decisions. His incarnate ministry demonstrates not only His love, but how we ought to love in response to Him. Actually, Christian ethics is not just a theory; it involves a relationship to the person of Christ. The casuistry that some seek to develop is dealt with in the gospels through the example of Jesus.

We live in a broken world. In this broken world conflict seems to force decisions when no option is without some moral difficulty. There may be times when choosing to uphold one moral principle entails violating another. For instance, consider the story of Anne Frank. Her decision to turn one over to the Nazi soldiers would uphold the principle of honesty, but it would seem to undercut the moral imperative of protecting life. Helmut Thielicke characterized this as a "compromise ethic," a concept which Dr. Strauss often made use of.

Using this word "com-promise" often causes resistance, but it is intended in its positive sense—"with promise." Decisions are sometimes made between two possibilities in light of a perceived purpose beyond the difficult circumstance. At times we are forced, in this broken world, to make choices which do not yield the moral confidence we crave. At those times we trust in a God who sees beyond our limitations and understands our intent to honor Him. When we make such choices, we seek God in His understanding and mercy while acknowledging our lack of insight. We seek His wisdom in decision-making and His forgiveness when our ignorance blinds us. Situations like this underscore the reality that we cannot save ourselves through perfect decision-making.

There are difficult situations which cause us to make choices. I would contend that such choices should be made in light of God's ultimate redemptive purposes. Biblical ethics not only reflects God's character and love, it anticipates the future Kingdom of God!

Note, for instance, the importance of the future for present Christian behavior in Colossians 3. Paul begins by telling his readers to keep their minds on things above. Paul clearly does not see this as escapism. He continues to describe the implication of this mind-set. Biblical values reflect what God has done, what He is doing, and what He will yet do in the future. He tells the readers to "put off the old behavior" of the earth and "put on the new," which reflects the age to come. In verse 10, Paul speaks of the need for a transformation in the very nature of the person. What other ethical theories merely presuppose (i.e., the *willingness* of humanity to seek to do "good"), Paul explains as made possible through our being made "new" in Christ. This transformation is not the product of man's competitive efforts; it comes through the grace of Christ. Paul alludes to this reality in Romans 6, where he speaks of dying to the old and rising into newness. This conversion is fundamental to following the Christian ethic. Having gratitude for the gift of God's grace through faith and exhibiting that faith to reflect His character are at the heart of moral commitment.

The realization that Christian behavior both reflects God's character and anticipates the coming newness of His kingdom is seen in Acts 4. In verses 32-37 we find the blending of themes related to present social concerns and to the reality of the resurrection. It may seem out of place for Luke to mention the proclamation of the resurrection in verse 33. But the transformation necessary to turn people from selfishness to selflessness is very much related to the resurrection. Social ethics, the concern for others, is based in God's concern for all, but it is made possible by the freedom that the resurrection hope brings. Greed is often the product of perverted efforts to establish one's identity by competing with others. The resurrection secures our identity and frees us from destructive possessiveness. The future and the present are bound together.

Accordingly, in Ephesians 5, Paul tells us to imitate God and to avoid immoral behavior by "walking as children of the Light." Christians pattern their behavior in light of the coming Kingdom. We ought not to act as those who have not seen the dawning of the coming Kingdom. This anticipatory ethic gives us the redemptive criterion necessary when we face moral conflicts. Christians should seek to make decisions consistent with God's redemptive purpose, since ethical decision-making is about witness, giving glory to God, and His redemptive purpose.

I conclude this essay by suggesting that a biblical ethic offers all the elements necessary to help us through the struggles of a broken world. The base, the rules, the principles, and even the models of specific cases are all present. It is true that the biblical world did not experience the specific technological issues confronting the twentieth century, but the base is there and the rules and principles are there to inform and guide our decisions. Ethical decisions are not always easy, and the infamous "slippery slope" must always be recognized. Yet the Christian is able to face those struggles with the assurance of God's gracious forgiveness and wisdom.

Our culture has been living on the memory of a moral base. But that memory has become blurred by the near-sightedness of a relativistic worldview. In the name of freedom and autonomy, the culture has been cut off from its base. Most ethical options of the day are selective and baseless. The twin questions "Why be moral?" and "How does one know what ethical choices to make?" render most ethical systems a precarious house of cards. Whether in science, politics, medicine, social ethics, or personal relationships, our culture must be pressed to consider the starting point or the base of ethical theory.

Every time there is a conflict in one of the levels of ethical theory, one is forced to seek resolution through reference to the next level. If the base of moral thinking is not present, there will be no ultimate resolution and no answer to the question, "Why be moral?" There are others in this culture with whom Christians may find agreement at times. It may be because of some form of natural revelation—the image of God in all people. If both Christians and non-Christians live in the world which God created, then it is not unlikely that even non-Christians would see some of the same human needs and realities which Christians do. Because God is the author of reality, Christians and non-Christians may become allies in facing shared concerns.

When Dr. Strauss, echoing Paul, contended that all things make sense in Christ, he highlighted the reality that morality makes sense in Him. Ethical behavior and moral commitment derive from God, are expressed in Jesus, and will be consummated in the new heaven and earth. Most contemporary discussions of ethics relate to damage control. The Christian supplies the needed values, purity, love, justice, and peace. Christian ethics, because it is grounded in the character of God, can and does challenge the "cut-flower" ethics of a baseless society. Ethics and moral commitment are matters which can witness to God's character and anticipate that day when "God shall wipe away all tears"—a day when conflict is ended!

RECOMMENDED BIBLIOGRAPHY

Abelson, Razel and Kai Nielsen. "History of Ethics." In *The Encyclopedia of Philosophy.* Edited by Paul Edwards, 3:81-117. New York: Macmillan, 1967.

This standard source will provide important information to the serious student. This is highly recommended.

Beauchamp, Toma and James Childress. *Principles of Biomedical Ethics.* New York: Oxford University, 1989.

The position taken by the authors suggests that, along with Ross, there are certain principles which, on face value, should obtain unless there is some very strong reason to overrule them. The book has become one of the standards in the teaching of medical ethics. It can be read easily, but to evaluate it would take at least moderate knowledge of the field.

Clements, Colleen and Roger Sider. "Medical Ethics' Assault Upon Medical Values." *Journal of the American Medical Association* (JAMA) 250 (October 21, 1983): 2001-2015.

An extremely helpful examination of the conflict between patient autonomy and the physician's commitment to the norms of good medicine.

Henry, Carl F. H. *Christian Personal Ethics.* Grand Rapids: Eerdmans, 1957.

This book has become a classic treatment of moral thought from one of Evangelicalism's most respected writers.

Jones, W. T., Frederick Sontag, Morton Beckner, and Robert Fogelin, eds. *Approaches to Ethics.* New York: McGraw-Hill Book Co., 1977.

This book is a collection of representative primary source articles. A very helpful way to enter the historical discussions.

Jonsen, Albert, Mark Siegler, and William Winslade. *Clinical Ethics.* New York: McGraw Hill, 1992.

A very helpful book which presents an overview of medical ethical principles and case analysis. Very helpful and moderate reading.

Nielsen, Kai. "Problems of Ethics. " In *The Encyclopedia of Philosophy.* Edited by Paul Edwards, 3:117-134. New York: Macmillan, 1967.

Smedes, Lewis. *Choices*. San Francisco: Harper & Row, 1986.
All of the listed books by Smedes are written on a popular level and reflect on Christian issues.

_____. *Mere Morality*. Grand Rapids: Eerdmans, 1983.

_____. *Sex for Christians*. Grand Rapids: Eerdmans, 1981.

Chapter 13:

The Cogito Meets the Imago:
The Image of God and the Concept
of a Person
by
Dr. James Sennett

James Sennett is presently Associate Professor of Philosophy at McNeese State University in Louisiana. He has also taught at Palm Beach Atlantic College, Pacific Lutheran University, and Northwestern College in Iowa.

He holds an A.B. in ministry from Lincoln Christian College, an M.Div. in Old Testament from Lincoln Christian Seminary, and an M.A. and Ph.D. in philosophy from the University of Nebraska.

His doctoral dissertation was published as *Modality, Probability, and Rationality: A Critical Examination of Alvin Plantinga's Philosophy* by Peter Lang Publishing. Journal articles have appeared in *Religious Studies*, *Faith and Philosophy*, *Philosophy and Phenomenological Research*, *International Journal for Philosophy of Religion*, *Logos*, *Southern Journal of Philosophy*, and *Auslegung*. Dr. Sennett has also published eight book reviews and given more than fifteen paper presentations at various conferences. He has worked as an editorialist for *The Wittenburg Door* and for *The Daily Nebraskan* newspaper. He is currently editing a book dealing with the philosophy of Alvin Plantinga which will be published by Eerdmans.

He is a member of the American Philosophical Association and the Society of Christian Philosophers.

Dr. Sennett has served the church as a Shelter Supervisor for a city mission, Campus Minister, Preaching Minister, Pianist, Choir Director, and Elder.

THE COGITO MEETS THE IMAGO:
THE IMAGE OF GOD AND THE
CONCEPT OF A PERSON

Introduction

In the movie *Raiders of the Lost Ark,* archaeologist Indiana Jones is racing against the Nazis to discover the resting place of the Ark of the Covenant. Whoever possesses the Ark, so the legend goes, possesses near omnipotent powers. The Nazis have obtained information regarding the location of the Ark, which they and Jones suppose to be complete, and have begun excavations in the suggested area. However, Jones and his associates soon discover that the Nazis lack an important piece of the puzzle. Upon realizing this, they look at one another in astonishment and delight, reciting in unison, "They're digging in the wrong place!"

This is the plight of anyone who attempts to discover the nature of persons without taking into account the biblical truth that human beings are created in the Image of God. Philosophy and the human sciences (psychology, sociology, and anthropology) are at a loss to give a full account of the phenomenon we call a person.[1]

---

[1]Throughout this paper, when I speak of philosophy and the human sciences, I am referring specifically to the practice of these disciplines from within a secular, non-theistic perspective—which is, in contemporary times, the most common perspective (by far!) from which they operate. I recognize, of course, that there are many outstanding Christians working in each of these fields, and that many of them are making significant contributions and playing redemptive roles in bringing their disciplines under the Lordship of Christ. In fact, it is a secondary purpose of this paper to function as an aid, resource, and encouragement to just such people as they carry on and redouble such redemptive efforts. No one knows better than they how

It is true that these disciplines have made a great deal of progress in understanding and explaining many of the issues related to and affecting persons. But, it seems, every time the attempt is made to move from explaining empirical data to encompassing such explanations in an overall theory, the result is nothing but dubitability, disagreement, and general frustration.

Over 350 years ago Descartes penned the famous words, *Cogito, ergo sum* ("I think; therefore, I am"). This dictum has come to symbolize the genius of the philosophical enterprise: the grounding of human knowledge in the cognitive capacities of that most mysterious of all phenomena, the perceiving, understanding self. It has long been the hope of philosophy (and always of the human sciences) that this thinking, knowing, self-aware individual—this *Cogito*—would lead the way to a thorough, and thoroughly secular, understanding of the world in which we live. Yet the more that is understood about persons, the more we find that we do not understand. As a result, the Cogito, its essential characteristics, and its cognitive powers have been the center of much philosophical and scientific bemusement over the centuries. I believe that such bemusement will remain so long as the Cogito is allowed to roam the earth alone, seeking its essence within the confines of the natural order. The Cogito must be introduced to the Imago—the existing self must meet the self-existent One—if it is ever to know, appreciate, and live up to its essence and purpose in the world.

---

dominant the secular, naturalistic perspective is in philosophy and the human sciences. I praise God for the courageous efforts of Christian philosophers and scientists, and hope this paper helps in some small way to bolster their commitment to Jesus in the intellectual Babylon that is American academia.

The Cogito Wanders Alone:
Personhood in Philosophy and the Human Sciences

One of the oldest and most persistent of philosophical problems is the nature of the human mind. Is it physical or not? How does it operate to produce such interesting phenomena as thoughts, beliefs, knowledge, emotions, decisions, actions, and the like? What is "the mark of the mental"—those distinguishing characteristics that identify an object as a mind and its activities as mental activities? The questions of mind are of particular interest when coupled with the question of personhood. It is commonly held that a being qualifies as a person if and only if it has a mind—or at least a mind with the kinds of capacities that the human mind normally affords to humans, such as freedom of action, deliberative capacities, and the ability to understand moral issues and make moral judgments.[2] So the question of the nature of mind is one directly related to the question of the nature of persons.

In my first college psychology class, the professor began the initial session by asking, "What is psychology?" Always eager to please (and impress), I

---

[2]This question takes on new and bewildering dimensions in this age when computer technology is advancing at logarithmic rates. I address the question of mind in my Introduction to Philosophy classes by asking, "Is Data a person?" Data is the lovable android on the TV series, "Star Trek: The Next Generation." Data can do virtually anything a human being can do, and most things much better than any of us. Data can enter into and develop relationships with human beings. He has friends. He deliberates, makes decisions, makes mistakes, and learns from those mistakes. He often feels challenged, sometimes appears puzzled, and communicates such inward experiences through facial expressions and other bodily behaviors— just like you and me. He even dreams. To claim that Data is a person is to commit to the astounding view (in theory at least) that human beings are capable of creating persons. To claim that he is not a person is to face the very troubling task of specifying exactly what it is that makes the difference between us and Data, and why that difference *is* the difference between persons and non-persons.

piped up, "Psychology is the study of the mind!" I was firmly chastised for so naïve a response. The mind, we were informed in no uncertain terms, is not an empirical object. Psychology is a science, and (as such) has as its subject matter only objects that can be investigated empirically. "Psychology," he informed us, "is the study of *behavior*." Couple these claims with the metaphysical assumption that the empirically accessible world is all the world there is, and two pivotal conclusions follow. First, mind (if there is such a thing) is ultimately reducible to behavior. Second, personhood—insofar as it is defined in terms of the phenomenon of mind—is also reducible to behavior. In short, if there is anything real, meaningful, or knowable about personhood, it is to be found in the study of human behavior.

But even as these words were leaving my professor's lips in the summer of 1975, the behavioristic models of psychology and philosophy of mind he was espousing had already crumbled under the weight of their own implausibility. Today only the staunchest and most unreasonable of die-hards insists on a behavioral theory of psychology or personhood. Current models tend rather to be functionalistic, neurophysiological, or biochemical. Still, these approaches share with behaviorism a critical assumption: any reality behind the phenomenon of personhood is a naturalistic, empirically verifiable, scientifically testable reality. To be a person, they all assume, is to be a part of the natural order. These theories, along with virtually all theories of mind prevalent in contemporary philosophy and the human sciences, fall into the category of *materialistic* (or *physicalistic*) theories.[3] A materialistic theory is one that holds that the phenomenon of mind is explainable solely

---

[3]I am speaking primarily of theories prevalent in the English speaking world. There are some non-naturalistic theories prominent in Europe and the Far East, but these have had little impact on the scientific worldview that dominates Western culture.

in terms of physical objects and physical events. That is, no non-naturalistic elements are needed in order to explain the mind or understand how it interacts with the world.

A major problem for materialism is that human beings do not talk as if our minds are naturalistic, material, or identical to any part of our bodies. The discourse in which we engage when we discuss mental phenomena is radically different from that with which we discuss physical phenomena. Words like 'think' and 'thought', 'decide' and 'decision', 'hope', 'contemplate', 'deliberate', 'choose', and the like have no counterparts in the vocabulary of physical objects and events. The materialist philosophy of mind has the task of accounting for what we might call "mind talk"—that discourse that entails or presupposes that human beings have minds and undergo mental events. Mind talk can be as sophisticated as the most technical articles in the latest issues of cognitive science journals, or as simple as the frustrated ejaculation, "I'm confused!"[4] The materialist philosopher owes the philosophical world an account of how such talk can be true or useful, given that it seems to be so different from any talk about physical objects and events we engage in.

To this end, a common strategy of materialists is *reductivism*. Reductivism is the view that, while mind talk is not apparently *about* physical objects and events, it is *reducible to* talk of physical objects and events. So it becomes the job of the philosopher of mind to specify what kinds of physical objects and events in the world exemplify the objects and events discussed in our mind talk. One such reductivist theory is behaviorism. The psychological theory of behaviorism mentioned above is grounded (historically, at least) in a more fundamental

---

[4]It is, of course, my sincere hope that none of my readers will exemplify this instance of mind talk (or any roughly similar to it) in their encounter with this chapter.

behavioristic theory of mind, which originated in the writings of the American pragmatists Charles Peirce and William James.[5] Behaviorism in the philosophy of mind is the theory that all mental phenomena (thoughts, beliefs, desires, decisions, etc.) are reducible to human behaviors and dispositions to behave (including verbal behaviors).[6] Hence, mind talk is reducible to talk about behaviors and dispositions to behave. One need postulate no activity other than that of the physical body in order to explain mental phenomena.[7]

---

[5]See, for example, Peirce's articles "The Fixation of Belief," *Popular Science Monthly* 12 (1877): 1-15; and "How to Make Our Ideas Clear," *Popular Science Monthly* 12 (1878): 286-302. Both are reprinted in H. S. Thayer, ed., *Pragmatism: The Classic Writings* (Indianapolis: Hackett, 1982). See also James, *The Principles of Psychology* (New York: Holt, 1890). Portions of this book are also reprinted in Thayer. Actually, Peirce proposed only a behavioral model for belief and doubt, and did not go on to formulate an entire behavioral theory of mind. James's theory was quite a bit more encompassing.

[6]The classic behavioristic theories of the late nineteenth and early twentieth-centuries fell on hard times, particularly because of counterexamples demonstrating the possibility of mental phenomena for which there was never any actual behavior to distinguish them from their opposites. Hard line behaviorists insisted that such phenomena were illusory. However, the theory gained new life with the emendation that some mental phenomena are accounted for by dispositions, rather than actual behaviors. "This salt is soluble" translates not as "This salt dissolves in water" (salt that is never actually placed in water is nonetheless soluble), but rather as "If this salt were to be placed in water, it would dissolve." So also, the emendation goes, talk of mental phenomena may translate not into talk of actual behaviors, but rather into talk of dispositions to behave under certain (counterfactual or subjunctive) conditions. The introduction of this emendation is traditionally credited to Gilbert Ryle in his seminal work, *The Concept of Mind* (London: Hutchinson, 1949), especially chapter 10.

[7]It would be an oversimplification and a mistake to suppose that the behaviorist holds that mind talk *just is* talk about behaviors and dispositions to behave. Philosophical behaviorism, and most other reductivist theories in contemporary philosophy, are *metaphysical* rather than *semantical* theories. That is, they hold that mind talk and the behavior talk to which it is reduced are both about the same

As I mentioned before, behaviorism has waned as a dominant theory, both in psychology and in philosophy of mind. However, the theories that currently dominate are no less adamant in their attempts to explain mind and mind talk in terms of purely natural phenomena. For example, many theories attempt to equate mental events with biochemical and electrical events in the brain and the neurophysiological system (so-called "mind-brain identity theories"). Under these theories, mind talk is useful and true because it reduces to talk about events in the brain.

Perhaps the most dominant view in contemporary philosophy of mind is *functionalism*—the view that mind is the conglomeration of processes, whatever their nature, that take us from given sets of perceptual inputs to given sets of behavioral outputs.[8] (The functionalist

---

objects and events in the physical world, but the *meanings* of mental terms are not the meanings of the behavioristic terms. In other words, while the mind talk and the behavior talk have identical reference, they are not synonymous. (Consider, for example, the terms "equilateral triangle" and "equiangular triangle." Necessarily, these terms will always pick out the same set of triangles; however, they do not have the same meaning.)

[8]A good, though overly simplistic, way to understand the emphasis of functionalism is to contrast it to behaviorism and mind-brain identity theories in the following way. Behaviorism errs in focusing only on the outputs of the functional systems. It attempts to encompass all the complexities of mind simply in terms of that which mind produces. Such a move will inevitably omit critical features of mental activity and thus fail in its attempt to encompass all the richness of mind in talk of behavior. Mind-brain identity theories, on the other hand, err in their concentration simply on the hardware of the system—on its biological machinery and defined circuitry. Again, these theorists pick out only part of the complex system and attempt to explain all mental phenomena in these terms; so again vital features of mind will not be accounted for by such an approach. The functionalist argues that the entire system, from inputs to processes to outputs, must be taken into account if a full picture of mental activity is to be gained. Clearly this is a more comprehensive program, and functionalism does stand as the most plausible of the naturalistic theories of mind available. But even here the "entire system" to be considered is entirely physical. Sensory inputs, neurophysiological

points to the computer as a handy, though somewhat inadequate, metaphor for the mind.) According to functionalism, the reduction of mind talk is not as simple as translation into talk about behaviors or brain events. However, all mind talk is reducible (in theory, at least) to talk about the complex interactions among sensory organs and systems, cognitive functions, and behaviors.

But the most radical of materialist theories are not reductivist at all. They are, rather, *eliminativist* theories. That is, they maintain that mind talk is fundamentally mistaken and obsolete, and that the "folk psychology" which uses "belief" and "desire" vocabulary should be, and eventually will be, supplanted by a new and more accurate vocabulary of neurophysiological processes.[9] When people thought the earth was flat, they developed a whole vocabulary based on the assumption that the earth is flat. When it was discovered that the earth is not flat, no one suggested that the flat earth talk was true and useful nonetheless, needing only to be reduced or translated into round earth talk. When it was discovered that the earth is not flat, flat earth talk was eliminated in favor of a whole new vocabulary that reflected the reality of a round earth.[10] Eliminativists claim that mind talk is no more

---

processes, and behavioral outputs are all features fully describable (theoretically, at least) in talk only of physical objects and physical events.

[9]See, for example, Stephen Stich, *From Folk Psychology to Cognitive Science: The Case Against Belief* (Cambridge, MA: MIT Press, 1985). Stich actually takes an agnostic stand on whether or not folk psychology is eliminable, but the book is an excellent example of the kind of research that leads many to believe that it is. For a very good response to both reductive and eliminative materialism, see Lynn Rudder Baker, *Saving Belief: A Critique of Physicalism* (Princeton University Press, 1987).

[10]This story is intended to be parabolic, and not strictly historical. Regardless of the actual linguistic consequences of the discovery that the earth is not flat, it is clear that many ways of talking previously considered indispensable to an adequate representation of the world were (gradually, anyway) recognized to be useless and

---

about the world we live in than flat earth talk was about the world we live in. In both cases, the old vocabulary is illusory. It is not about anything that is really true about the world. Like flat earth talk, mind talk will eventually be eliminated, and the cognitive and neurological scientists will aid us in developing a new vocabulary to talk about what is really going on—the complex physical reactions and interactions of the neurophysiological system.[11]

Eliminativism is, at once, the most dangerous and the most honest of the materialist theories. Behaviorism, mind-body identity, functionalism, and other kinds of reductivist theories all face insurmountable frustrations in trying to account for mind talk.[12] The ultimate naturalistic response to such pervasive frustration is to conclude that the failure of reductivism indicates that the presumed reduction is illusory, and that mind as we know it is a fable. This is the charge of the eliminativist. The eliminativist recognizes that the attempt to construct a materialist theory of mind will always end in frustration. However, she does not admit that such frustration indicates that she has been digging in the wrong place. From the

---

misleading, and consequently discarded. However, the process was not nearly so obvious and explicit as would be indicated by the artificial manner in which the story is given in the text. My parable is an example of what Daniel Dennett calls "just so stories" (with apologies to Rudyard Kipling). See Dennett's *Elbow Room: The Varieties of Free Will Worth Wanting* (Cambridge, MA: MIT Press, 1984), p. 38.

[11]This position has most recently been proposed by Francis Crick, the Nobel Prize winning chemist who, together with James Watson, discovered the double helix structure of the DNA molecule. Crick offers his eliminativist theory in *The Astonishing Hypothesis: The Scientist's Search for the Soul* (New York: Scribners, 1994).

[12]Space does not permit even an overview of such problems, though they are readily available in any good topical introduction to philosophy that has a section on philosophy of mind or the mind/body problem. See, for example, Robert Solomon, *Introducing Philosophy: A Text with Integrated Readings,* 5th ed. (Fort Worth: Harcourt Brace, 1993), pp. 420-540.

materialist point of view the natural world is the only place to dig. If we cannot find an answer to the question of mind by digging in the natural world, then this can only mean that there is no answer to be found. And cognitive scientists, philosophers of mind, and neurophysiologists are coming to such conclusions with increasing frequency.

The Cogito Fades Away:
Materialism and the Elimination of Personhood

What is true in the philosophy of mind is true in every other category essential to personhood—knowledge, free will, morality, and the like. Across the board, philosophers and human scientists assume that human capability and activity are to be understood on a physiological model comparable to that of any other animal.[13] Despairing of any success in explaining what is so special about persons, contemporary philosophy and the human sciences are adopting the task of explaining personhood *away*. They are not seeking explanations of why humans are so special. Rather, they are seeking explanations of why we *think* we are so special when, as a matter of fact, we are no more special than anything else in the natural order.[14] Given the scientific cast of

---

[13]See, for example, Fred Dretske, *Explaining Behavior: Reasons in a World of Causes* (Cambridge, MA: MIT Press, 1991) and Daniel Dennett's *The Intentional Stance* (Cambridge, MA: MIT Press, 1987) and *Consciousness Explained* (Boston: Little Brown, 1991). In a recent review of this last book (*Journal of Philosophy* 90 (1993): 181-193), Ned Block quipped, "In some ways, this is an extraordinary book, though *Consciousness Ignored* would have been a more descriptive title."

[14]One popular area in which this sentiment is rampant is the animal rights movement. When animal rights advocate Peter Singer coined the term "speciesism," he did so explicitly to assert that the attitude that human beings are ontologically superior to other animals is no more justifiable than, and every bit as sinister as, the attitude that some human beings are ontologically superior to other human beings, as in racism and sexism. See "All Animals are Equal," in

---

such theories, "sophisticated moderns" are often intimidated into giving them more credibility than their evidence or level of plausibility deserve. We mistake explanations of what would have to be the case if naturalism were true for explanations of what actually is the case.[15]

G. E. Moore, one of the most important philosophers of the twentieth century, was fond of rebutting skeptical arguments with the simple pronouncement that it is more obvious to him that he knows (for example) that he is holding a pencil than it is that any argument for skepticism is sound. That is, he always has better reason to doubt skepticism than he does to doubt the knowledge skepticism questions. Thus, the rational thing for him to do is to deny skepticism, even though he may have no incontrovertible arguments against it.

James E. White, ed., *Contemporary Moral Problems* 3rd ed. (St. Paul, MN: West, 1991), pp. 340-348. For a defense of a less radical, though still thoroughly naturalistic, thesis, see Bonnie Steinbock, "Speciesism and the Idea of Equality" in the same volume, pp. 364-371. It is imperative that Christians realize that one need not adopt an egalitarian position with regard to humans and animals or conjure up the highly problematic notion of animal rights in order to defend the ethical treatment of animals. It is the fact that we are image bearers and stewards of all creation that grounds our obligation to see after the needs of, and refrain from cruelty to, other sentient beings. Our obligations to humane activity originate not in any moral rights that animals have, but in the moral duties that human beings have.

[15]Noted Christian philosopher Alvin Plantinga has devoted much of his most recent work to pointing out the importance of this distinction for Christian scholarship. For example, he argues that Darwinism, far from constituting a good reason to accept naturalism, is a feasible theory only if naturalism is true. A scholar operating from a non-naturalistic worldview has no logical or scientific compulsion to accept Darwinism as a theoretical base for his work. See "When Faith and Reason Clash: Evolution and the Bible," *Christian Scholars Review* 21 (1991): 8-32. For further work by Plantinga on related issues, see "An Evolutionary Argument Against Naturalism," in Elizabeth S. Radcliffe and Carol J. White, eds., *Faith in Theory and Practice: Essays in Justifying Religious Belief* (Chicago: Open Court, 1993), pp. 35-66; and *Warrant and Proper Function* (Oxford University Press, 1993), chapters 11 and 12 (pp. 194-237).

William Rowe has dubbed this dialectical maneuver "the G. E. Moore Shift."[16]

The G. E. Moore Shift has critical application to the current efforts in philosophy and the human sciences to reduce personhood to naturalistic and physicalistic phenomena. The assumption of naturalism leads inevitably to the conclusion that human beings are not unique or qualitatively different from any other part of creation. As a result, we are asked to believe that, despite our first impressions, it is false that there is something special about being human. Yet it seems far more obvious to me that human beings are unique and qualitatively different from all the rest of creation than it is that naturalism is a viable metaphysical theory. Chimpanzees may be taught to use sign language. But until a chimpanzee delivers the Gettysburg Address, I will not accept ontological parity. Baboons may be observed using tools. But until baboons build the Taj Mahal, I remain unimpressed. Humpback whales may engage in mysterious and intricate songs of communication. But until a school of whales performs the "Ode to Joy" from Beethoven's ninth symphony, I hold fast to my conviction.

Given that the qualitative uniqueness of persons is so obvious, why should I not consider the fact that naturalism leads to a denial of that uniqueness as evidence that naturalism is false? It seems that the rational thing for me to do—à la G. E. Moore—is to deny naturalism, even though I may have no incontrovertible arguments against it. Yet, in the name of academia and intellectual sophistication, many are far too willing to reject the obvious truth that we are unique, in order to

---

[16]See *The Philosophy of Religion: An Introduction,* 2nd ed. (Belmont, CA: Wadsworth Publishing, 1993), pp. 86f. Rowe makes an important application of the G. E. Moore Shift to that philosophy of religion conundrum known as the problem of evil.

accept materialistic theories of mind that are plausible only if naturalism is true.

The history of philosophy and the human sciences is a dialectical nightmare. The quest for an answer to King David's age-old question "What is Man?" has produced only inadequate theory after inadequate theory. I maintain that a key reason for this unending cycle of vacuity is the presupposition that the nature of persons is explainable in terms of the natural order alone. Such an approach assumes that being human is being merely a part of nature, and that the study of the nature of persons is simply a segment of the study of the nature of nature. Therefore, if one is to understand personhood, one must investigate the natural order and find the naturalistic slot into which human beings fit. But all the slots are square, and the concept of personhood is perfectly round. There is no fit. The very methodologies of philosophy and the human sciences rule out the most essential piece to the puzzle. They're digging in the wrong place!

It is my contention that a proper understanding of the doctrine of the Image of God is the only way to make sense out of the phenomenon of personhood. It is the only way to give proper due to all those miraculous facets of humanness that we so often take for granted. Without taking the Image into consideration, we doom ourselves to the fate shared by so many in the history of thought—we explain nothing. We only explain away truths that are, in our genuinely reflective moments, wholly undeniable.

The Primacy of the Imago:
A Prolegomenon to Biblical Anthropology

Genesis 1:26 announces that human beings are made in the "image" and "likeness" of God (the *Imago Dei*). What this claim means is, of course, a matter of great debate. However, it is not my aim to adjudicate that debate or to offer a theory of what the Image of God is.[17]   Rather, I would like to make a few brief observations concerning this passage and draw a very important conclusion—a conclusion which, while consistent with any plausible theory concerning the Image, nonetheless has far reaching implications for philosophy and the human sciences.

The only other place in the Old Testament where the words translated "image" and "likeness" in Genesis 1:26 appear together is Genesis 5:3, where Adam had a son "in his own likeness, in his own image; and he named him Seth."[18]   In the South where I grew up, we used to speak of children being the "spittin' image" of their parents. This expression was used to indicate more than mere family resemblance. To be the spittin' image was to be the very reincarnation of the parent at an earlier age. I believe that Genesis 5:3 is telling us that Seth was the spittin' image of his daddy. Although Adam had other sons, it was Seth who had his father's

---

[17]Of all the theories I have heard, I think I like that proposed by Dorothy Sayers the best. She notes that, at this point in the Bible, all we know about God is that he is a creator. We are witnesses to his handiwork, his orderliness, his powerful imagination. We are overwhelmed by his creative activity, and that alone is in focus. So when we are told that human beings are created in the Image of God, the simplest and most natural interpretation is that we, like God, are creators. She believes that the Image is our creativity—our power literally to bring something into existence where previously there was nothing. See *The Mind of the Maker* (San Francisco: Harper & Row, 1979), pp. 21ff. As one who believes that the first question in biblical interpretation must always be, "What does the text say?"   I am attracted to the directness of Sayers' theory.

[18]The Hebrew here is *tselem* ("image") and *demut* (likeness). The reason for the two-fold description is debated.   Keil and Delietzsch propose that the two words "are merely combined to add intensity to the thought" (*Commentary on the Old Testament in Ten Volumes, Volume I: The Pentateuch* [Grand Rapids: Eerdmans, 1978], p. 63). This is probably as good a theory as any, and better than most. So Luther translates the phrase, "An image which is like Us," and the Today's English Version combines both words into a single thought: "So God created human beings, *making them to be like himself*" (my emphasis).

mark.[19]   In Genesis 1:26, God says, "Let's make somebody who is our spittin' image." To be in the Image of God is to be a creature so like God and so different from all else around that there can be no rational denial of the divine parentage.

This observation is supported by the creation story in Genesis 2. While the human body is formed from the earth, that body does not become a living being until it receives the divine in-breathing.[20] That which makes it alive could not be drawn from the created order, like that which makes the plants and animals alive. That which makes it alive is the very breath of God. God brings the human being to life literally by

---

[19]Undoubtedly, the fact that Seth is singled out as Adam's image and likeness is related to the fact that it is through his line that the nation of Israel comes. Also, Seth is the child of Adam's maturity, the son who follows the fall from grace, the loss of innocence, the abandonment of hope. Adam was in God's image and likeness, but Seth is in the image and likeness of his father—the fallen, disobedient man now in need of redemption.

[20]Some might see the translation of the Hebrew *nephesh* as "being" to be inadequate. After all, many of us were weaned on the power of the King James Version: "And man became a living soul." With all the theological implications that have been poured into the concept of *soul* over the centuries, the KJV leaves us with the impression that what was imparted by the breath of God was something ethereal, mysterious, and other-worldly—surely more than the mundane, workaday "living being." Unfortunately, the loftiness of this sentiment is unsupported by the linguistic facts. *Nephesh* is just the word used to denote that to which we refer by the English word "person." It is associated with breath, with blood, with appetite, with animals, and even with corpses. It can be used literally as a personal pronoun (cf. Gen 27:25; Jer 3:11). So the result of the God-breathing is simple: the body came to life. He began to live. He was transformed from a lifeless lump of clay into a dynamic, vibrant, living person. However, while God was able to bring the animals to life with a word from his lips, his plans for human beings required that the breath in us be from his own. But this point is made by the context, not by the word *nephesh*. See Edmond Jacob, *Nephesh* (s.v. *psyche*), in G. Kittel and G. Friedrich, eds., *Theological Dictionary of the New Testament*, tr. by Geoffrey Bromiley (Grand Rapids: Eerdmans, 1974), IX: 617-620.

putting a part of Himself into the body of clay. It is His breath that imparts the Image. Prior to the breathing, there is lifeless earth, even less significant than the grass pressed beneath it, the insects buzzing around it, or the chipmunks approaching it cautiously. What makes the human being a human being at all is that which makes him fundamentally and undeniably distinct from the rest of creation. It is that which makes it impossible to understand him without understanding his God.

The irony of this point for contemporary naturalism must not be missed. Biblically, the human being without the divine breath is *less than* the other living things. If God had simply formed the body, then gone off to other activities, nothing would have ever happened. The body would have remained lifeless, nudged occasionally by curious wildlife until worn away by the elements. We do not have the option of simply *equating* ourselves with other living things. If we are not in the Image, if we are not *much more* than other living things, then we are only lifeless clay—of *even less* importance or metaphysical stature than the lowest living creatures.

These observations, along with many others to be made from these and related passages (e.g., Psalm 8:4-6), lend credence to a claim that I wish to make the centerpiece of this essay. Whatever else it might mean to be in the Image of God, I propose the following:

**To be in the Image of God is to be more like God
than we are like anything
in the created order.**

I will call this principle "The Likeness Principle." The attribute it names—that is, the attribute of being more like God than like anything in the created order—I will call "The Likeness Factor."

Notice that the Likeness Principle does not say simply that we are more like God than anything else is.

That is certainly true. But this claim is a stronger, bolder one. It is not just that, if we order everything in terms of likeness to God, human beings come out on top. Rather, the idea is something like this. Imagine a continuum whose end points are full divinity and utter creatureliness. That is, on one side of the continuum is God in all His fullness, and on the other side is anything that is so much a part of the world that there is no mark of the divine, the eternal, the transcendent in it. The claim of the Likeness Principle is twofold: (1) that the place human beings occupy on that continuum is closer to the divinity end than to the creatureliness end; and (2) that the place of human beings is closer to the divinity end of that continuum than it is to the place of any other created object on that continuum.

To see these claims more graphically, consider the following illustration:

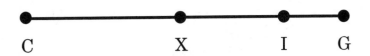

Point C represents total creatureliness, devoid of any divine being. Point G represents total divinity—God Himself. Point I represents the Imago—human beings created in the Image of God. Point X represents that part of creation that is next in line in terms of participation in divinity—whatever it may be.[21] The two claims of the Likeness Principle mentioned above can now be cashed out as the following two respective claims:

---

[21]It may very well be that the rest of creation is total creatureliness, that there are no degrees of divinity beyond that given to human beings (see next footnote). I tend to doubt this point (puppies and dogwood blossoms come to mind), but I don't see how it can be settled this side of heaven, and it is immaterial to my point anyway. Even if points C, I, and G are the only points on the continuum, the claims of the Likeness Principle still hold.

(1*) the distance from point I to point G is smaller than the distance from point C to point X; and (2*) the distance from point I to point G is smaller than the distance from point I to point X. Not only is humanity closer to God than to total creatureliness, we are closer to God than we are to anything else on the continuum. The closest thing to being God is being human, *and* the closest thing to being human is being God. We are more like God than we are like anything else God has created.[22]

This point cannot be stressed enough. To be in the Image of God is to be made (*contra* Carl Sagan) of "God-stuff."[23] As noted in the discussion of Genesis 2:7

---

[22]I am not sure how literally I want this metaphor of a continuum between absolute creatureliness and absolute divinity to be taken. On the one hand, I am concerned by the Medieval overtones it has, smacking of such esoteric and troublesome concepts as degrees of reality or the balance between potentiality and actuality. On the other hand, I am quite attracted to a metaphysic that permits continuous, unbroken connection between creator and created. Besides, it makes a lot of sense to me to speak of humans as being like created things and being like God and being more like God than they are like created things. The continuum is the best metaphor I can come up with to explicate what seems to me to be a strikingly plausible intuition. So I present it here, and allow the metaphysical chips to fall where they may.

[23]It must be emphasized how different this doctrine is from contemporary teachings within the so-called New Age movement." The claim of scripture is that we are divine Image bearers. This fact emphasizes both our close affinity with, *and* our metaphysical distinction from, the Godhead. One cannot be the image of that with which one is identical. The traditional Judaeo-Christian doctrine of the objective distinction between creation and creator is not only consistent with, but entailed by, the point I am making here (although it may allow more mystical interpretations of the relationship between God and persons than many are comfortable with, but resolving that matter would require another paper). Eastern pantheistic doctrines and the New Age perversion of them into a "we are all gods" mentality are diametrically opposed to any anthropology true to the biblical text. But the church must not be intimidated into suppressing or avoiding powerful doctrines like the Image of God for

---

above, that which made the human being alive is different from that which made the animals and plants alive. Without the breath of God we are even less than they—just lifeless clay on the banks of the primordial Euphrates. It is the God-breathing that makes us who we are and what we are. Our essence, our nature as human beings has its origin in the nature and essence of God himself. Nothing else in the created order has hold on such a claim. Everything else was either created, spoken into being, or made. Only we were sent out from the "lungs" of the Creator. Only we were given dominion over other created things. We are the Ambassadors, the Viceroys, the Chief Managers of the Estate. Such a station requires one capable of functioning in the capacity of the Creator and on His behalf. Our meager and tragic record in carrying out this mandate is too obvious (and painful) to mention. But our failure at the task does not alter the fact that we, and we alone, are worthy of being given the task. God needed someone with divine breath to crown His creation. We are that someone. We are more like God than we are like anything in the created order.

To be a human being is to be in the Image of God. To be in the Image of God is to be more like God than we are like anything in the natural order. Therefore, to discover what it is to be a human being, one should not investigate the natural order, as philosophy and the human sciences do. That is digging in the wrong place. To discover what it is to be a human being, one must investigate what it is to be God. It is a corollary of the Likeness Principle that anthropology is a branch of theology. The proper understanding of personhood requires a prior understanding (as much as can be ascertained) of Godhood.

Over my years of studying and teaching philosophy, I have become firmly convinced that the

---

fear of being misunderstood and interpreted as promoting New Age nonsense.

most persistent and intractable problems in the history of philosophy are so persistent and intractable precisely because they address features of personhood that are not explainable by the natural order. These features (e.g., mind, freedom, knowledge, and moral responsibility) are those that make us more than the world we occupy. They are attributes we have because we have the Likeness Factor. They are *divine* attributes, not natural ones. They will never be understood or explained without taking the Likeness Principle into consideration. Anthropology is essentially a branch of theology, and understanding persons requires understanding God.

But as the Apostle Paul is quick to remind us, we do have this treasure in vessels of clay (2 Cor 4:7). It was into a physical body that God breathed divine life. We are, literally, *in* the world but not *of* it (John 17:11,14,17). This is why philosophy and the human sciences can have such success in explaining certain facets of personhood, and fail utterly in developing a theory to encompass it. Certainly we know much more about the workings of the human psyche, about the dynamics of human relationships, about the concepts critical to studying personhood, than we did just a few decades ago. There is much to be learned from the analytical discipline of philosophy and the empirical disciplines of psychology, sociology, and anthropology. Yet the fact remains that the attempt to sum up these findings under an umbrella theory of persons is and always has been a dismal failure.

On the one hand, human beings are *in* the world. We are, in a very important respect, part of the created order. We are *on* the continuum mentioned above, but in this sense we are not at the divinity end of it. We have physical bodies that are subject to the laws that govern interactions among physical bodies. If we are cut, we bleed. If we step off a building, we fall to the ground. Furthermore, we are affected by events in the physical world. The way we were raised, the values of those important to us, and the developmental history and limitations of our physical bodies all have powerful effects on our emotions, our intellect, and our potential for growth. We are in the world and affected by the world. So it is only to be expected that the empirical study of that world will yield much information regarding our behaviors and tendencies. To the extent that we are *in* the world, studies of that world will reveal much about what it means to be a person.

But we are not *of* the world. Our present state is much affected by the world, but our essence is not determined by the world. While we can learn much about being human from studying the world, we can never thereby exhaust the subject. More importantly, from the standpoint of being merely *in* the world, we can never get at the essence of personhood. We can never uncover that which makes us unique in the world—that without which we would not be human. If we think we have a total explanation of humanness devoid of the Image, we fool ourselves. Any such attempt is not *explaining* personhood, but explaining it *away.* We do not discover what is special about personhood. Instead, we wind up giving explanations for why we think we are special when, as a matter of fact, we are not. As Dr. Jones would put it, "We are digging in the wrong place!"

The Imago Ventures Forth:
Preaching and Teaching the Image of God

I will close this essay with a few observations on some familiar passages of scripture, attempting to bring a dimension to them that would be missed without paying proper respect to the doctrine of the Image of God. I offer these insights as but a sampling of the power this doctrine has for preaching, teaching, and motivating a church that will face the greatest materialistic challenge in all of history over the next few generations.

In Colossians 2:18 Paul writes, "Do not let anyone who delights in false humility and the worship of angels disqualify you for the prize. Such a person goes into great detail about what he has seen, and his unspiritual mind puffs him up with idle notions." The phrase translated "unspiritual mind" here is literally, "mind of flesh" or even "mind of body" (*nous sarkos*). Perhaps a better translation would be "natural mind" or "naturalistic mind." Just a few verses earlier Paul had issued another warning to the Colossians: "See to it that no one takes you captive through hollow and deceptive philosophy, which depends on human traditions and on the basic principles of this world rather than on Christ" (2:8). The mind of flesh just is that mind that is taken captive through hollow and deceptive philosophy— dependent on *human* traditions and on the basic principles of *this* world. The mind against which we are being warned is the mind that seeks to explain everything it encounters in terms of the world in which it lives. One prominent place where the mind of flesh is exemplified today is in those who attempt to explain what it is to be a person by looking at the natural order—those who are digging in the wrong place. Paul uses the term "mind of flesh"—an astoundingly appropriate label for a mind that has relegated itself to the body.

This total surrender to the mind of flesh contrasts sharply with the struggle to which Paul confesses in Romans 7:21-23: "So I find this law at work: When I want to do good, evil is right there with me. For in my inner being I delight in God's law; but I see another law at work in the members of my body, waging war against the law of my mind ...." Paul here equates God's law, in which he delights, with the law of his mind. This law is opposed to the law at work in the members of his body which makes him "a prisoner of the law of sin." He exclaims, "What a wretched man I am! Who will rescue me from this body of death? Thanks be to God through

Jesus Christ our Lord! So then, I myself, in my mind, am a slave to God's law, and in the sinful nature [*sarx*] a slave to the law of sin" (v. 24-25).

That which is supposed to control and motivate us as mental beings—that to which we are supposed to be bound—is the law of God, which is the law of the mind. But we are constantly frustrated in our efforts to give ourselves over completely to such control, because we are constantly tempted by the idea that we are purely natural beings. We easily buy into the idea that who and what we are is simply a part of the world we live in, reducing so much of what we are to that which is purely physical. The issue is not merely theoretical or metaphysical; it is eminently practical. The struggle Paul describes in Romans 7 is a struggle for holiness, for righteous living, for a life worthy of the calling issued by God. Only subservience to the law of the mind (as it accords with the law of God) grants power to live so pleasing a life. Adherence to the law of sin and its accompanying mind of flesh yields what contemporary evangelical theology calls "carnality." Carnality is not simply, or even primarily, indulging our occasional prurient interests. Carnality is a matter of giving ourselves over to being nothing more than something in the world. To be carnal is to be a mind of flesh. It is the decision that allows the world to define everything we are. Carnality is the biblical contrast to the Image.

The doctrine of the Image and its opposition to carnality give new insight into the familiar words of Romans 12:1: "Therefore, I urge you brothers, in view of God's mercy, to offer your bodies as a living sacrifice." We are told to offer our *bodies*—the *natural* part of what we are—as a sacrifice that is "holy and pleasing to God." How do we do that? How do we redeem the body and make it a sacrifice? This question is answered in the next verse: "Do not conform any longer to the pattern of this world." The words "pattern of this world" echo the warning in Colossians 2:8 against philosophy based on "the basic principles of this world." The pattern of this world calls not for presenting the body as a holy sacrifice, but for exalting the body as the sum total of what we are. We are, according to that pattern, entirely body. If we are mind as well, it is only because mind is part of the body.

So the behaviorist and functionalist say that we can exhaustively explain mind by talking about body. The eliminativist says that we cannot explain mind by talking about body; therefore, mind has to go. The one thing they all have in common is the claim that the body is *all* we are. Certainly we fit into the natural order, because our bodies are physical. But according to these theorists, we are *only* physical things, and anything else we "think" we are can be explained in purely physical terms. Any claim of what we are that cannot be so explained is thereby inferred to be false or meaningless.

But Paul says, do not conform to that pattern. "But be transformed by the renewing of your minds, that you may be able to test and approve what God's will is: his good, pleasing, and perfect will" (Rom 12:2). We are to renew our minds—to make them over into something other than minds of the flesh. We are to make them over into the Image. We are to recover, through relationship with Christ, who we really are—primarily mental beings, not primarily physical objects.[24] That is what we really are. That is what makes us more like God than we are like anything around us.

Finally in this famous passage, we are told to renew our minds so that we may test and approve what God's will is. Just before this, in Romans 11:34, Paul

---

[24]The doctrine of the Image of God takes a dramatic turn from Old to New Testaments. In the former it is the human being who is the primary Image bearer. In the New Testament, however, it is Christ who is the perfect Image of God (cf. 2 Cor 4:4-6; 1 Cor 15:45-49; Heb 1:3; Col 1:15,19; 2:9). We recover (or rediscover) that Image by seeing God in Christ and allowing ourselves to be drawn away from the mind of flesh back to the mind of Christ.

quotes from Isaiah 40:13: "Who has known the mind of the Lord?" In verse 33 Paul speaks of "the depths of the riches of the wisdom and knowledge of God," saying that "His judgments are unsearchable, his paths cannot be traced out." Yet we are commanded to test and approve what God's will is—that will that Isaiah has told us cannot be known!

The solution to this mystery lies elsewhere in Paul's writings. In 1 Corinthians 2:14 he notes, "The man without the Spirit does not accept the things that come from the Spirit of God. They are foolishness to him and he cannot understand them, because they are spiritually discerned." Paul is certainly talking here about moral truth and about the divinity of Jesus Christ. But he is also talking about other phenomena that people have futilely spent their lives trying to understand—phenomena like mind, knowledge, freedom, and morality—because they were digging in the wrong place. These are the things of God. Once we set our minds against Him, it is no wonder we keep running up against roadblocks with our explanations. It is no wonder that some finally throw up their hands and say, "It must all be myth." 1 Corinthians 2:15 says, "The spiritual person makes judgments about all things, but he himself is not subject to any person's judgment." Then, in verse 16, Paul uses the exact passage he quoted at the end of Romans 11: "'For who has known the mind of the Lord, that he may instruct him?'" And then Paul says, "But we have the mind of Christ."

The answer to the question "Who knows the mind of the Lord?" is simply this: Christ does. And now Paul says that by having the mind of Christ we can, in very significant ways, know the mind of the Lord. We can test and approve what God's will is. We can learn what it is to be a person; we can understand that to be a person is primarily to be a mental being, like God, and not primarily to be a body, like the objects in the natural world. As mental beings—as living beings with the very breath of God—we are closer to being like God than we are to being like anything in the world.[25]

EPILOGUE: A TRIBUTE

I first began contemplating the notion of the Image of God while a student at Lincoln Christian Seminary, in the theology and philosophy classes of Dr. James D. Strauss. It was he who instilled in me the idea that anthropology is essentially a branch of theology—that we do not properly understand what it is to be human unless we understand what it is to be God. This paper can (and should) be seen as the initiation of a project in philosophical theology: the redefinition of the problems of philosophy in terms of a quest for understanding God and his relationship to persons—that is, an exercise in anthropology as theology. So conceived, this project is Dr. Strauss's, not mine. I engage in it because he envisioned it. I therefore dedicate this project and whatever useful work might come from it to my first philosophy teacher—the man who, more than any other, taught me (by word, but especially by example) how to be a thinking Christian. God bless you, Jim.

---

[25]It is important to understand this point correctly in order to avoid the kind of destructive dualism of the Middle Ages that led to an abhorrent asceticism. Paul is not saying that the body drags us down and must be kept in subjection. Rather, he is saying that if we allow the body to be the primary image of what we are, we will degenerate into the mind of flesh. But if the mind is renewed—if we have the mind of Christ—then we begin to see that it is the features of personhood that cannot be explained that make us who we are, that set us apart from the world, and make us more like God than we are like anything created or natural.

RECOMMENDED BIBLIOGRAPHY

Allen, Ronald B. *The Majesty of Man: The Dignity of Being Human.* Portland, OR: Multnomah Press, 1984.

   Allen uses Psalm 8 as a basis for exploring the ramifications of an unashamedly biblical humanism. Allen argues that the proper response to secular humanism is not the degradation of persons, but the legitimate understanding of the origin and nature of human grandeur. Such an understanding enables us at once to revel in our glory as the crown of God's creation and to bow contrite before the Creator in whose Image we are. [Beginning]

Berkouwer, G. C. *Man: The Image of God.* Grand Rapids, MI: Wm. B. Eerdmans, 1962.

   This work, by one of the most renowned Reformed theologians since Barth, constitutes perhaps the most comprehensive development of a biblical anthropology of this age. Chief among the many valuable aspects of the work is its unwavering dedication to the teachings of scripture, rather than to the pronouncements of historical and systematic theology. [Advanced]

Blamires, Harry. *The Christian Mind: How Should A Christian Think?* Ann Arbor, MI: Servant Books, 1963.

   I first read this book as a student under Dr. Strauss,. and it changed my life. Blamires plots the demise of the Christian mind into secularism, then discusses six distinguishing characteristics of the Christian mind and offers admonition to recover these characteristics in our thought patterns, value systems, and decision making processes. Many of these themes are reintroduced and updated in Blamires's more recent work, *Recovering the Christian Mind: Meeting the Challenge of Secularism* (Downers Grove, IL: InterVarsity Press, 1988). [Intermediate]

Dennett, Daniel C. *The Intentional Stance.* Cambridge, MA; MIT Press, 1987.

   This is a collection of essays presenting some of the most important ideas from one of the leading voices in contemporary materialism. Dennett is a thorough and witty writer who presents his secular agenda in a clear and very persuasive way. It is his general thesis that the traditional concept of mind has nothing to fear from the advancement of cognitive science, and presents a very optimistic brand of reductivism. [Advanced]

Lewis, C. S. *The Abolition of Man.* New York: Macmillan, 1965.

Perhaps Lewis' most purely philosophical work, this book explores the ramifications—and dangers—of contemporary educational theory, including its corollary theory of moral anti-realism (the view that there is no genuine moral truth, only personal preferences or societal conventions). Lewis argues that such theories constitute not the coming of age of persons, but the removal of personhood as a unique ontological category. [Advanced]

_____. *The Weight of Glory and Other Addresses.* New York: Macmillan, 1965.

I once heard Dr. Strauss describe Lewis as "that weaver of words that once in a generation God grants to the church." Nowhere does Lewis weave his words with more eloquence or profundity than in this collection of sermons. Of primary importance for the subject at hand is the title essay, "The Weight of Glory," in which Lewis presents the grandest picture of personhood that I have ever encountered. [Intermediate]

MacKay, Donald M. *Human Science and Human Dignity.* Downers Grove, IL: InterVarsity Press, 1979.

MacKay argues that Christianity has nothing to fear from the development of the human sciences when properly understood and applied. He approaches the issue, in his own words, "from a standpoint which unites a concern for the integrity of science with a conviction of the truth of the biblical Christian faith." Until his death in 1987, MacKay was one of the world's leading brain physiologists and a pioneer in artificial intelligence research. Many of his most important papers relating these fields to the Christian faith have been collected in *The Open Mind and Other Essays: A Scientist in God's World,* edited by Melvin Tinker (Downers Grove, IL: InterVarsity Press, 1988). [Intermediate]

Moltmann, Jurgen. *Man: Christian Anthropology in the Conflicts of the Present.* Translated by John Sturdy. Philadelphia: Fortress Press, 1974.

Father of the so-called "theology of hope," Moltmann offers here a powerful application of his theology to the question of philosophical anthropology. He examines and criticizes many current models of personhood—including those arising from the human sciences and from ideologies like capitalism and Marxism. He then offers a biblical anthropology grounded in the person of Jesus Christ and fleshed out in terms of the tensions and conflicts that arise from redeemed persons at work in an unredeemed world. [Advanced]

Randall, John Herman. *The Making of the Modern Mind.* New York: Columbia University Press, 1976.

This is another book I first encountered while a student of Dr. Strauss. In it Randall offers an in-depth look at the ideas in Medieval, Renaissance, and modern philosophy, theology, and science that have made the contemporary mind what it is. Especially helpful is Randall's treatment of the great ideas of the Western World in terms of their historical context and their interplay with one another. [Intermediate]

Rudder Baker, Lynne. *Saving Belief: A Critique of Physicalism.* Princeton, NJ: Princeton University Press, 1987.

This volume represents perhaps the most important and persuasive rebuttal of reductive and eliminative materialism in print. Rudder Baker argues that the concept of mind is both essential to a proper understanding of persons and not reducible to any purely physicalistic model. Her book stands as a provocative attack on many of the most popular approaches in contemporary psychology and cognitive science. [Advanced]

Sayers, Dorothy. *The Mind of the Maker.* New York: Harcourt and Brace, 1941.

Sayers, the famous mystery writer and companion of C. S. Lewis and J. R. R. Tolkien, develops a theory of the Image of God as the creative power of human beings. Sayers then applies this theory to a number of theological issues. This book is primarily an examination of the human creative process in light of its divine origins, coming from the viewpoint of one of the most creative minds of this century. [Intermediate]

Chapter 14:

A Ministry of Words:
A Bibliography of the Works of
Dr. James D. Strauss

Compiled by
Bill Redmond and John D. Castelein

Bill Redmond is involved with a variety of ministries, community services, and political organizations. He is the founding (and current) minister of the Santa Fe Christian Church; Manager of the Santa Fe Youth and Family Roller Rink; and Adult Basic Education Instructor for the University of New Mexico at the Los Alamos County Detention Center and UNMLA campus. He is also a member of the Republican State Central Committee in New Mexico and is the 1996 Republican Candidate for U.S. Congress from New Mexico District 3.

Mr. Redmond holds degrees from Murray State University, Lincoln Christian College and Lincoln Christian Seminary. While at Lincoln, he served as President and Vice-President of the Chi Lambda Student Fellowship and as a founding member of the Imago Dei Task Force, a student organization devoted to pro-life concerns.

Having achieved the honor of Eagle Scout, he has worked as a Scout Master for the Cub Scouts and Boy Scouts. His commitment to young people is also evident from his service as a foster parent, a big brother, and a participant in youth drug prevention programs.

Mr. Redmond's concern to "take every thought captive to the obedience of Christ" prompted him to begin the "Megaviews Forum," a discussion group primarily for scientists at the Los Alamos National Laboratory.

He is married and has one daughter and one son.

A MINISTRY OF WORDS:
A BIBLIOGRAPHY OF THE WORKS OF
DR. JAMES D. STRAUSS

Compiled by Bill Redmon and John Castelein

T he words of Dr. James Strauss, both oral and printed, have inspired thousands of Kingdom servants worldwide. His work spans five decades and has set many voices preaching and many pens writing! Below is an inventory of his more publically available words. Many of his sermons and addresses are available through the Media Center at Lincoln Christian College and Seminary. Their impact for the Kingdom of Christ continues to be immeasurable. May God continue to use them in a mighty way!

I. Published Works

Books and Book Parts

Newness On The Earth Through Christ. Lincoln, IL: Lincoln Christian College Press, 1969.

CHALLENGE!!! RESPONSE???: World-wide Missions in Light of the Nature of the Church. Lincoln, IL: Lincoln Christian College Press, 1969.

The Seer, The Savior and the Saved: The Lord Of The Future. Joplin: College Press, 1972.

Birth of a Revolution. Cincinnati: Standard, 1974. Co-authored with Dr. Wayne Shaw.

The Shattering of Silence: Job, Our Contemporary. Joplin: College Press, 1976.

"Ethical Relativism," "Honesty," "Maturity," and "Nihilism." In *Baker's Dictionary of Christian Ethics.* Edited by Carl F. H. Henry. Grand Rapids: Baker, 1973.

"God's Promise and Universal History." In *Grace Unlimited*.
Edited by Clark H. Pinnock, pp. 190-208. Minneapolis:
Bethany Fellowship, 1975.

"A Puritan in a Post-Puritan World—Jonathan Edwards." In
Grace Unlimited. Edited by Clark H. Pinnock, pp. 243-
264. Minneapolis: Bethany Fellowship, 1975.

Articles in *Christian Standard* (Cincinnati, Ohio)

"Three Titles for Christ" (March 29, 1958).

"The Scriptures and Illness" (November 1, 1958).

"The Gospel and Non-Christian Religions" (November 7, 1959).

"The Calendar and Special Days" (April 9, 1960).

"What Is Man That Thou Art Mindful of Him?" (September 24,
1960).

"The Bible and Politics" (October 22, 1960).

"When The Pope Speaks" (October 29, 1960).

"The Miracle of His Coming" (December 24, 1960).

"What Is Revelation?" (April 22 & 29, 1961).

"Translators and Their Theology" (October 7, 1961).

"The Need of the Hour: Revival Among The People of God"
(October 21, 1961).

"Songs For A New-Born King" (December 16, 1961).

"Race, Redemption, Responsibility" (February 10 & 17, 1962).

"The Nature of the Gift" (March 2, 1963).

"Death Be Not Proud" (April 6, 13, & 20, 1963).

"Handel's *Messiah*" (June 22, 1963).

"A Most Disturbing Book!" (November 9, 1963).

"The Master Blessing" (December 12, 1964).

"Seeing Cities Through the Tears Of Jesus" (May 24, 1969).

"Resurrection Living and the Growth of the Church" (March
21, 1970).

"The Fellowship of the Forgiven" (April 25, 1970).

"The World Tomorrow" (November 14, 1971).

"Isaiah Revisited" (December 5, 1971).

"The Crucified God and Man's Search for Justice" (April 8, 1979).

"A Time for Laughter" (July 8 & 15, 1979).

Articles in *A Journal for Christian Studies* (Chi Lambda Fellowship, Lincoln Christian Seminary)

"The Christian World View and the Rise of Modern Science." Vol. 1, no. 2 (March 1982).

"Carl Sagan's Cosmic Connection." Vol. 2, no. 1 (August 1982).

"Conversion: Horizons on Personal and Social Transformation." Vol. 3, no. 1 (August 1983).

"The World-view of Karl Marx: Contemporary Communism's Challenge to the Church." Vol. 4, no. 1 (October 1983).

"The Gospel Commission and Marxism." Vol. 4, no. 1 (October 1983).

"God's Authoritative Word and the Gospel According to Gallup." Vol. 4, no. 1 (Summer 1984).

"Study Guide for the Inspiration of Scripture." Vol. 4, no. 2 (Summer 1984).

"Community and Cross-Paradigm Communication." Vol 6, No. 1 & 2 (Winter 1986/87).

"Conflicting Models of Constitutional Hermeneutics." Vol. 8 (Fall 1988).

"The Future Isn't like It Used to Be (Bibliography)." Vol. 9, (1989/90).

"Anthony Thiselton in the Hermeneutical Maze." Vol. 12 (Fall 1993).

Booklets

"Race, Redemption and Responsibility."

"The Christian and the 20th Century Attack on His Faith."

"Restoration Principle in the Light of Restructure."

"The Virgin Birth of Our Lord."

"Children Choose you Parents Wisely: Responsibility of Christian Parents in Our Age of the New Morality of

Maturity Regarding T.V., Tobacco, Narcotics, Sex, Pornography, and Alcohol."

"The Word of God and Resurgent Glossolalia (Speaking in Tongues Today???)."

II. Unpublished Works

Academic Theses

"Hermeneutics and Anthropology of Karl Barth's Theology." M.A. thesis, Butler University, 1960.

"Heilsgeschichte and Its Facticity: Faith, History, and the Believer." Th.M. thesis, Chicago Graduate School of Theology, 1971.

"Theology of Nature and the Ecological Crisis." D.Min. thesis, Eden Theological Seminary, 1974.

Tracts

"The Word of God and the Jehovah's Witnesses."

"The Mormons: Have they Restored the Biblical Church?"

"Seventh-Day Adventists: The Lord's Day-Sabbath."

"Is Christian Science Christian?"

"Evangelism and Adherents of the Cults."

III. Collected Notes, Key Syllabi, and Projected Books

The History, Logic, and Sociology of Western Science: In a Christian Perspective (with Special Attention to the Theory of Thomas Kuhn).

The Word of God in a World of Words: Theological Essays From The Johannine Epistles.

Grace for a Fractured World.

The Promise of God in a Culture of Victims: A New Testament Theology of Promise.

A Christian Stake in the Maze of Meaning.